Understanding Christian–Muslim Relations

Also available from Continuum:

Muslims and Modernity, Clinton Bennett
In Search of Jesus, Clinton Bennett

Understanding Christian–Muslim Relations

Clinton Bennett

continuum

Continuum

Continuum International Publishing Group

The Tower Building
11 York Road
London SE1 7NX

80 Maiden Lane
Suite 704
New York NY 10038

www.continuumbooks.com

British Library Cataloguing-in-Publication Data
A catalogue record for this book is available from the British Library.

ISBN-10: HB: 0-8264-8782-3
         PB: 0-8264-8783-1
ISBN-13: HB: 978-0-8264-8782-7
         PB: 978-0-8264-8783-4

Library of Congress Cataloging-in-Publication Data
Benett, Clinton.
  Understanding Christian-Muslim Relations / Clinton Bennett.
    p. cm.
  Includes bibliographical references.
  ISBN 978-0-8264-8782-7 — ISBN 978-0-8264-8783-4 1. Christianity and other
religions—Islam. 2. Islam—Relations—Christianity. I. Title.

  BP172.B48 2008
  261.2'7--dc22
                2007036198

Typeset by Free Range Book Design & Production Limited
Printed and bound in Great Britain by Cromwell Press Ltd, Trowbridge, Wiltshire

To the faculty, board members and students – past and present – of the Centre for the Study of Islam and Christian–Muslim Relations (CSIC), University of Birmingham at Selly Oak, Birmingham, UK

Without such a centre, progress in Christian–Muslim understanding would be even harder to identify

Contents

Acknowledgements

Over the years, many Muslims and many Christians have contributed to my understanding of Christian–Muslim relations. It would be impossible to mention all of these people. However, among Muslims I especially wish to acknowledge my former teacher Hasan Askari, Farid Esack, Ataullah Siddiqui and the late Zaki Badawi. Among the Christian contributors I have met, Kenneth Cragg has been the most influential on my thinking.

I also wish to acknowledge my former teacher and doctoral mentor David Kerr, my former fellow student Hugh Goddard and Tom Michel of the Pontifical Council for Interreligious Dialogue. Ataullah, Farid, Hugh and I were all part of an annual consultation which met under the auspices of the Church Mission Society at Leasow House, Selly Oak, where we were joined by other leading contributors to Christian–Muslim understanding, including David Thomas, Michael Nazir-Ali, Christopher Lamb (who convened the gathering) and Nancy Lambton. I met Tom when we were both involved in drafting *Issues in Christian–Muslim Relations* for the World Council of Churches. I draw on his scholarship of Ibn Taymiyyah, based on his own doctoral work, in this book. I have also made use of an article by David Kerr.

Zaki and I co-drafted several press releases during my tenure as director of inter-faith relations for the British Council of Churches. He kindly hosted several visits at the Muslim College, Ealing from my students and invited me to share the breaking of the fast there during Ramadan. At times, in the face of what some people do in the name of Islam, I have felt that in promoting a sympathetic approach to Islam, I am defending the indefensible. My denial that Islam permits or encourages acts such as the destruction of the Twin Towers has been met by incredulity. Many persist in seeing Islam as a violent, anti-free speech, women-oppressing religion. At such times, I have considered channelling my energy into a different field but then I have remembered the generosity, the humanity and the compassion of Muslims such as Zaki, who was appalled, sickened and ashamed by association at what others do in the name of his religion. Then, my commitment to improving Christian–Muslim understanding has increased.

Research for this book used the World Wide Web and the libraries of Birmingham University, UK, UTS, Barrytown, NY and Harftord Seminary, Harftord, CT. The latter gave me access to an original edition of Sir Sayyid Ahmad Khan's 1870 text. Final revisions and checking of sources was carried out in the Sojourner Truth Library of SUNY New Paltz, of which I am a Sponsor, and in Kingston Public Library, Kingston, NY. Bible verses cited derive from the Hebrew and Greek guided mainly by the New King James Version (1982) while Qur'anic verses are derived from the Arabic guided by Ali (2002).

I am, of course, indebted to all the authors of the books and articles which I consulted in writing this guide to Christian–Muslim understanding. I hope it will encourage better relations between members of the two largest religions in the world. Hugh Goddard's *A History of Christian–Muslim Relations* (1995) complements my more detailed analyses of the texts, while Ataullah Siddiqui's *Christian–Muslim Dialogue in the Twentieth Century* (1997) proved invaluable for more recent encounters analyzed from a Muslim perspective. Books not cited in my text have also informed my thinking, for example María Rosa Menocal's *The Ornament of the World: How Muslims, Jews and Christians Created a Culture of Tolerance in Medieval Spain* (2002) and Rollin Armour's *Islam, Christianity and the West: A Troubled History* (2002). Menocal supplements my brief discussion of Andalusia's *convivencia* in Chapter 4 of this book. Armour graciously makes some positive comments on my writing as 'sensitive to the religious aspects of Islam' (183).

In the background of my thinking, as always, lurks the presence of a pioneer Baptist contributor to Christian–Muslim understanding, Lewis Bevan Jones (1880–1960), whose legacy, alongside Kenneth Cragg, helped me to overcome my initially negative understanding of Islam as mechanical, cold and legalistic, and of the God of Islam as distant and remote. Instead, I learnt to see Islam as a faith that sanctifies, for Muslims, the whole of life, enabling them to develop a sense of intimacy with God in their daily lives.

Much of what follows represents the fruit of hours of reading and book-based research but what I write is also stimulated by my years of personal involvement in Christian–Muslim encounters. In addition to visiting various Muslim-majority countries and taking part in various formal dialogues, I have assisted mosques with planning applications, obtaining charitable status and funding. I have taken Christians to visit mosques. As associate pastor of a Baptist congregation, I hosted visits from Muslims. I have led 'Islamic collective worship' in a Muslim-majority state school, at the invitation of Muslim teachers who included me on the roster of worship leaders. I have presented prizes for Qur'anic recitation in a Mosque school. I have served alongside Muslim colleagues on school boards, not-for-profit agency management committees and on a city-wide Community Relations Council. I have made common cause with Muslims in a drugs and HIV–AIDS awareness and prevention campaign. At times, the task of promoting Christian–Muslim dialogue has become one and the same as that of encouraging a more accurate, sympathetic and informed view of Islam, which is still demonized. Space placed certain restrictions on what could and could not be included in the following pages, so the dialogue of life and action does not receive the attention it deserves.

I would like to acknowledge Rebecca Vaughan-Williams and her team at Continuum for encouragement and constructive criticism. Nancy Abdel Khalek and Chipo Muzorewa assisted me with reading and commenting on draft chapters, and both more than deserve my gratitude. Errors of commission or omission, though, are all mine. My former Graduate Assistant, Ravil Kayumov, aided this project immeasurably by taking other burdens off my shoulders. My wife Rekha Sarker Bennett and our son George gave me much needed moral support throughout this project, for which I am very grateful.

Finally, I dedicate this work to the Centre for the Study of Islam and Christian–Muslim Relations, Selly Oak, Birmingham, UK, and to its faculty, board members and students past and present for their outstanding contribution to the subject of this book. It was there that I first started to study Islam and its relationship with Christianity. It was there that I later completed my MA and PhD. It was there that I have had the privilege of meeting some of the most distinguished contributors, both Christian and Muslim, to a better understanding of Islam and Christianity.

Clinton Bennett
Sojourner Truth Library, New Paltz, NY
13 August 2007

Introduction

Confrontation versus Conciliation,
Debate versus Dialogue

The Problem of Progress

This book analyses and discusses contributions to Christian–Muslim relations from both traditions. Contributors discussed include writers of historical as well as of contemporary significance. Any analysis of Christian–Muslim encounters will be interested in asking what kind of progress has been made over time, which begs the question, 'How is progress judged?' For many on both sides progress would seem to be the other's[1] conversion, or even capitulation. For some, progress is simply a better understanding of the Other's religion and a resolution of some of the traditional points of disagreement between Muslims and Christians, which often results in collaboration in common social and ethical action. The difficulties involved in defining and judging progress are such that this book is unlikely to be able to offer a satisfactory answer to the question. It will, however, delineate what changes have occurred and what new arguments have developed in response to the issues, problems, questions and challenges that Christians and Muslims confront when they consider their relationship. Christians and Muslims have encountered each other for almost 1400 years. This book explores that encounter. In the process, it aims to shed some light on the main issues, debates and agendas that feature in the story of Christian–Muslim relations, with a view to improving understanding of the issues involved.

Examining Categories and Exploding Preconceptions

It is almost certainly true that millions of Christians and Muslims today think that their religion is superior and would like to see the conversion of the Other. It is also likely to be true that most Christians and most Muslims have relatively little knowledge of or contact with the Other but think that their own faith and world-view is somehow threatened by the Other's existence. Many Muslims equate the Western world as Christian, or as a post-Christian civilization that owes much to its Christian past, and see it as ill-disposed towards Islam. Some go so far as to talk of a Western conspiracy or crusade against Islam.[2] From the Western point of view, many books discuss Islam as a 'threat'. Samuel P. Huntington's 'Clash of Civilizations' thesis, for example, predicts a conflict between the Western and Muslim worlds in alliance with neo-Confucian states (see 1993: 48). Bush's 'Axis of Evil' speech of 29 January 2002 employed similar rhetoric when it pitted the Muslim countries of Iraq and Iran (together with North Korea) over-and-against the 'free world' in a simplistic 'us' and 'them' divide. Libya and Syria as well as Cuba were later added to the list of 'rogue' or terrorist-sponsoring states. The war against terror (officially 'Operation Enduring Freedom'), said Bush, was waged to 'save civilization itself' (9 November 2001). As US troops supposedly rooted out al-Qaeda and Osama bin Laden in Afghanistan, America, he said, was responding to terrorism with 'courage and caring'.

However, any simplistic division of the world into an 'us' and 'them', 'Axis of Evil' against the 'coalition of the willing', or into a Western and Muslim polarity is problematic. There are millions of Muslims living in the so-called West, including communities that are hundreds of years old in the Balkans. Christian communities in the Arab world represent a sizeable minority and have been there since ancient times. One third of the population of Lebanon, about 6 per cent of Egypt, 10 per cent in Syria and 4 per cent of Iraq is Christian. Indonesia, the world's largest Muslim country, has a 10 per cent Christian minority, while large migrant Muslim communities of more recent origin reside throughout Western Europe, including 7–10 per cent of the French and 6 per cent of the Dutch populations. Estimates of the number of Muslims in the USA range from 3 to 6 million (from 0.5 to 1 per cent). One of the largest Muslim communities, in India, lives in a country that is majority Hindu. Nor should Christianity be identified quite so comfortably with the 'West' or with the 'North', since it flourishes in parts of Africa, in South America and also in parts of Asia, such as South Korea and the Philippines, while Christians may be as many of 8 per cent in China. The so-called Christian West also contains significant numbers of Buddhists, Hindus and Sikhs, while the influence of other non-Western religions and philosophies on countless individuals who do not associate with any organized religion is incalculable.

Siddiqui (1997) asks, 'How far is the West going to recognize or ignore Islam's long presence in Europe? . . . Will the people in the West . . . accept this third heritage?' (199). In both so-called worlds, communities of the Other are well established and by no means everyone in the majority regards the Other as different from themselves, or as being on another 'side'. As Prince El-Hassan bin-Talal of Jordan, who moderates the World Conference on Religion and Peace (WCRP), has pointed out, Christian and Muslim Arabs share a common culture and lifestyle, as do Christians and Muslims in many other parts of the globe.[3] Arguing that Christians have made invaluable contributions to Muslim-Arab life in the past, Hassan rejects the contention that either Muslims or Christians have anything to fear from the other, and calls for continued co-existence, friendship and collaboration (Bin-Talal, 1995).

Nonetheless, while talk of a 'frontier' between the Muslim and non-Muslim worlds may misrepresent reality, the notion has considerably currency in academic and political discourse (see Apostalov, 2004: 10). As few as 5 per cent of Europeans regularly attend Church but as many as 52 per cent of Americans regard themselves as Christian, and 40 per cent are said to be conservative evangelical Christians. Phillips (2006), in his detailed analyses of the interplay between politics, the oil industry and religion in the USA, argues that the Bush-led administration of the early 2000s was a 'theocracy' in all but name. Under Bush, he says, the USA has been 'in the grip of a . . . powerful religiosity' and of 'constituency pressure' from right-wing Christians whose 'biblical worldview' impacts on policy (262). He details this impact, not least on policy in the Middle East where war and conflict represent for many signs of the 'End': 'As the forces for the Iraq invasion gathered . . . many Christian fundamentalists dismissed worries about oil or global warming out of belief that the end times were under way' (95). The peace initiative is of less interest to many fundamentalists than an escalation of conflict (88). It is theology, not science, which informs Washington's anti-climate change stance (174).

The West and the Muslim World

Yet there is a political and social reality out there that can be called 'Muslim'. This exists in Muslim-majority countries, many of which can be identified as politically distinct from the West, yet it also exists in the West itself. Many who live in this world do not think that the West serves their interests, or that global institutions such as the World Bank and the World Trade Organization address their needs fairly. On the other hand, there is also a dominant culture in the West. Some Muslims who reside within its sphere are critical of its ethos and accepted moral practices and, often, of its political and economic stranglehold on the rest of the world. Many Muslims don't like what they see in the West and do see it as somewhat opposed to or incompatible with Islam. The idea that the Muslim world, which is militarily and economically much weaker than the West, presents a strategic threat, however, is absurd. Even the oil-rich nations of the Gulf have to sell their oil to the West, and will only remain rich while their reserves continue or while they can trade with the industrialized nations of the West, in which they also have considerable investments. Saudi Arabia has invested roughly 860 billion dollars in the USA, which represents 6–7 per cent of Wall Street equity.

Nineteenth-century Western writers on Islam in particular, and on the non-Western world generally, depicted it as chaotic, immoral, in need both of Christianity and of colonial rule. Much scholarship, as Said (1978) argued, was placed at the service of Empire to justify colonial rule and attitudes of racial or civilizational superiority. Sir William Muir (1819–1905), who combined high colonial office with scholarship and evangelical Christianity, depicted Islam as incapable of progress or change (1924: 601). Islam retarded Muslim society, while Christianity encouraged progress. Orientalists, said Said, created a *homo islamicus* who was the same everywhere and at all times: and thus Islam's variety and diversity was denied. Islam was effectively 'essentialized'. These Orientalists described an 'Other', who, so that they could be dominated, were inalienably different from and inferior to themselves. However, this description did not correspond to any actual reality. There is little doubt that the

Orientalists' portrayal of the Muslim world as chaotic still rings true for many Westerners. They see a reality in which many regimes seem dictatorial or undemocratic. They see some very rich nations and some of the world's poorest nations, where the level of corruption is cited as among the worst in the world. For example, Transparency International names Bangladesh, the second largest Muslim country, as the world's second most corrupt country. Nigeria, with a large Muslim population, is sixth, Sudan is eleventh, Pakistan fourteenth and Indonesia twentieth. Oman and the United Arab Emirates score as the least corrupt within the Muslim world (29 and 30) (Global Corruption Report, 2005).

Another colonial administrator, Lord Cromer (1841–1917), drawing on first-hand experience in Egypt, summed up how many non-Muslim Westerners regard Muslims:

> The European is a close reasoner . . . The mind of the Oriental, on the other hand, like his picturesque streets, is eminently wanting in symmetry. His reasoning is of the most slipshod description . . . They are often incapable of drawing the most obvious of conclusions. (1908: 2: 146)

Cromer coined the phrase 'Islam reformed is Islam no longer'. For their part, the writings of Sayyid Qutb (1906–66) and Abu'l A'la Mawdudi (1903–79), two of the most popular twentieth-century Muslim thinkers, demonstrate popular Muslim perceptions of Westerners. Qutb described 'Free sexual intercourse and illegitimate children' as the basis of Western society, where women's role 'is merely to be attractive, sexy and flirtatious' (1988: 182–4). Mawdudi characterized the West as full of 'nude pictures, sexual literature, love romances, nude ballroom dancing and sex-inciting films' (1972: 15). Ahmed (1992) describes the image painted by one popular Muslim commentator in the United Kingdom, now deceased, as an 'Occidental stereotype', which portrayed Western women as 'waiting for sex on car bonnets' (178). He was referring to Kalim Siddiqui (1931–96), founder of the Muslim Parliament in the UK. Then Britain's 'best known radical Muslim' (160), Siddiqui advocated a separate political and social order for Muslims in Britain. In his *Islam Under Siege: Living Dangerously in a Post-Honor World* (2003), Ahmed argues that Muslims feel dishonoured by the process of globalization that threatens to turn their countries into satellites of the West, while the West has also forsaken honour in its relentless pursuit of free-market-driven economic and political hegemony over the rest of the world and in choosing to respond to violence with more violence. 'Paralyzed in the face of Muslim suicide bombers', he says, the USA and other countries 'had no answer to the violence except more violence' (24). Indeed, the West's strategy in dealing with Islam seems to be to use even more force, and to inflict even 'more pain on the opposite side' (24). Globalization is regarded as 'created and sustained in order to serve the American economy and politics', not as an opening up of the world system to make possible fairer access to its limited resources (52). It has been described as 'McDonaldization' (Ritzer, 1993; Barber, 2001; see Ahmed, 1992: 53). Muslim leaders, too, have largely 'lost the capacity to respond effectively to the challenges of the world and have 'abandoned the idea of pride, dignity and honor (*izzat*)' (46). Ahmed draws on anthropology for the importance of maintaining a people's sense of honour (1). The psychological processes we use to set up 'us' and 'Other' categories often ascribe all the best virtues to ourselves, and all the worst to the Other.

Borders as Zones of Cooperation or Conflict

In passing moral judgement on the political maturity of many Islamic states, non-Muslims overlook or forget that the 'nation state' is a relative newcomer in the Islamic world. Many modern states were once provinces of the Ottoman Empire, governed for centuries from the imperial centre. Others were for 200 years or more subject to European colonization, also ruled from imperial centres. In neither case did indigenous governmental institutions evolve or develop, nor were local people allowed much if any say in governance. Many borders were artificially created by the imperial powers and reflect their political interest more than linguistic, ethnic, religious, social or historical realities on the ground.[4] Some Muslims regard the nation state as a Western imposition, which for them is alien and alienating. Few Muslim nation states have evolved from the bottom-up as coherent, natural entities. The ideal of a single, united, trans-racial caliphate or global entity remains potent. Westerners need to be reminded that their own institutions, generally speaking, took hundreds of years to evolve and that it is misleading to speak of 'democracy' as a single, easily transferable commodity. In practice, there are a wide range of democratic practices in the

West. As several eminent Muslim scholars point out, there is a real question about who wields power in the West – the common people who vote, the politicians, or those who bankroll their campaigns and lobby for special and powerful interests? Western forms of democracy, it is argued, may not be the best or most appropriate for Muslim countries where, for example, the isolation of religion from the public square might not be tolerated. This book takes the view that there is merit in speaking of inter-civilizational dialogue between Islam and the West, an approach which Siddiqui (1997) also favours. He comments that if indeed the 'fault lines of civilizations' are going to be the future battle grounds, then 'Western and Islamic civilizations have many fault lines to mend', and dialogue between them is an essential block on the road to global security (199).

Siddiqui further points out that 'the dialogue between' Christianity and Islam 'is not simply a dialogue between religions, but a dialogue of two civilizations' (198). Apostolov takes the bold step of suggesting that the nation state may not be, as most take it to be, 'the only rule in the structure of world society' (165). Federalism, though regarded as having failed in various parts of the world such as the Balkans post-Tito, has much potential for 'bargaining and compromise about government' with a view to ensuring equal rights and opportunities for all (79–80; see also 41). The existence of civilizations, religions and cultures that are trans-state, too, means that other 'actors' and 'relationships' need to be taken into account. Apostolov (2004) points out that, where borders exist, and communities mix and mingle and 'shade off' into each other, just as Christians and Muslims have historically done in various border zones, these spaces have the potential to be either 'barriers' or 'bridges' (185). That they serve to buttress the two larger communities against each other, or to keep them apart, is not inevitable. Such zones can also become bridges. Their spaces can be manipulated to either 'encourage cooperation or conflict – the choice lies with the power-brokers' (185). International relations can be conceived in cooperative not combative terms. Political borders are marked, patrolled and guarded but civilizational ones are more malleable and can be imagined either as 'a bridge, or a supporting wall in the edifice of world society'. Sells (1998), in his analysis of the Bosnian conflict, hopefully suggests that in a world where some sort of geo-political war or conflict between the 'increasingly polarized spheres of East and West' seems likely, 'Bosnia-Herzegovina could be a bridge between the majority Christian world and the majority

Islamic world' (148). Our Christian and Muslim memories are historically selective. We choose to remember battles and hostility, not what the Spanish call '*convivencia*', that is 'eras of co-existence and intermingling' (O'Shea, 2006: 8). We can choose to overcome what O'Shea refers to as 'selective, agenda-driven amnesia' and, by reconstructing the past more accurately, we can imagine, and create, a different Christian–Muslim future (9).

Confrontation v Conciliation, Diatribe v Dialogue

This book takes the view, on the one hand, that the most meaningful dialogue between Christianity and Islam takes place when individuals or groups of Christians and Muslims meet face to face and discuss their faith, hopes and dreams, problems and successes. Such dialogue or conversation occurs in concrete situations between real people, who do not so much represent all Christians, or Christianity, or all Muslims, or Islam, but themselves. On the other hand, while it is true that no abstract, ideal Islam or Christianity exists, this type of scholarly exchange does, and will continue to, happen and is not without merit. Muslims and Christians really do believe that what they hold to be true corresponds with a template, with a genuine expression of Christianity or Islam that is universally, not just locally, true. Therefore an attempt to create discourse between these two ideological abstractions is just as valid as an academic discourse between Marxism and capitalism, or between Freudian and Jungian psychology. While this book focuses on examples of actual encounter and on what exchanges took place between Christians and Muslims, it also discusses points of a more abstract theological or ideological nature

In that this book begins with initial encounter, it adopts a chronological approach to its survey of Christian–Muslim relations. It discusses key contributions from a range of Christian traditions, Orthodox, Roman Catholic and Protestant, and of Muslims from Sunni and Shi'a background, with both pro-Sufi and anti-Sufi stances. However, it will be noted from the outset that arguments and counter-arguments used centuries ago remain popular today, on both sides. Largely, this is because whether Christianity and Islam do or do not exist as abstract categories, the reality is that both traditions' scriptures contain material that sets the agenda for encounter. This book uses two categories, conciliatory and confrontational, to characterize approaches, a categorization I developed in my 1992 book. A conciliator will usually find a conciliator on the other side to talk with, while a confrontationalist will talk, or rather debate with, another confrontationalist. Whether Christian or Muslim, conciliators share a more irenic or peaceful view of Christian–Muslim relations, and confrontationalists a polemical, antagonistic view. Conciliation rarely impacts on confrontation and vice versa, since exponents of each start off with different agendas and goals and prefer different methods. These can be characterized as dialogue or diatribe. Actual meetings between Christians and Muslims may result in a change of heart and mind. More often than not, however, in this writer's experience, it confirms our prejudices, which it has to be said is one of the biggest problems involved in Christian–Muslim encounter. Conciliators may not be put off by encounter with confrontation, since they can excuse this on the grounds of ignorance. On the other hand, confrontationalists on either side may be hostile towards conciliators on both sides, dismissing them as innovators or heretics who forfeit the right to represent or speak for their religion. Sadly, although conciliation has a long history, confrontation has dominated both sides.

Conciliatory Muslims and Christians risk the charge that they only converse with those Others who share their 'liberal' views. Yet some Muslims who subscribe to a conciliatory Christian–Muslim understanding represent a more conservative, traditional version of Islam, and cannot be accused of holding ideas akin to those of Western liberalism, such as that truth is relative or that religion should be confined to the private sphere.[5] Confrontationalists and conciliators usually operate with preconceptions that determine the way in which they view the Other. The former believe that they already possess truth and that they possess this exclusively, so the Other cannot possibly have anything valuable to offer. They may also believe that they know all about the Other's beliefs before the encounter, and consider them to be wrong. At best, this may be due to human error. At worse, a more sinister explanation is available. When Others are encountered, polemic, diatribe and debate follow. The aim of such debate is to convince the Other to change their minds, to admit that their religion is wrong. They will then be expected to convert. Confrontationalists may compare their own best practice with the Other's worse, or ignore planks in their own eyes.[6] For example, Christians may accuse Islam of having spread violently while totally ignoring episodes in Christian history when force was used, or when Christian monarchs acquired huge empires at the expense of other people's territory, sometimes with Papal sanction. Muslims may accuse Christians of neglecting social and political aspects of life, forgetting that in their own tradition those who exercise power often marginalized Islam's political influence so that it too was largely a private faith. Goddard (1995) comments that 'the two communities bitterly resent the other's caricature of themselves, but only rarely does this affect their continuing love of their own caricature of the other, which they love because it makes them feel superior' (9). Zebiri (1997) writes that too often 'Christians and Muslims talk past each other' (230). From the earliest encounter until today, Christians and Muslims have consistently thrown the same darts at each other, convinced that they will reach the target, demolish the Other's credibility and result in capitulation. Yet this dart-throwing has invariably failed. The criticism of the Other that is meant to completely undermine the ground beneath them rarely causes them to stumble.

When a conciliator approaches the Other, their aim is to listen, to learn and also to share. They assume that their religion is indeed true but not exclusively true, thus other religions can also contain truth. When a conciliator looks at the world of many faiths, they see God's hand behind them all. Conciliators are generally more likely to regard their scriptures as documents that witness human experience of the divine than as infallible documents of completely divine origin. Christian conciliators will most likely regard their scriptures as human attestation to the divine. Muslims have traditionally admitted that while the Qur'an is divine and infallible, it must be read and interpreted in a specific context and through human mechanisms. However, the hope expressed by some Christians that Muslims will abandon belief in an infallible and divine Qur'an and apply to its text the same sort of analysis, form, source and redaction criticism that Christians apply to the Bible and to the Qur'an, is problematic given the centrality of belief in the absolute nature of the Qur'anic revelation within Islam. In response to Hans Küng's suggestion that Muslims adjust their view of the Qur'an so that it conforms more closely to the Christian understanding of scripture, thus allowing for form, source and redaction criticism, S. H Nasr responds that this overlooks the 'beliefs of a billion Muslims concerning the nature of the Qur'an and its relation to the prophet' (1987: 98). Nasr states that for Muslims the whole of the Qur'an and 'not parts of it' is

God's word, without any human element whatsoever (1987: 99–100). Muslims do analyze the language and grammar of the Qur'an and identify the context in which revelations were received in order to shed light on their meaning. It can be argued that the absolute nature of the Qur'an protects it from being undermined by critical analysis. However, to argue that the Qur'an is a human composition or that its context determined its content goes beyond what most if not all Muslims find acceptable.

Conciliators on both sides are less certain that a clear distinction can be drawn between religion and revelation, since the latter can only be accessed through the former, that is, through the minds of women and of men, who have to interpret what revelation says. Many Muslims dislike calling the Qur'an a 'text', because it treats it as if, like other texts, it had a human author. Belief, too, that the language of the Qur'an is divine means that applying linguistic analysis to the Qur'an or comparing how it uses words with other 'texts' is similarly problematic. Esack points out that belief in the Qur'an's eternal nature meant that its 'language came to be viewed as equally timeless and independent of any "non-divine" elements' (2005: 69). While not wishing to offend any Muslim reader, I do refer to the Qur'an as Islam's primary text. Conciliators are likely to regard 'the truth' as, ultimately, beyond all of us, so in dialogue the aim is not horizontal conversion from my faith to yours but the vertical conversion of all participants towards a fuller understanding of the truth. At the Tambaram Missionary Conference in 1938, at which Hendrik Kraemer presented his *The Christian Message in a Non-Christian World*, A. G. Hogg (1875–1954), a life-long missionary in India (born in Egypt where his father was a missionary), rejected Kraemer's contention that there was no such thing as non-Christian faith, arguing: 'I have known and had fellowship with some for whom Christ was not absolute Lord and only Saviour, who held beliefs of the typically Hindu colour, and yet who were no strangers to the life "hid in God" ' (1939: 110).

For Kraemer, other faiths could only represent a seeking, never a finding of God. For Hogg, the answer to the question 'may we meet' in non-Christian faith, 'something that is not merely a seeking but in real measure a finding, and a finding by contact with which a Christian may be helped to make fresh discoveries in his own finding of God *in Christ*', was 'yes' (103). Hogg referred to Mahatma Gandhi as deriving his 'spiritual nourishment . . . through Hindu forms, thus it would be idle to suggest that he is not a Hindu but an un-professed Christian' (112). Kraemer disapproved of Gandhi's opposition to conversion (1938: 238–9) and saw his 'sympathetic attitude towards' Jesus' 'personality and teaching' as irrelevant, since Gandhi did not break from his Hindu past. According to Kraemer, his motive, too, was more nationalist than spiritual, although he did draw 'strength from the noble and pure elements in the Indian religious and ethical heritage' (242). From a Muslim perspective, Esack also regards 'faith' as an inner quality that Christians and Muslims and Jews and others may genuinely possess, regardless of their external religious identity. Thus, being a *kafir* (denier, rejecter, ingrate) or a *muslim* (submitter to God) is not a nominative but a verbal matter: 'it is not labels that are counted by God, but actions that are weighed (Q2:177, 99: 7–8),' he says (1997: 116).

The confrontationalist looks at religious pluralism and asks, 'How can I prove that my beliefs are right and all others wrong?' The conciliator asks, 'How can I integrate all these beliefs, or harmonize them?' For confrontationalists, only 'un-belief' can be found in other religions, while a conciliator is willing to see genuine 'faith' in the heart of the other. Sometimes, the conciliator may agree to differ while still respecting the other's perspective. For example, a Muslim might, after conversation with a Christian, still find the Trinity unacceptable, even though the Christian has tried to explain that Christians believe in one God, not in three Gods and do not think of Jesus as physically God's child. He may accept that Christians believe in One God but remain unconvinced that God can properly be spoken of as a 'Trinity'. A confrontationalist will find it much harder to respect their opponents' viewpoint. They aim to win an argument, not to agree to differ. Often, following a debate, both sides claim victory. In dialogue, in contrast to debate, neither side sets out to win so neither claims victory. Some sort of acceptance of pluralism might be a precondition for engagement in genuine dialogue.

Debaters or confrontationalists speak in propositional terms, the dialogian or conciliator in subjective, experiential, even provisional terms. Conciliators, says Zebiri (1997), are more comfortable with 'mystery', 'ambiguity', 'tension' and 'paradox' (175). No movement towards the truth can take place for the confrontationalist because truth is a commodity they already possess. However, the dialogian can move towards truth because they understand truth as being always beyond us, as external to us, as ever beckoning us forward. Christian conciliators will almost certainly be familiar with and make reference to the several guidelines on dialogue that have been issued by such bodies as the World Council of Churches (WCC) and the Pontifical Council on Inter-religious Dialogue, such as *Guidelines on Dialogue*[7] (1979), *Issues in Christian–Muslim Relations*[8] (1992) (both from the WCC) and *Dialogue and Proclamation*[9] (1991) from the Vatican, for which the Vatican II document *Nostra Aetate*[10] (1965) remains authoritative.

This book concentrates on theological issues, analyzing primary texts in detail. There is also what has been called the 'dialogue of life and action', in which some of those discussed have also engaged.[11] Chapters 1 and 2 examine the role of Bible and of the Qur'an in encounter. Chapter 3 discusses traditional Christian confrontational contributions, while Chapter 4 discusses classical Christian conciliators. Chapter 5 discusses traditional Muslim confrontation, while Chapter 6 discusses classical Muslim conciliators. Chapters 7 and 8 parallel contemporary Christian and Muslim confrontational and conciliatory contributions respectively. The conclusion summarizes what lessons have been learned.

Chapter 1

The Bible:
An Agenda for Dialogue or Diatribe?

The Bible's Primacy

Scriptural passages largely determine the issues that form the agenda of Christian–Muslim relations. Scripture informs the attitude each adopts towards the Other. With their respective theological and hermeneutical traditions, scriptures provide ready-made points of debate, as well as of apparent convergence and divergence. More often than not, these 'points' have formed the substance of debate, discussion, dialogue, apology and polemic. Christians regard the Bible, especially the New Testament, as the primary source of information about God. When seeking guidance on any subject, or trying to determine what position a Christian ought to take, whether the issue is care of the environment, homosexuality, abortion or attitudes towards other religions, it is first of all to the Bible that most Christians turn. Obviously, all Christians do not agree on every issue. The Bible can be used to support different, even opposing, opinions. On the question of what attitude should be adopted towards people of other faiths, conciliators and confrontationalists have favourite 'proof texts'. Understood at what might commonly be called a 'literal' level, these texts appear to support their respective positions. This means that each side also has to come to terms with verses that seem to 'prove' the opposite position, arguing that they in fact support their own.

In theory, for Christians, the primary revelation is Jesus Christ, to whom scripture bears witness; thus scripture is not itself identified as 'the revelation'. In practice, however, almost all Christian thought starts with scripture. Christian thought may be stimulated by a spiritual experience or by a sense of direct personal communion with

Christ, but in order to make sense of and to reflect on that experience, it is to the Bible that a Christian turns. Christian opinion on whether the Bible is the exclusive channel through which revelation can be accessed, whether God also speaks through human reason or through the world of nature, or indeed through 'non-Christian' scriptures, is subject of debate. Generally, though, conciliators are much more likely to accept the validity of other sources than confrontationalists. Confrontationalists often believe in the plenary inspiration of the Bible, that it is infallible and word-for-word divinely inspired (see I Timothy 3:16). This is closer to a Muslim view of the inimitability ('*Ijaz*) of the Qur'an. For Muslims, the Qur'an is the uncorrupted word of God transmitted through a process of revelation. In this view, there is very little difference between how Jesus and the Bible are understood in terms of their 'revealing' truth about God. Conciliators, for their part, are likely to believe that the Bible is a mix of human attestation and divine inspiration.

Early Encounters with Religious Pluralism

In contrast to the Bible, where neither the words 'Muhammad' nor 'Muslim' occur, the Qur'an contains explicit references to Jesus, to Christians and to aspects of Christian belief. This is because the Qur'an post-dates the Bible. There are at least 110 verses of specific relevance to Christian–Muslim relations in the Qur'an. On the other hand, many Christians believe that the Bible does refer to Islam and, historically, they have had no difficulty applying texts to both Muhammad and to Islam. From their earliest encounter with other religions, Christians found guidance in the Bible. Indeed, just as the Qur'an contains material that describes some of Muhammad's actual dealings with Christians and Jews, so the Bible contains material describing how the early Church dealt with Judaism and paganism, much of which has been applied to Islam. A dominant issue in the Book of Acts and in some of St Paul's epistles concerned the status of the Jewish religion. Did Jews need to convert to Christianity? Must Christians be circumcised? This material is widely thought to describe a struggle between 'Judaizers' who stressed continuity between the primitive Jesus movement and Judaism, and 'Hellenizers', for whom the 'old covenant' was now obsolete.[1] The persistence of Judaism as a separate religion has long been problematic for Christians. Similarly, Islam acknowledges a prophetic relationship with both Judaism and Christianity and unambiguously locates itself within the same story of divine–human encounter, stressing Abraham's providential role. Abraham was 'sound in faith' (3:89; 6:162) and received a revelation (2:130). He is properly understood as a Muslim because he surrendered to the Will of God; 'Abraham was neither Jew nor Christian . . . but a Muslim' (3:60). Islam sees itself as replacing, fulfilling or superseding the earlier religions (Q2:3; 5:48) and finds their continued existence problematic. Christianity has traditionally been supercessionist vis-à-vis Judaism; Islam is supercessionist vis-à-vis both Judaism and Christianity. Some Christians extend the supercessionist argument further, arguing that any value that may be contained in other religions finds completion or fulfilment in Christianity.

The typical Muslim view is remarkably similar: God revealed himself through the earlier Abrahamic faiths but now the complete, perfect and final revelation has come. In many respects, the conservative Christian view of the Bible as infallible and as inspired word for word is closer to how Muslims view the Qur'an than to the liberal Christian view of the Bible as a potentially fallible, human response to experience of the divine. On the Muslim right, the Bible is regarded as so corrupt that it no longer has any value. On the Christian left, an attempt is made to understand how the Qur'an can be accepted as 'revelation'. One difficulty is that Christians who deconstruct the Bible are likely to transfer this approach to the Qur'an as well, which is unacceptable, even to more liberal Muslims. Yet despite each side's views of the Other's scripture, Christians and Muslims from both the 'right' and the 'left' cite from the Other's scripture to support their views. Christians have their favourite Qur'anic passages while Muslims have favourite Bible passages. More often than not, when Christians and Muslims use each other's scriptures, they do so in a manner that ignores or refutes how Christians and Muslims understand the passages concerned. This is an interesting point, because when they use their own scriptures, both tend to do so within an interpretive history. That is, they do not separate verses from traditional understandings, yet when they use the Other's scripture, they rarely refer to an interpretive tradition, of which they are usually quite ignorant. For example, Christians on the right cite Q5:51, 'do not take [Christians] as your friends' as representative of how Muslims regard Christians (and also widely cite Q9:5 as supporting unlimited aggression), while Christians on the left cite Q5:82–3 which says that Muslims will find Christians the 'closest in affection' as evidence of Muslim friendship towards Christians, and Q 2:190 ('fight those who fight you') to point out that only self-defence in permitted. What is more pertinent is how both sets of texts are to be understood and how they can be reconciled (see Chapter 2). Favourite among Bible texts for Muslims are Deuteronomy 18:15–18, which they believe prophesies the birth of Muhammad and Genesis 17:4, God's promise that Ishmael would father many nations, which they say was fulfilled through Muhammad.[2] Many Muslims also believe that Muhammad is the 'Paraclete' (Comforter) promised by Jesus at John 14:15–25, which for Christians refers to the Holy Spirit.[3]

Common Ground

Both Bible and Qur'an condemn idolatry. The Old Testament does so in the Ten Commandments:'thou shall not make any graven image' or 'bow down to them' (Exodus 20:4–5); while the New Testament describes Gentile offerings to images as a defilement (I Cor 10:20). The Qur'an describes the 'Taking of images as gods' as 'manifest error', and singles out associating partners with God as the gravest sin: 'Verily, God will not forgive the union of other gods with Himself.' Q 29:17 says to idolaters: 'For you worship idols besides God, and invent falsehood. The things that you worship besides God have no power to give you sustenance: then seek sustenance from God, serve Him and be grateful to Him, for to Him will be your return.' Bible and Qur'an both proclaim that there is but One God. The Old Testament declares this in the *shema* at Deuteronomy 6:4: 'Hear, O Israel, the Lord our God is one Lord' while the New Testament affirms monotheism at, for example, Mark 12:29, Matthew 23:9, 1 Timothy 2:5 and 1 Corinthians 7:6. The Qur'an does so in such verses as those in Surah 112: 'Say: God, He is alone and none is comparable to Him'; and in numerous verses that condemn any association of a partner with God. People have mistakenly adopted 'gods besides Him which have created nothing, but were themselves created' (25:3). Christians, though, cannot but read many of these verses, including Surah *Al-Ikhlas* (112, a succinct statement of how God neither begets nor is begotten), as criticizing Christian doctrine. The verse appears to refer directly to Christian belief in Jesus as God's son. This verse was probably revealed during debate between Muhammad and Christians. Other verses include 4:171 'say not

"Three" (there is a Trinity) – forbear – it will be better for you. God is only one God! Far be it from His glory that He should have a son'; and 5:72 reads: 'the Messiah said, "O children of Israel! Worship God, my Lord and your Lord. Whoever joins other gods with God shall be forbidden entry to the garden".' This is followed by, 'surely they are infidels who say, "God is the third of three", for there is no God but God' (which forms the Muslim *shahadah*, or testimony of faith, 'there is no God but God', the first pillar of Islam, or the doctrine of *tawhid*). Q5:116 implies Christian belief in the divinity of the Father, Son and Mother: 'O Jesus, son of Mary, did you say to mankind, "take me and my mother as two Gods besides God?",' to which Jesus answers that he did not, but taught 'worship God, my Lord and your Lord'. Trinity will be discussed many times in this book. At the very least, the Qur'an is suspicious about the validity of Christian monotheism, strongly suggesting tri-theism, although verses also affirm that Christians and Muslims do worship the same God, such as 29:46.[4]

The Bible and the Confrontational Approach to Islam and to Other Traditions

In addition to specific texts used to support the view that there is only one valid 'religion' that God intends for all people, and that all other religions are either human effort, or diabolical, the general tendency of the Biblical narrative towards exclusivity is recruited to justify the 'one and only' view. For example, when the children of Israel were claiming their Promised Land, they were commanded to destroy the altars and images of the Hittites, Girgashites and others who had been living there, to 'smite them, and utterly destroy them', showing no mercy (Dt 7:2–5). Their allegiance to God was to be so total that they must not deal with these people, intermarry with them or seek any form of treaty with them. Thus, in 1 Samuel 15 when Saul, instead of completely destroying the Amalekites, spares some of the best sheep and cattle and King Agag, he is rebuked: 'rebellion is as the sin of witchcraft and stubbornness is as iniquity and idolatry' (23). Deuteronomy 28:1 promises Israel that if she is faithful to God, she will be 'raised above all nations of the earth'. Other verses speak of Israel's enemies being vanquished, 'through God we shall do valiantly, for he it is that shall tread on our enemies' (Psalm 108:13; also 60:12). Leviticus 26 assures Israel that their enemies will fall before them provided they 'keep God's statutes and reverence His sanctuary' (2:7). Christians regard the Church as the New Israel, hence some do not hesitate to transfer to Christianity the same claim to be superior to all other religions, and the goal is to bring all other religions into submission to Christ. A number of verses support this view. The Great Commission, when before his Ascension Jesus commands his disciples to 'go therefore and teach all nations', implies a claim to universal allegiance (Mtt 28:20). Verses referring to the fullness of God dwelling in Jesus and to all principalities and powers being subject to him (Eph 1:21) under whom 'all things' have been placed suggest that Jesus' claims are absolute. Perhaps the most commonly cited verses used to support exclusivism are John 14:6, Acts 4:12 and Romans 10:9. Moreover, this Jesus is both the 'author and finisher' of Christian faith (Hebrews 12:2), therefore any claim to be a successor to Jesus or a completer of his message and mission (claimed by Islam for both the Qur'an and Muhammad) is redundant.

Religious inclusivism/confrontation	
John 14:6	'I am the way, the truth and the life, no one comes to the Father except through me'
Acts 4:2	'Neither is there salvation in any other name under heaven given among men whereby we must be saved'
Romans 10:9	'If you confess the Lord Jesus with your mouth, and believe in your heart . . . you will be saved'

An Exclusivist Approach[5]

Kraemer (1938), whose primary academic field was Islamic studies (he was a missionary in Indonesia), cites both John 14:6 and Acts 4:12. 'God sent Jesus into the world as The Way, the Truth and the Life' (49, 106), he wrote, and 'the only possible basis' for Christian mission 'is the faith that God has revealed *the* Way, and the Life and *the* Truth in Jesus Christ and wills this to be known through all the world' (107). Against the background of a world in which other 'Lords' claimed to offer salvation, the above sounds very much like a claim to be the one and only way by which people can enjoy a proper relationship with God, placing their trust and faith in Jesus. All three verses imply that some explicit recognition of Jesus' status viour is a condition for salvation, and that merely to regard as a good man, whose teachings contain ethical guidance, is inadequate. Against the argument that good men and women who continue to wear a different religious label, such as Muslims who pray regularly and live righteous lives, are actually Christians even though they do not publicly acknowledge Jesus, Romans 10:9 is used as a trump card because of its reference to confessing with the mouth. Others point to a verse such as Ephesians 2:8–10, 'for by grace you are saved through faith, and not of yourself . . . not of works, lest anyone should boast' to claim that however good or righteous a person may appear to be, their own good deeds cannot save them because 'we have all sinned and fallen short of the grace of God' (Romans 3:23).

The theology of salvation developed in the New Testament says that all humans are sinful, and sinful people cannot save themselves. Only faith in Jesus (*sola fides*), the perfect human who had no sin, yet died for the sake of our sinfulness, shedding his innocent blood 'as a propitiation for our sins', can justify us before God (Romans 3:25). This demands conscious recognition of Jesus' sacrifice on our behalf, and explicit faith in him, a 'with the lips' confession. Therefore, a Hindu or a Muslim who does not believe that Jesus died for their sake, and who does not confess that Jesus has wiped out their past sins, cannot stand in a right relationship with God (Romans 3:26). Hence, the conviction that faith which saves an individual from eternal punishment or estrangement from God must be linked with Jesus; 'the righteousness of God is by faith of Jesus unto all and upon all who believe' (Romans 3:22). In this view, those who do not 'believe' do not have access to God's gift of righteousness. Such people, including Muslims, however pious, humane or generous, must call on the 'name' of Jesus in order to be 'saved', for 'whoever shall call on the name of the Lord shall be saved' (Acts 2:21). Those who do not call on his name, who reject his claim to be Saviour (which includes Muslims who say that Jesus did not die on the Cross) or who call on a different 'name', such as Ram, Krishna, Isis or Mithra, cannot be saved. I John 3:23, which also refers to 'believing on the name of Jesus', suggests that explicit recognition of Jesus' role in mediating salvation is required for divine–human reconciliation. As shall be seen in this book, Muslims disagree with Christian insistence on the total depravity of humanity due to original sin, and therefore with the idea that some sort of sacrificial atonement is needed for salvation. This is one reason why

Jesus' crucifixion is problematic in Islam and is another recurrent theme in this book. Paul described the Cross as folly to the Greeks and as a stumbling block to Jews, but for him it was the power and wisdom of God and the centre-piece of his preaching (I Cor 1:23–24; cited by Kraemer, 1938: 70). Zwemer (1912),[6] citing 1 Corinthians 1:23–24, argues that by preaching Christ crucified, Christians supply Muslims 'the one thing lacking in their faith and the unfulfilled desire in their lives'. 'The Cross' is 'the missing link', and preaching it will prove to be among Muslims the wisdom and power of God (181). Deedat (1984) found such preaching obnoxious, commenting that all the missionaries offered 'mankind' was 'the blood and gore or Jesus . . . for all your good deeds, says the Christian dogmatist, "are like filthy rags"'. In his opinion, 'Jesus was not crucified, and did not die for our sins', thus such Christian preaching collapses, since if there was no crucifixion, there is no Christianity (1–4). Deedat is discussed in Chapter 7.

The Missionary Imperative

For most exclusivists, the above theology of salvation informs their belief in the urgency of the missionary task, that is, in the task of preaching faith in Jesus and of inviting non-Christians to believe in Him. Matthew 24:14 says, 'and this gospel of the kingdom shall be preached throughout the world for a witness unto all nations, and then the end shall come', so many exclusivists believe that the task of preaching to Muslims is an urgent one, since the Muslim world represents a largely 'un-reached' constituency. Hence, what is called the missionary imperative. Among confrontationists and exlusivists there is a great concern for numbers and for tactics to reach the un-reached, reminiscent of the more recent Church growth movement. Zwemer's books contain statistical data on Muslim populations, maps and identify strategic centres where missionary activity can best penetrate into the Muslim world, which remained 'one of the great unsolved missionary problems of the twentieth century' (1909: vii). The Missionary view holds that until 'un-reached peoples' are reached with the Gospel, the 'End' will be delayed. Church-growth expert Donald McGavran (1897–1990), founder of the School of World Mission at Fuller Seminary, Pasadena, CA, who was a missionary in India 1923 to 1957, wrote that 'church growth' as a 'theological stance' holds that 'belief in Jesus Christ is necessary for salvation' (1990: 8) and that 'the long-range goal of church growth is the discipling of *panta ta ethne* (all peoples), to the end that rivers of the water of eternal and abundant life flow fast and free, to every tongue and tribe and people in all the earth' (xv). McGavran's definition of 'mission' is 'an enterprise devoted to proclaiming the good news of Jesus Christ, and to persuading men and women to become his disciples and responsible members of his Church' (24). He identified the number of un-reached people as '3.4' billion (49), including 'the 100-million non-Christians living in Bangladesh (a statistic now closer to 150), 900 million in the Muslim world and 950 million in China (44). Such exclusivists do not necessarily regard Islam, or other religions, as altogether negative. Many will speak of Islam's strengths and weaknesses and of how the Christian can build on Islam's strengths, such as Muslims' desire to develop a spiritual life, to point towards the 'one' in whom this desire can be fulfilled. William St-Clair Tisdall (1859–1928) dealt with what he called the strengths and weaknesses of Islam in his *The Religion of the Crescent* (1895), writing that, 'Islam contains many noble truths mingled with much that is erroneous. Its strength lies in these truths, its weakness in its false doctrines and its imperfect moral system' (9).

Dennis (1897), a missionary in Lebanon, argued that other religions 'are as a whole . . . so dominated by error and corrupted in practice that the modicum of truth they contain has been neutralized' (460–61). Other exclusivists, though, find Biblical grounds for seeing Islam not as human effort, or as a benign though misguided religion, but as actively obstructing the 'truth' of the Christian gospel. In this view, Islam's origin lies, at worse, in satanic inspiration, at best in Muhammad's misconceived human lust for power and influence. Either way, Islam is regarded as having no connection at all with God. An early Christian view of Islam was that it is a type of Christian heresy. Muhammad qualifies in this view as a 'false prophet' or even as a 'false-Christ', deceiving people with his claim to complete what Jesus had taught (Mtt 24:5). Verses such as Matthew 24:11, Mark 13:22; Matthew 7:15, Matthew 24:24, II Corinthians 11:13-14, Revelation 13:6, I John 4:1–3 that warn of false Christs and false prophets were also applied to Muhammad.

A Satanic Origin?

Justin Martyr (d. 165), who attributed the Marcionite heresy to the 'devil', argued that pagan religions, especially when they appeared to have beliefs or practices that were similar to Christianity, were counterfeits produced by Satan:

> But the evil spirits were not satisfied with saying, before Christ's appearance, that those who were said to be sons of Jupiter were born of him; but after He had appeared, and been born among men, and when they learned how He had been foretold by the prophets, and knew that He should be believed on and looked for by every nation, they again, as was said above, put forward other men, the Samaritans Simon and Menander, who did many mighty works by magic, and deceived many, and still keep them deceived. (First Apology, Chapter LV1)[7]

Such inventions or counterfeits were, at least superficially, ingenuously similar to Christianity in order to attract people while actually catering to their lusts or ambitions: hence the early assertion that Islam met people's sexual or material desires. Muir, who more than hinted at a satanic origin for Islam, put it this way: 'Barely so much of virtue and of spiritual truth was retained to appease man's religious instincts and his inward craving after the service of his creator while the reigns of his passion and indulgence [were] relaxed to the utmost extent compatible with the appearance of Godliness' (1858, V2: 94).[8]

Islam has thus been described as a 'counterfeit', for example, by Sam Shamoun in several articles at www.answering-islam.org. He writes of 'Muhammad the compromiser and doubter' as having rejected the real Jesus for a 'counterfeit Isa who cannot save'. In 'Jesus or Muhammad: Who is God's true seal of prophecy', he suggests that as the angel of revelation presented Muhammad with a false message, he must have been a 'counterfeit angel'. Shouman has debated with the webmaster of answering-christianity.com, Osama Abdullah (see Chapter 7). Similarly, Muir wrote:

> it is incumbent on us to consider this question from a Christian point of view, and to ask whether the supernatural influence which acted upon the soul of the Arabian prophet may not have proceeded from the Evil One . . . May we conceive that a diabolical influence and inspiration was permitted to enslave the heart of him

who had deliberately yielded to the compromise with evil. (1858: Vol 2, 90f.)

According to Muir, Islam was 'designed with . . . consummate skill for shutting out . . . the light of truth' (1894: 506–7).

More recently, the influential American evangelical Pat Robertson, a 1988 Presidential candidate and founder of the Christian Coalition, applied 'satanic inspiration' not only to Islamic origins, but to Islamist terrorists:

> . . . these people are crazed fanatics, and I want to say it now: I believe it's motivated by demonic power, it is satanic, and it's time we recognize what we're dealing with. . . The goal of Islam, ladies and gentlemen, whether you like it or not, is world domination. (*700 Club* TV show, 13 March 2006)

Other Christians have recognized God's hand behind Islam but in a somewhat negative sense similar to God's use of Babylon to punish the Israelites, as Zwemer (1909) remarked: 'centuries before the Crusades, Islam was considered a scourge of God for the sins and divisions of the Church, each party considering the Saracens as a special avenger for their rivals' (187). An early example of this attitude is suggested by words of Emperor Heraclius (610–41) who is reported to have told his generals not to fight the Muslims because 'God had sent this misfortune upon men, who should not oppose the will of God' (Sweetman, 1955: 9).

Extra Ecclesiam Nulla Salus

The Old Testament image of Noah's ark served as a symbol of the medieval church; all who were baptized and safely aboard the good ship, the Church, were saved, all others were perishing in the deluge. The formula, *extra ecclesiam nulla salus*, that is, no salvation outside the church, became official Roman Catholic dogma, remaining so until the Second Vatican Council. Originally, as expressed by Origen (185–254) and St Cyprian of Carthage (d. 257), the dogma referred to schismatics, rather than to people who belonged to a religion other than Christianity. By the time of Pope Boniface VIII (1294–1303) and the Lateran Council it emphatically included all who did not identify with the Catholic Church: 'We declare, say, define and pronounce that it is wholly necessary for the salvation of every human creature to be subject to the Roman Pontiff' (*Unam Sanctam*, 302 CE). Pope Eugene IV (1431–47) pronounced that the Church firmly believes, professes and proclaims that none of those outside the Catholic Church, not only pagans, but neither Jews, or heretics and schismatics, can become participants in eternal life, but will depart into everlasting fire which was prepared for the devil and his angels (Mtt 25:41) unless before the end of life they have been added to the Church.

Verses cited with specific reference to Islam/Muhammad	
Matt 7:15	'Beware of false prophets who come to you in sheep's clothing'
Matt 24:11	'and many false prophets shall arise, and deceive many . . .'
Matt 24:24	'there shall arise false Christs and false prophets . . . They shall deceive the very elect'
Mark 13:22	'for false Christs and false prophets shall arise, to deceive even the elect . . .'
II Cor 11:13–14	'for such are false prophets, deceitful workers . . . and no marvel, for Satan himself is transformed into an angel of light . . .'
1 John 4:1	'believe not every spirit, but try the spirits whether they are of God, because many false prophets are gone out into the world . . . every spirit that does not confess that Jesus Christ is come in the flesh is not of God, and this is the spirit of the Antichrist . . .'
Rev 13:6	'and he [the beast] opened his mouth in blasphemy against God . . .'

An Eschatological Perspective

Given the end-time, or eschatological setting of many of these verses, another early view of Islam was that it was a sign of the 'End', and even a mechanism for punishing Christians for their unfaithfulness. During the early Moorish period in Spain a group of Christians, looking at their Bibles, came to the conclusion that Muhammad was the beast of Revelation 13 (they thought he had been born in the year 666) and the Little Horn of Daniel 7:8. From this they calculated that Islam would flourish for three and a half periods of 70 years each, that is, for 245 years, then the Day of Judgement would dawn. Bishop Eulogius of Toledo (d. 859) and his friend Alvarus encouraged some 48 Christians (between 850 and 859) to insult Muhammad and Islam publicly so that they attracted the death sentence and were martyred (known as the martyrs of Cordoba). They stood outside Mosques or attended Islamic courts and shouted out statements that they knew were offensive to Muslims, such as that Muhammad was an imposter, a false prophet who had composed the Qur'an and a lecher who lusted after women. Much of this is gleaned from a brief Life of Muhammad, the *Istoria de Mahomet*, known to be in circulation in Spain at the time (see Wolf, 1997[9]). They believed that their voluntary martyrdom would hasten the coming of the End. One of the earliest criticisms of Muhammad, reflected in the text of the Qur'an, was that he had composed the Qur'an from pre-existing composite sources with the aid of deviant, or heretical, Christians. Christians were aware of the story that Muhammad had met with several monks, possibly Nestorian, who according to Muslim tradition had affirmed his mission (see Chapter 3). This, according to some, qualified him as a deceiver, as in Matthew 24:24.

The designation anti-Christ was especially reserved for those who questioned the deity of Jesus or the Trinity (Sahas, 1972: 69). Muhammad, as far as Christians were concerned, blasphemed against God because he denied both Jesus' deity and the Trinity. He also claimed to have received a revelation that superseded Jesus. Thus, he sounded like the anti-Christ, since he did not confess that Christ 'had come in the flesh', and could not be inspired by the Holy Spirit. Polemicists concluded that if he was inspired, his inspiration must be Satan. Another Bible text that has been negatively applied to Islam is from the Old Testament story of Isaac and Ishmael – John of Damascus referred to the acknowledged Ishmaelite ancestry of Muhammad. Genesis 16:12 says of Ishmael that 'his hand will be against every man, and every man's hand will be against him'. As early as 731, the Venerable Bede, in his *Historia ecclesiastica*, referred to Muhammad (probably borrowing from John of Damascus, on whom the Spanish may also have drawn) as a 'wild man of the desert' who, like his ancestor Ishmael, was 'outside the covenant'. The Saracens (John also used this term to describe Muslims) were 'rude, war-like and barbarian' (Reeves, 2000: 85). Muhammad's motive had been lust for power, and his religion was strongly associated, suggested Bede, with 'war and destruction'. Bede linked this with Genesis 16:12, as does a much more recent writer, Hal Lindsey, one of the most widely read end-time analysts, described by the *New York Times* as a best-selling author of the 1970s. Citing the same passage, Lindsey (2002) writes: 'Islam literally resurrected the ancient enmities and jealousies of the sons of Ishmael . . . towards Jews and enshrined them in religious doctrine' (127). Moreover, Lindsey also refers to Daniel 7 and Revelation 13:7–8 with reference to Islam's role in the end-time battle: 'The initial attack is led by the Arab-Muslim confederacy . . . the Muslims are immediately joined by the Russians in an all out assault on Israel' (240–1). Islam, according to Lindsey, is 'nothing less than a religious-cultural imperialism that wants to take over the world' (129). Antagonism between Jews and Muslims goes right back to Genesis and we can gain insight into views of Muhammad from 'his forebears, Ishmael and Kedar', which is another example of how the Bible is recruited to inform Christian attitude towards Islam.

The Bible and a Conciliatory Approach to Islam

Conciliators, inclined to an inclusivist or pluralist theology of religions, also have favourite texts. In addition to the texts listed below, it is possible to identify another general trend in the Biblical narrative that expresses God's concern for all people, not just for his 'chosen people'. Chief Rabbi Jonathan Sacks refers thus to the Noahide laws:

> As Jews we believe that God has made a covenant with a singular people, but that does not exclude the possibility of other peoples, cultures, and faiths finding their own relationship with God within the shared frame of the Noahide laws. These laws constitute, as it were, the depth grammar of the human experience of the divine: of what it is to see the world as God's work, and humanity as God's image. *God is God of all humanity* . . . (2002: 53)

Indeed, the Noahide laws are described as an 'everlasting covenant' between God and 'every living creature', symbolized by the rainbow. Abraham, called to become father of a chosen nation, is promised that through him all people will also be blessed (Genesis 12:3).

The most frequently cited verses supporting conciliation	
Matt 7:16	'you shall know them by their fruits'
Matt 7:21	'not everyone who calls me Lord will enter the kingdom of God, but those who do the will of my father'
John 1:9	'the true light that enlightens all men cometh into the world'
John 3:8	'The wind blows where it will, you hear the sound of it but you do not know where it came from or where it is going . . . so everyone who is born of the spirit'
John 10:16	'I have other sheep also that are not of this fold, I must bring them also'
John 14:2	'in my father's house are many mansions'
Luke 6:46–9	'Why do you call me, Lord, Lord, and not do what I say?'
Luke 9:50	'He that is not against us is for us'
Luke 13:22	'. . . and people will come from east and west, from north and south and sit at table in the kingdom of God'
Acts 14:17	'He had not left himself without witnesses . . .'
Acts 17:23	'As I walked along and saw your devotion, I found an altar with this inscription, "To an unknown God". Whom you ignorantly worship as unknown, I now declare to you'
Romans 3:15	'When the gentiles, who do not have the law, do by nature the things that are contained in the law, they are a law to themselves'
Romans 11:32	'For God has committed them all to disobedience, that he might be merciful towards everyone'
Col 4:17	'Whatsoever things are true, whatsoever things are honest, whatsoever things are pure, whatsoever things are lovely, whatsoever things are of good report, if there be any virtue, and if there be any praise, think on these things'
I Cor 13:6	'Rejoice in the truth'
Philippians 2:10–11	'At Jesus' name, every knee will bow and every tongue will confess that he is Lord'
Titus 1:16	'Unto the pure, all things are pure'

In addition to these verses, conciliators understand many of the verses that exclusivists use as supporting their position, just as confrontationalists interpret many of the above in a way that does not conflict with their theological stance.

The Inclusivist Approach

Inclusivist refers to those who believe that it is possible for someone who identifies with another religion, and who does not make an explicit confession of Christian faith, to nonetheless benefit from the salvation that is available through Jesus. Muslims are thus 'included' in rather than 'excluded' from the grace of God, which operates in their lives as Muslims. Jesus retains a unique role as Saviour of humanity but faith is regarded not so much as an activity of individual human hearts and minds than as God's free gift, regardless of religious affiliation. Such texts as 'faith is the gift of God, not of works, least any should boast' (Eph 3:8) can be cited to support this view. The reference to an explicit confession in Romans 10:9 still stands, since those who do make such a confession will indeed be saved, but all those whom God chooses to save, Muslim or Christian, are saved by the power that resides in the 'Name' of Jesus. As Cracknell (1986) put it, referring to Acts 4:12, 'Jesus is the name by which the nature and activity of God is fully revealed . . . His name is the saving name because it affords the means by which human beings share in the grace and love that is the nature of God himself' (108). Acts 4:12, therefore, is transformed into an inclusive text. Others point to Philippians 2:10, which says that 'at the Name of Jesus every knee shall bow, and every tongue confess that Jesus Christ is Lord' to suggest that the saved will indeed make a 'with the lips' confession at the End. For some, confession is in the here and now, for others it will be an eschatological act. Origen (d. 254), who first coined the dictum 'outside the church no salvation', actually advocated universal salvation, believing that only thus would God's love be unlimited, and God truly omnipotent. In his view, people continue to be born, in different realities, or ages (*aiônes*), until they allow God's love to penetrate their hearts, and all resistance to God subsides. Satan himself will have a chance to repent, then the very gates of hell will be thrown open and all people will enjoy eternal harmony with God. Then, all things will be restored (*apokatastasis*). Acts 3:20–21 reads, 'and he shall send Jesus Christ . . . whom the heaven must receive until the times of restoration of all things'.

The very concept of universal salvation is sometimes referred to as 'Origenism'. Origen wrote:

> The process of amendment and correction will take place imperceptibly in the individual instances during the lapse of

countless and unmeasured ages, some outstripping others, and tending by a swifter course towards perfection, while others again follow close at hand, and some again a long way behind; and thus, through the numerous and uncounted orders of progressive beings who are being reconciled to God from a state of enmity, the last enemy is finally reached, who is called death, so that he may also be destroyed, and no longer be an enemy. (*De Princ.* 3: 6: 6)

Kraemer also believed that God is love, but did not see universal forgiveness as a necessary outcome of God's love:

God is love, perfect love, and is not then forgiveness not the most obvious thing to happen? It is not . . . God's love is holy love, and therefore radical love. Because God loves man, the sinner, radically, He condemns him radically . . . disregarding the reality of sin would be indulgence, not love. It would mean destroying holiness, on which depends the validity of all moral life . . . (1938: 79)

A Finding and a Seeking

Hogg, who was cited in the Introduction, can be classified as an 'inclusivist'. He refers to both the John 16:6 and the Acts 4:12 passages as 'proof-texts' against his position but interprets these differently. Jesus did say that he was the way, the truth and the life and that 'no one cometh to the Father but through him', but he did not say, 'that apart from faith in the Christ who once walked on earth, no degree of fellowship, no really two-sided commerce is possible between God and man' (1939: 114). Nor did Hogg think that 'a willingness to admit the possibility of a life "hid in God" but not rooted in faith in Christ' prevented him from affirming the truthfulness of Acts 4:12. Rather, 'if God be willing and able to hide "in the secret of His tabernacle" some perhaps many – who have not yet 'learned Christ', this graciousness of God towards men, like all his graciousness, is morally conceivable only because of the Name that is above every name (115). For Hogg, other religions could contain the experience of 'finding' as well as seeking God. Properly speaking, it is God who finds people, rather than people who find God, so it can be argued that, from the human side of the divine–human chasm, there is, as Kraemer says, *only ever a seeking*. Others who adopt an inclusive or pluralist approach point out that many New Testament scholars are sceptical that the 'I am' sayings of John's gospel can properly be attributed to Jesus. Rather, they represent back-projection onto Jesus by the early church of its own theology. If this is true, then Jesus never said, 'I am the way, the truth and the life' and it cannot be used as a proof-text against the possibility that non-Christians can be saved. On the other hand, explicit faith in Christ could be after death, as suggested by Philippians 2:10–11. Karl Rahner (1904–1984), the Catholic theologian whose thought influenced Vatican II's document *Nostra Aetate*, is usually associated with the inclusivist position. Like Origen, Rahner could not believe that a God of love, who wills the salvation of all people, would allow evil-minded, stupid men and women to thwart his salvific plan:

> We have every reason for thinking optimistically that God and his salvific will . . . is more powerful than the extremely limited stupidity and evil-mindedness of men, However little we can say with certitude about the final lot of an individual inside or outside the officially constituted Christian religion . . . we have to believe that every human being is really and truly exposed to the influence of divine supernatural grace . . . (1966: 123)

In 'spite of' people's apparent estrangement from God, it must, said Rahner, be possible for people outside the Church to experience God's grace, and to accept its gift. Such people can be called 'anonymous' or un-baptized Christians (a term Kraemer rejected; 1938: 29), since they have been touched in some way 'by God's grace and truth' (123–4). When Rahner first used the term he had in mind secular humanists, but by the time he wrote 'Christianity and the Non-Christian Religions' (1966) he was also applying the term to people who identify with other faiths. Rahner did not dismiss the need for conversion or for proclamation, since he argued that what he called 'reflective Christian faith' (that is, a 'faith fully conscious of itself') brings us closer to God. The Church, though, should not 'regard herself . . . as the exclusive community' of the saved 'but rather as the historically tangible vanguard and the historically and socially constituted expression of what the Christian hopes is present as a hidden reality even outside the visible Church' (133). 'God', says Rahner, 'is greater than man and the Church' (134). The church's attitude should be that of St Paul, when he said, 'What therefore you do not know and yet worship (and yet worship!) that I proclaim to you' (Acts 12:23), citing thus one of the favourite inclusive verses. Rahner hints, when he wrote that we may be able to say little with any certitude about the 'final lot of an individual inside or outside' the church, that, as Augustine taught, even in the visible church there are those who will, and those who will not, be among the 'saved'.

Nostra Aetate (In Our Time)

Rahner's theology influenced the official teaching of the Roman Catholic Church, represented by *Nostra Aetate*, promulgated 28 October 1965 and passed by a vote of 2,212 to 88 of the assembled bishops. The work of Louis Massignon (see Chapter 5) was also influential. The Church, declared the document, 'rejects nothing that is true and holy in' other religions but regards 'with sincere reverence those ways of conduct and life, those precepts and teachings which, though differing in many aspects from the ones she holds and sets forth, nonetheless often reflect a ray of that Truth which enlightens all men'. The reference here is to John 1:9, which an exlusivist such as Tisdall could also cite (1895: 8). In this view, then, what is 'true and holy' in other religions can be understood as also a result of divine revelation, since it is a product of that light, which is Χριστός (Christ), or the λόγος (Logos) that enlightens all people. Or, Acts 14:7 can also be applied. This understanding of the origin of what Christians recognized as 'true and holy' in non-Christian thought or religions or philosophy was actually articulated very early in Christian history. Philosophy, Islam, Hinduism, are thus pointers to Christ. A verse such as 'I have not found so great a faith, no, not in Israel', spoken by Jesus of a Roman Centurion, testifies to the possibility of faith outside the formal Church, since the narrative is silent on whether the Centurion actually became a follower of Jesus (Luke 7:9).

Natural Theology

Inclusivism argues for a degree of continuity between God's revelation of God's-self through nature, the human conscience (Romans 3:15) (sometimes referred to as general revelation) and the fuller, indeed the full, revelation in Christ. Kraemer rejected this concept of continuity, arguing for discontinuity. Traditional

Catholic and mainstream Protestant theology accepted 'nature' alongside Scripture as a valid source of knowledge of God, again drawing on Romans 3:15. Classically, this was the position of Thomas Aquinas (1227–1274), for whom there were two sources of revelation, the Scriptures and the tradition of the church, and reason. Both originated from a single source. Reason for Aquinas represented the fountain of natural truth (hence the term 'Natural Theology'). He could therefore take seriously Muslim thought, and in his *Summa Contra Gentiles* attempted to bring the best of Muslim philosophy within the scope of Christian thought. Faith, for Aquinas, had less to do with trusting in Jesus as a personal saviour than with accepting the propositional truths concerning the nature of God, of humanity and of the Man-God. Only the latter, what Aquinas took as truth concerning Jesus as both human and divine, obviously excluded Muslims. Aquinas believed that the self-evident truths of reason could always be harmonized with the truth of revelation. His maxim was '*Gratia non tollit sed perficit naturam*' (grace does not abrogate but perfects nature) (Kraemer, 1938: 115). Luther and Calvin both affirmed nature as a source of revelation. Calvin wrote:

> In reading profane authors, the admirable light of truth displayed in them should remind us that the human mind, however much fallen and perverted from its original integrity, is still adorned and invested with admirable gifts from its Creator. If we reflect that the Spirit of God is the only fountain of truth, we will be careful, as we would avoid offering insult to him, not to reject or condemn truth wherever it appears . . . (*Institutes*: 2. 2. 15–16)

Calvin said that all people, 'however barbarous and even strange', are 'touched by some idea of religion', since 'we are all created in order that we may know the majesty of our creator' (Fosdick, 1952: 215). For Calvin, salvation did not involve a 'with the lips' confession because God has already saved the elect and condemned the damned. Calvinists, though, would engage in mission, since Calvin also believed that the elect should grow in their knowledge and understanding of God and in their spiritual relationship with Him, which requires nurture. Wherever 'truth' is, there is the Christ, perhaps hidden from sight. Christians can thus claim 'whatever is rightly said', for 'whatsoever things are true, whatsoever things are honest, whatsoever things are pure, whatsoever things are lovely, whatsoever things are of good report' emanate from the One who is Truth (Col 4:8). Truth encountered among non-Christian writers can be understood as a product of the human conscience, or as the fruit of the Spirit of God blowing, like the wind, wherever it will.

Kraemer rejected 'nature' as a source of revelation. This doctrine, 'from the standpoint of revelation', is 'a failure and an error' (1938: 115). 'Reason' and 'history' might express human longing for God, but it is 'mistaken to describe the religious pilgrimage of mankind as a preparation or as leading up to a co-called consummation or fulfillment in Christ' (1939: 3). The 'fundamental discontinuity of the world of spiritual reality . . . to the whole range of human religion, precludes the possibility and legitimacy of a *theologica naturalis* . . .' (4). To represent other religions as somehow a 'schoolmaster to Christ' is, he continued, 'a distorted perception of these religions and their fundamental structures and tendencies' (6). True Christian thought, or what he called 'biblical realism' (which begins with the uniqueness of the Christian revelation), 'stresses discontinuity, and takes this as its starting point'. 'This involves', he continued, ' the . . . rejection of all "natural theology" and a vehement . . . abhorrence of terms such as "fulfilment" or "general revelation"' (15).[10]

Clement[11] and *Nostra Aetate* were also informed by St Paul's attitude towards the Jews, his own (and Jesus' own) people. Speaking about how the law functioned before the coming of the new covenant of grace (John 1:17), Paul, who agonized over the fate of all people, prayed from the depth of his heart that they may be saved (Romans 10:1) and spoke of the law as a 'schoolmaster' to 'bring us to Christ' (Gal 3:24). Thus, Greek philosophy, or Islam, serves a function, pointing people in the direction of Christ. Describing the Church as having been 'grafted on' to the original covenant between God and the Jews, Paul said that, when 'the gentiles come in', God would re-graft the Jews onto the covenant so that all will be saved; 'for I would do not want you to be ignorant of this mystery . . . all Israel will be saved' (Romans 11:25–6). God could not 'cast away His people', nor had he (11:1–2). Some Jews and Muslims may come to explicit faith during their earthly life but for many it will be an eschatological happening. Isaiah 60:7 predicts that, on the day when peace dawns, the sons of Ishmael will flock to Mount Zion, where their worship will be accepted by the Lord. Of course, Christians should not expect Muslims, who regard their salvation to be independent of and unconnected with Jesus, to approve of such a view. On the other hand, Christians can believe that it does not really matter how an individual thinks he or she will be saved, if it is really true that Jesus is the saviour of all people. Newbigin writes:

> we do not presume to limit the might and the mercy of God for the ultimate salvation of all people, but the same costly act [the cross] . . . which gives us that assurance and promise also require that we share with our fellow pilgrims the vision that God has given us. (1989: 182–3)

Nostra Aetate parts company from exclusivists in inviting Christians to 'recognize, preserve and promote' the good things, spiritual and moral, as well as the socio-cultural values, found in non-Christian religions. Kraemer saw any such positive aspects as so entrenched in a misdirected system that converts have to make a complete break with their past. Specifically referring to Muslims, the declaration states:

> The church holds with esteem . . . the Muslims. They adore the One God, living and subsisting in Himself, merciful and all powerful, the creator of heaven and earth . . . Though they do not acknowledge Jesus as God, they revere him as a prophet. They also honor Mary . . . value the moral life and worship God especially ardently through prayer, almsgiving and fasting.

Acknowledging that historical 'quarrels and hostilities between Christians and Muslims' damaged relations, the Declaration calls on 'all to forget the past and to work sincerely for mutual understanding and to preserve as well as to promote together for the benefit of all mankind justice and moral welfare, as well as peace and freedom'. Christians, the Declaration concludes, should recognize all people as brothers and sisters, for all are made in the image of the One Father, and maintain 'good fellowship among the nations' (I Peter 2:12). Several of the passages cited above as supportive of a conciliatory approach suggest that not all who call Jesus Lord will be admitted to the Kingdom, but those who do what Jesus said, namely, feed the hungry and visit the imprisoned. This opens up the possibility that a Muslim who lived a righteous life might gain entry, whereas a self-proclaimed Christian who never helped anyone in need might be refused. Such verses as Luke 9:50 and James's 'faith without works is dead' (James 2:20) suggest that anonymous Christians who live Christ-like lives may enter the kingdom ahead of baptized Christians who call Jesus Lord but who oppress the poor and neglect the needy. 'Be doers of the word, not hearers only', says James (1:22). Jesus' words that he has other sheep also, and that there are many mansions in his father's house, can also be applied to anonymous Christians. Further, *Nostra Aetate* does not state that the un-baptized are damned, which appears to contradict the earlier teaching of 'no salvation outside the church'. However, Catholic theologians argue that the 1965 Declaration is consistent with earlier doctrine, since those who have a genuine 'faith', which is gifted by God, are implicitly Christian, and implicitly baptized. The same formula was used to explain how the billions of people who have never had an opportunity to respond to the gospel may still be touched by the grace of Christ. Those whose hearts and souls conform to the will of God have implicitly expressed a desire for baptism and for Church affiliation, even though they are unaware of the existence of either. Inclusivists often go further, since they also want to affirm that Muslims and others who have heard the gospel but who have not accepted baptism may still be saved as a result of their implicit faith. In its official attitude towards other Christians, previously labelled as schismatic or heretics, the Catholic Church has also reformulated its teaching. While it still identifies itself as the true Church, post Vatican II it no longer says that it 'is' (*est*) the true church but that the true church subsists in it (*subsitit in*). Thus, the 'church' can not be identified with any single sociological manifestation, and consequently other 'churches and ecclesial communities' which are no longer called sects may 'contain significant elements of the true church, and members of these communities come to salvation through the mediation of their communities, and not in spite of them' (Gros et al., 1998: 68). Extended to include the 'wider ecumenism', that is, other faiths, this means that Islam for Muslims can be the religious system through which God's saving grace operates in their lives.

The Pluralist Approach

The 'pluralist' view says that no single faith can claim to be uniquely legitimate, so all can be regarded as valid. John Hick has been an influential exponent of this theology. Sometimes, pluralism is characterized as the typically Hindu concept of different paths leading by various routes up to the same mountaintop, but properly understood pluralism allows for the diversity of goals that religions actually aim towards, that is, they may not all set out to reach the same destination or to meet the same human needs. The Hindu 'different paths up the same mountain' is arguably inclusivist. Inclusivism seeks to 'include' non-Christians within God's salvific work but reserves a central role for Jesus as the mechanism by which salvation has been achieved for humankind. For Newbigin, unless Jesus' death has universal significance, the Cross becomes a mockery:

> If it is true that almighty God, creator and sustainer of all that exists in heaven and on earth, has – at a known time and place in human history – so humbled himself as to become part of our sinful humanity and to suffer and die a shameful death to take away our sins . . . then to affirm it is no arrogance . . . if it is a fact it cannot be slotted into some way of understanding the world based on other presuppositions, it can only be the starting-point, the presuppositions of all our struggles to understand the world of history. (1989: 328)

John Hick (born 1922) was raised as an evangelical Christian, and had assumed that salvation derives from explicit Christian faith. After moving to his teaching post in multi-cultural Birmingham in 1967, he began to question this assumption as he met and became friends with people from many faiths. In *God and the Universe of Faiths* (1973) he advocated a paradigm shift, from a Christ-centric to a theo-centric emphasis, one that moves Christ from the centre to the circumference, positing that it is the Absolute, or the Real that occupies the centre. Later, Hick tended to avoid the word 'God', preferring 'the Real' as a more inclusive term, embracing non-theists as well, such as Buddhists. He compared this with the Copernican revolution, which moved the earth from the centre. It is also referred to as a crossing of the Rubicon. All religions revolve around the centre, and represent culturally mediated responses. Hick does not claim that every religion is necessarily equally efficient in enabling adherents to achieve their goal but he says it would be invidious to pass any type of judgement, since religions are culturally embedded. However, he does suggest that the degree to which a religion brings about individual transformation from self-centre-ness to Other centre-ness (which can include transformation from selfishness, to living for the sake of others) is a reasonable guide to their value and worth. Like Rahner, it was conviction of the love of God that caused Hick's own paradigm shift. He wrote (1973):

We as Christians believe that God is the God of universal love. That he wills the ultimate good and salvation of all. And yet we also know that the large majority of the human race have lived outside the borders of Christendom. Can we accept the conclusion that the God of love who seeks to save all mankind has nevertheless ordained that men must be saved in such as way that only a small minority can in fact receive this salvation? It is the weight of this moral contradiction that has driven Christian thinkers in modern times to explore other ways of understanding the human religious situation. (122–3)

Pluralism privileges neither Christianity nor Christ nor any other religion and, to cite Küng (1993), it not merely recognizes the existence of other religions but their intrinsic equal value (180). Pluralists generally share Ernest W. Hocking's conviction that co-operation in humanitarian, social justice, social welfare and peace-making work is the common task to which all people of good faith are called. Many pluralists, as did Hocking, believe that a single world civilization will evolve, which will build on the best of all faiths and cultures. Hocking[12] identified this coming world civilization with the Kingdom of God (1956: 118) and believed that Christianity had a special role to play in assisting other faiths to re-conceive themselves in universal terms (230, 277). Pluralists regard inclusivism as another name for exclusivism, since inclusivists still claim that salvation is only through the Cross.

Chapter 2

The Qur'an and Christianity:
Affection or Hostility?

Approaching the Qur'an

For Muslims, the Qur'an is God's comprehensive, definitive, immutable self-revelation. Many Muslims believe that the Qur'an is the source of all knowledge (*'ilm*). Every aspect of Islamic thought begins with the guidance that is found in this book. Von Denffer describes *tafsir* (Qur'anic exegesis) as 'the most important science for all Muslims' since 'all matters concerning the Islamic way of life are connected with it in one sense or another' (1983: 123). Some Qur'anic passages regarding other religions were 'revealed' to Muhammad in the context of direct encounter with Christians and Jews. Next in authority to the Qur'an, for Muslims, is the collection of Muhammad's saying and doings, the *hadith*, which also contains material directly related to Christian–Muslim encounter. On the one hand, Muslims believe that the Qur'an is God's eternal word and therefore pre-existed its sending down, piece by piece, to Muhammad between 610 and 632. On the other hand, Muslims believe that the Qur'an sometimes addressed specific situations or circumstances in the life of Muhammad, known as 'occasions of revelation'. The Qur'an repeatedly asserts its Arabic-nature, for example, 12:2; 13:37; 46:12. As a consequence, the vast majority of Muslims assert its untranslatability, which also produces a miss-match between Christians, who probably have no knowledge of biblical languages and who have no objection to Muslims using a translation of the Bible, and Muslims, who insist that an English, or a French 'rendering' of the Qur'an is *not* the Qur'an.

Kabbani comments that she feels that a non-Muslim or a non-Arabic speaking Muslim reading the Qur'an in translation read a *different text.* The 'screen of imperfect translation', she says, prevents them from apprehending 'this linguistic triumph'. For those who do not know Arabic, it remains a 'silent text' and 'attempts to analyze it cannot amount to anything' (1989: 34). This means that a prerequisite tool in the kit of a serious Christian participant in dialogue is at least a rudimentary knowledge of Arabic. Christians should also try to identify Qur'anic chapters by their Arabic names, such as *al-Fatiha* (the opening, Chapter 1), or *al-Nisa* (women, Chapter 4) as these are more familiar to Muslims than the numerical system of identification.[1] The division into verses is a convention of Western scholarship. Numbering varies from edition to edition, which can make tracking references difficult. Rodwell (1955), for example, only identifies every tenth verse. This writer recommends the revised edition of Ali (2002). Many Muslims are in fact more familiar with a quite different system of identifying verses, of which few non-Muslims have much knowledge. This is the *Juz'* (part, or portion) system, which divides the Qur'an into 30 portions of roughly equal length. Often, this system is sub-divided into four sections (*hizb*), which in turn divide into four, facilitating 'recitation over seven days' (Denffer, 1983: 68–9).

An aspect of the Qur'an that baffles and wrong-foots non-Muslims is that it is primarily intended to be recited and heard, rather than picked up and read. Arguably, the Biblical books tell a story from creation (Genesis) through the narrative of God's covenant and dealing with the Hebrews, to the life and times of Jesus, through the spread of Christianity and the Epistles dealing with issues of faith and order to the Book of Revelation, which concludes with the Day of Judgment. Although this narrative is sometimes interrupted by legal, devotional and wisdom literature, it can be read as a whole, from beginning to end. The Qur'an, revealed to Muhammad piece by piece between 610 and 632 CE, is ordered differently. It is not chronological in terms of a narrative stretching from creation to judgement (both, of course, are described in the text) but is arranged, roughly, according to the size of its chapters. Shorter chapters are at the end, larger (except Chapter 1) towards the beginning. Chapter 2 is thus the longest. Different types of material – some legal, stories of the prophets, accounts of creation, references to Judgment and to Paradise, regulations on prayer and on fasting – are spread across its 114 chapters. There is a chronological aspect, since the shorter chapters tend to be from early in Muhammad's career (revealed at Makkah), while longer chapters tend to be from later in his career (revealed at Madinah). Traditionally, Surahs (chapters, literally a row or a fence) are identified as Makkan or Madinan. Makkan chapters typically challenge hearers to desist from idolatry, to uphold justice, care for the oppressed and to embrace Islam and Muhammad as God's true revelation. Makkan material more explicitly addresses the social and religious organization of the *ummah*, legal issues including crime and punishment, rules concerning marriage, inheritance, divorce as well as setting out what emerge as distinctive to Islamic religious identity, the *fard* (obligatory) responsibilities of prayer, fasting, pilgrimage and *zakat*. This scheme is not perfect, since 'surahs may sometimes be composite astride that radical divide' (Cragg: 2005: 12). Esack (2005) commented how, after 9/11, sales of translations of the Qur'an rose dramatically. People presumably wanted to know what the book that, allegedly, had sent young men to their deaths really said. Yet, wrote Esack, most probably gave up after a 'few pages, for the Qur'an is a difficult book for "strangers" . . . to negotiate'. Mawdudi, from the opposite spectrum of Islam, similarly wrote: 'a stranger to the Qur'an, on his first approach to it, is baffled when he does not find the enunciation of its theme or its divisions into chapters and verses' (1967: 1:7). In my experience, without preparation and guidance, many non-Muslims find the Qur'an at best opaque, at worst a book that, to put it bluntly, confirms their negativity towards Islam. The challenge to learn some Arabic is thus joined by one to persevere with reading the Qur'an. Any serious participant in Christian–Muslim dialogue will need to develop a rapport with the Qur'an, which is by no means an easy task.

Occasions of Revelation (Asbab al-Nuzul)

Muslims use knowledge of the 'occasions of revelation' to decide whether a Qur'anic verse is meant to be understood as being of universal or of limited applicability. For example, permission at Q33:50 for Muhammad to marry more than the four wives that 4:3 allows other Muslims is not applied universally. Many Muslims interpret 4:3 as only permitting polygamy in limited circumstances and argue that the weight of Qur'anic verses support monogamy (see 30:21). While the message of the Qur'an is universal (7:158), and also definitive, Muslims do not regard every single verse as necessarily binding for all time. Some were revealed to deal with specific incidents in the life of Muhammad. This means that knowledge of the *Sira* (Life of Muhammad) is also involved in studying and understanding the Qur'an. The verse at 5:41 prescribing amputation as the penalty for theft was 'revealed concerning a specific person who had stolen a piece of armour' but this penalty has been taken as universally applicable (Denffer, 1983: 102). There is debate about the general applicability of such verses as 33:55 (on *Purdah*) 33:59 (on *hijab*). Some Muslims understand them to mean that all Muslim women should be veiled and secluded. Others interpret these verses as applicable only to the wives of the Prophet. A major concern of missionaries towards the end of the nineteenth century and at the beginning of the twentieth was that Christians intending to evangelize Muslims be adequately prepared for the task. This need for preparation also applies to Christians who engage in dialogue with Muslims, rather than in polemic or debate.

Most Muslims approach the text from within a history of interpretation, although there is an increasing tendency for some to ignore or by-pass this tradition, especially those often described as 'fundamentalist'. There is a surprising similarity between how some Christians cite the Qur'an and how fundamentalist Muslims use the Qur'an; both understand texts literally and neither refer to the tradition of *tafsir*. This approach was pioneered by two of the most influential Muslim scholars of the twentieth century, Abu'l A'la Mawdudi (d. 1979) and Sayyid Qutb (d. 1966), who 'dismissed much of the exegetical elaboration of the intervening centuries as an unnecessary, or even misleading, accretion of attitudes and opinion . . . what matters is a direct application of the text . . .' (McAuliffe, 2005: 623). Christian conciliators and confrontationists both employ this approach and are often unaware of how Muslims traditionally understand the verses they cite. From the point of view of Christian–Muslim relations, reference to *tafsir* does not necessarily produce a result that is more favourable to a positive attitude, although it can do so. One exegetical device widely used in *tafsir*, although not universally, is *naksh*, the mechanism by which some early Qur'anic verses are cancelled by later revelations. This is based on Q2:106: 'Any message which we annul or consign to oblivion we replace with a better or similar one.' Traditionally, many exegetes have taken the earlier, more sympathetic verses in the Qur'an vis-à-vis Christians and Jews to be cancelled by later, more critical verses.

Three categories

There are upwards of one hundred verses that are directly relevant to Christian–Muslim relations, and many others that have indirect relevance. Three categories of verses can be identified. The first speak of the role of Jesus (or Isa, عيسـى) and of other prophets, identifying their true message as identical with Muhammad's and with that of the Qur'an. The second speak about the role of the earlier *kitab* or scriptures revealed by God through the Prophets, including Jesus. The third category of verses refers directly to Christians and to their deviation from Jesus' message, to their false claims and beliefs. These verses have as their backdrop the Qur'an's own affirmation that it is the criterion of right and wrong, in which there is no doubt, that it represents the complete testament of God's will (see Q3:3–4; 2:2), that Islam is the 'perfect religion' (5:3) and the Muslim *ummah* the best people '*khair umma ukhrijat li*' (3:110). The claim that Islam 'confirms' what was sent before (3:3) and that the Qur'an 'guards' Jesus' 'gospel' (5:48) sounds like an affirmation of the continued validity of Christianity; but 5:48 also says that Christians have departed from their true faith, 'following their vain desire', which represents a negative judgment on Christians. 10:37 describes the Qur'an as a 'fuller explanation' than 'that which went before it' and informs the traditional Muslim view that Islam came to *complete and perfect* Christianity, which means that it cannot be as adequate as Islam. This suggests that Islam supersedes Christianity, in the same way that traditional Christian displacement theology saw itself as superseding, or replacing, Judaism. 3:110 cited above also impacts on Christian–Muslim relations even though it makes no explicit reference to Christians, since, if Muslims are the 'best community evolved for mankind, enjoining what is right and forbidding what is wrong', Christians *are not the best community*. When the same expression 'enjoining what is right and forbidding what is wrong' occurs just a few verses earlier (3:104), there is specific reference to Christians and Jews. They had their 'signs' (see 3:98; 3:105) but 'fell into disputations' and even 'obstructed those who believe'. 3:102 declares, 'O ye who believe, fear Allah as He should be feared, and die not except in a state of Islam', which implies that only Muslims will inherit salvation. 2:145 describes the *ummah* as 'justly balanced' so that it might witness 'over the nations', which also implies superiority, not equality.

The Qur'anic Jesus

The first category – verses that refer explicitly to Jesus – allows the construction of a 'view' of Jesus as a prophet of Islam. While, as Chapter 1 showed, Christians find guidance in the Bible to inform and shape their view of Muhammad, he is not mentioned by name (setting aside Muslim understanding of John 14:16). Many Christians use the biblical texts identified in our last chapter to vilify Muhammad. For Muslims, Jesus is a revered and honoured prophet, after whose name they will say, '*sallahu alayhi wa sallam*' ('Peace Be upon Him') as a mark of respect. Muslims may draw a distinction between the Jesus in whom Christians believe, which many regard as a mythical figure, and the Qur'anic Jesus and some may be much less respectful towards the former Jesus. Deedat, for example, more or less ridicules the Jesus of Christian belief as shall be seen in Chapter 7. Generally, though, Muslims are respectful of Jesus, less respectful towards Christianity.

The Qur'anic verses relating to Jesus are usefully identified and discussed in Parrinder (1977). A popular Muslim discussion of Jesus as Prophet of Islam is 'Ata-ur-Rahim (1977) while the more recent and arguably more scholarly Ruqaiyyah Waris Maqsood, herself a former Christian, wrote *The Mysteries of Jesus* in 2000. Maqsood draws on the controversial scholarship of Kamal Salibi (see 1992) to at least entertain the possibility that the Jesus in whom Christians believe and the Qur'anic Jesus are not identical. Since Muslims almost unanimously believe that the four canonical gospels are not the *Injil* (إنجــيل or Gospel) referred to in the Qur'an, this is an open possibility. Rahim and Deedat accept the authenticity of the Gospel of Barnabas, which they say was written by Paul's companion. Maqsood is less convinced that this document is genuine but considers it to be 'a beautiful and interesting document' (229). However, she does think that the Jesus of Christianity may actually have been derived not from Jeshu of Nazareth (whose existence she does not deny) but from Isa of Arabia, of whom Paul learnt while spending fourteen years there (Galatians 2:1). In Arabia, he 'may have acquired a copy of the Aramaic Gospel which spoke of the Jesus who was 'Isa, a Messiah of the House of Aaron, not the Davidic Jeshu, perhaps one of the precious books of parchment he was so anxious to have sent him in prison in his last years' (2 Timothy 4:13) (154). This would explain the different teachings of Paul and of the Jerusalem leadership and why 'in Paul's writings the historical Jesus is only a shadowy figure, reduced to unimportance by Paul's vision of the Living Christ' (153). Given the common Muslim conviction that the four gospels are not to be confused with the original gospel, Muslim's derive their view of Jesus, whether or not he is identified with the Jesus who at least can be said to stand behind Christian dogma, from the Qur'anic account.

What Jesus Taught

There are references to 'Isa by name, and also as the 'Son of Mary'. He has a number of titles, including *al-Masih* (المسـيح, Messiah), *nabi* (نَـبــي, prophet), *rasul* (رسول, messenger) and *Word* (كلمة, Kalimat). He is also a sign (آيـة, ayah). Like other prophets who were also *rasul*, he was given a *Kitab* (the *Injil*) and Signs to confirm the truthfulness of his message. Q61:6 is an important verse, because it summarizes the orthodox Muslim view of Jesus. It reads:

> And remember Jesus [this is Allah's direct speech to Muhammad] the son of Mary, said, 'O Children of Israel! I am the messenger (*rasul*) of Allah sent to you, confirming The Law [of Moses] which came before me, and giving Glad tidings of a Messenger to come after me, whose name shall be Ahmed.' But when He came to them with clear signs, they said 'This is sorcery'.

5:46 describes Jesus as following in the footsteps of earlier prophets, and as receiving from God the *Injil* wherein was 'guidance and light and confirmation of the Law'. This places Jesus in a sequence of Book-receiving prophets, each of whom conform with the message of their predecessors, since God's will is the same from eternity and for eternity. The Qur'an states at 2:136, referring to Abraham, Ismail, Jacob and the descendants of Jacob, Moses, Jesus and 'all the prophets' as equal in status, 'we make no difference between one and another of them'. Each community of people have messengers (Q22:34), and Allah has sent such messengers in succession. Many have been rejected: 'every time their messenger came to a people, they accused him of falsehood' (23:44). Jesus experienced this, and had to rebuke people. In several passages, Jesus says that he attested or witnessed to the truth of the Law 'which was before' him, and to preach obedience to Allah, thus 'it is Allah who is my Lord and your Lord, so worship Him. This is a way that is straight' (3:50).

The expression 'straight path' (*sirat-ul-mustaqeem*) is a synonym for Islam (see Q 1:6); thus Jesus' true, uncorrupted message was identical with Muhammad's. Jesus' helpers are described as Muslims (Q3:52). At Q43:64 Jesus says, 'For Allah, His is my Lord and your Lord, so worship Him: this is a straight way'. The fairly lengthy treatment of Jesus between verses 42 and 62 concludes with the *shahadah*, Islam's first pillar, 'This is the true account, There is no God except Allah', making it absolutely clear that Jesus was a monotheist who pointed his hearers towards God, not at himself. In the Qur'an, the *shahada* serves an almost sacramental function (to borrow language from Cragg), restoring 'life' to those who utter it. At Q15:29 God breathed his 'spirit' into Adam which, says Ali (2002), represents 'The faculty of God-like knowledge and will' (625, n. 1968). Dulled by the human tendency towards forgetfulness (*nasiyaan*), this 'spirit' is revived by reciting the *shahadah*. The tendency to forgetfulness resulted from Adam's 'slip' or 'lapse' (*zallat*) (2:36). Q3:79 explicitly rejects the possibility that a true prophet could have invited people to worship himself. It is not possible that a man, to whom is given a Book and the office of Prophet, should say to people, 'Worship Me'. On the contrary, he would say, 'Worship Him Who is truly the Cherisher of All'. Nor would a true prophet, such as Jesus, have urged people to take 'angels and prophets for lords and patrons'. This could be a reference to Christian veneration of saints, although this is not clear. Alongside 9:31, which says that as well as taking Jesus as their Lord, Christians also take 'their priests and anchorites' (or monks), it could be a criticism of Christians being overly deferential to their clergy, bishops and archbishops (see Parrinder, 1977: 33). What is clear is that the Qur'anic Jesus did not expect anyone to worship himself. Q4:171 describes him as 'no more than a messenger of Allah (see also 5:75 and 43:59) and His Word which he bestowed on Mary, and a Spirit proceeding from Him (*ruhun minhu*)', so Christians should 'believe in Allah and His messengers, and not say "Trinity"'. They should 'desist' from this. The verse then refers to Christian belief in Jesus' sonship: 'far exalted is Allah above having a son.' He is above the 'partners ascribed to Him' (7:190). Jesus had not 'disdained from serving Allah', so neither should those who claim to be followers of Jesus (4:172). Q5:116–117 removes any doubt that Jesus could have claimed to be God's son, or a partner with him in a Trinity of Gods:

Allah will say, "O Jesus . . . did you say unto men, Worship me and my mother . . ." [and] he will say, "never could I say such a thing . . . You know what is in my heart . . . Never did I say anything to them except what you commanded . . . I said, Worship Allah, my Lord and Your Lord."

5:73 says that those who say 'Allah is one of three' blaspheme, for 'there is no God but God'. Note, though, the association of Mary, Jesus and God as partners, not Father, Son and Spirit, which has led to speculation that some Christians in Arabia may have worshiped such a Trinity, accepted by W. H. T. Gairdner (1873–1928). Gairdner argued that the only way by which Christianity of the time of Muhammad had reached Arabia was through false gospels and other literature of some heretical sects, which denied the divine sonship and the redeeming death of Christ (1920: 39). Tisdall agreed that Muhammad never had contact with pure gospel Christianity and that it was largely due to the false forms which the faith had then almost universally assumed in the Arabian peninsula, isolated from mainstream Christianity, that the rise of Islam is really due (1905: 140). The source of Jesus creating a bird from clay (see Q3:49), suggested Tisdall, was the Arabic *Gospel of the Infancy* (175: see *Gospel of the Infancy*: 36).[2] What these verses show is a Jesus who faithfully proclaimed the message of obedience to One God, and the distinction between right and wrong that God demands. He never asked people to worship himself; he never described himself as the 'Son of God'; nor did he speak of a Trinity.

What Jesus Did

The above-cited verses present the Qur'anic version of what Jesus said. Other verses in the Qur'an describe some of the works of Jesus: what he did. Here, he is described as performing miracles, including the bird-miracle mentioned above. This occurs both at Q3:49 and at 5:110. 3:49 also describes him as healing lepors and as restoring sight to the blind (as he does in the four gospels) although he does so 'by Allah's leave'. 13:38 says that all signs are given by Allah's leave. This could be emphasized to avoid the impression that Jesus is superior to Muhammad, who was not given leave to perform miracles. Although the biographical material records many miracles, in the Qura'nic response to the demand that Muhammad prove his claims by performing a miracle is the assertion that it is itself a miracle and requires no such supernatural confirmation (2:23). The Qur'an suggests that people who require supernatural signs before they will believe can only have a shallow faith, not one grounded in reason. Muhammad, says 29:50, is a 'plain Warner', not a worker of portents. When people ask 'why he does not come with a Sign', he is to say that Allah 'has made clear The Signs to those who hold firmly to Faith in their hearts' (2:118). Belief rests on inner conviction, not on external miracles. Muhammad was a Warner who summoned people with 'wisdom and beautiful preaching' (16:125). It is enough that God 'has sent the scripture.' This description of Muhammad implies that, unlike Jesus, he did not require miracles. Of course, in the canonical gospels, when Jesus was challenged to perform a miracle, he refused to do so just to save himself or to impress King Herod (Luke 23:8). The Qur'an may seem to possess what Cragg calls 'a belligerence, a will to dominate and Islamise the world' (2005: 10) but it also appeals again and again to human reason. The demand for spectacular proof, such as the causing of a spring to gush, or a river to suddenly appear in the middle of a garden of date trees, is ridiculed (17:90f.). The Qur'an is itself sufficient if people read and study it; 'the whole of mankind and jinns could not produce the like of this Qur'an, even if they backed each other up with mutual support' (17:88). Moreover, it is plain and easy to understand (44:58). Muhammad, says Q5:19, was sent by God as a Messenger after a break in the succession of Prophets, least any one say that 'no bringer of glad tidings came to us, no Warner from evil'. He is a 'bringer of glad tidings and a Warner'.

Like Jesus, Muhammad receives a Book that confirms previous scriptures; 'the Revelation to thy heart', brought down 'by Gabriel' by 'Allah's will is a confirmation of what went before, guidance and glad tidings for those who believe' (2:97). Only the perverse reject the Signs that God has sent down (2:98). Muslims regard all prophets as equal but revere Muhammad as *primus inter pares*, first among equals. This is based on the understanding that prophecy ended with him, since he is the seal of prophecy (33:40). His life is also the best guide (33:21). Several verses of the Qur'an, though, speak of 'some' being 'raised in degrees' above others (see 6:165; 12:76; 43:32; 58:11) which leaves open the possibility that Muhammad is more exalted than other prophets, as well as that some people within the Muslim community might command more respect than others, or claim to speak with special authority.

Esack points out how *Ulama* (religious scholars) have claimed the exclusive right to interpret the Qur'an and he is quite open about the influence of Christian liberation theology on his own thinking. He encourages lay people to read the Qur'an for themselves, to re-think its message and meaning in their own context, so that they can 'forge hermeneutical keys that will enable' them 'to read the text in such a way as to advance the liberation of all people' (1997: 78)

Jesus is also described as feeding people, at his mother's request, by asking God to send down a Table, which God did so that the people might believe, and to show that he is 'the best of providers' (5:114–15). This has been compared with the Feeding of the Five Thousand (see Parrinder, 1983: 88, referring to the Muslim scholar Tabari. Tabari (d. 923) was an eminent historian, jurist and exegete whose work still carries considerably weight). Some Christians take this as a reference to the Lord's Supper. The story at 5:114 is also reminiscent of John 2, where Jesus turns water into wine after his mother drew his attention to the fact that the wine had run out at the wedding party. Q5:110 reads: 'I [Allah] strengthened thee with the Holy Spirit so that thou didst speak to people in infancy and in maturity.' At Q19:28–30, Jesus speaks from the cradle, saying 'I am indeed a servant of Allah, who has given me a revelation and made me a prophet'. The child continued:

> He has made me blessed . . . and has enjoined on me prayer and charity as long as I shall live . . . he has made me kind to my mother . . . so, peace is on me the day I was born, the day that I die and the day that I shall be raised to life again. Such was Jesus [the passage continues] . . . it is a statement of truth, about which they dispute in vain.

The latter clearly refers to Christian belief in Jesus' divinity, because verse 35 says, 'it is not fitting that Allah should beget a son'. Jesus is described as *'abd* (عبد, servant) in several passages, which stresses that he is subject or subordinate to God, not equal with Him.

Reference to the Word and to the Holy Spirit appear at Q4:171 and in a number of other passages, such as 2:87, 'we strengthened Jesus by the Holy Spirit', and 3:40, where in the annunciation account Mary is told that she will give birth to 'Jesus' who will be 'held in honour in this world and in the next'. The angels tell her that they have 'Glad tidings of a Word from Him', whose name is Jesus. Incidentally, most Muslims accept the Virgin Birth of Jesus,

based both on the following verse, when Mary asks how can she
have a son when no man has touched her, and Allah replies that
He only has to say, 'be', and it is; and also on Q3:59, which says
that the likeness of Jesus before Allah is 'that of Adam', whom he
'created from clay'. This implies that neither Adam, nor Jesus, had a
human father. Adam had no human mother either. God in the Qur'an
enabled Mary to conceive without having sexual intercourse but God
is not Jesus' father. The Qur'an's characteristic description of Jesus is
as 'Son of Mary', a designation rarely used in Christianity (Parrinder,
1977: 23), which perhaps serves to emphasize his humanity. Jesus'
virgin birth is therefore upheld by most Muslims (although not by
all) but for them it does not mean that Jesus' status was ontologically
different from that of any other human being. There has been much
discussion about the meaning of references to Jesus as a 'word and
a spirit' (روح, ruh) from God. The description of Jesus as 'Word'
sounds like John's pre-existing Logos. It would be more usual for
the Qur'an to describe Jesus not as a Word but as receiving a Word,
which is how the first Prophet, Adam, is described: 'then Adam learnt
from his Lord Words of Inspiration' (2:37). Parrinder comments that
the description of Jesus as a 'spirit' from God (4:171) sits oddly with
Christian belief that Jesus was guided by the Spirit, blessed by the
Spirit at his baptism, but that the Spirit is not identical to him. He
remarks that one Muslim understanding of Jesus as both 'word' and
'spirit' from God is that he came with a word (47) or that he 'is a
prophecy' and that the word ruh (spirit) could also mean 'mercy',
thus 'Jesus is a mercy from God' (49). Cragg points out that it does
not help dialogue when well-meaning Christians try to find 'more
theology in the Qur'an than it actually yields', such as seeing there
a Christian view of Jesus as the 'word of God', which is not present
(cited by Zebiri, 1997: 216). Jesus as servant of God fits Jesus' self-
description at Q19:30, that he is 'a servant of Allah, who has given
him a Book and made him a prophet'. Jesus is also called al-Masih,
which occurs in eleven passages. 5:17 describes as blasphemy the
view that Allah is the Messiah (see also 5:72). Christians do not call
God Messiah but the logic is clear: if Jesus is God and the Messiah as
well, then God is also Jesus and Messiah. Here, the Qur'an conflates
Jesus as Messiah with Jesus as the second person of the Trinity.
The Qur'anic use of al-Masih appears to be a title rather than a
reference to Jesus as the apocalyptic Messiah expected by some
Jews. Commenting on the title al-Masih, Parrinder (1977) remarks:
'the interpretation of the Messianic concept in a special kingly or

historical manner' has hardly been discussed 'in the Muslim world'. He continues to point out that in popular 'usage the name Messiah is prefixed with the word al-Sayyid, "the Lord", which is a mark of honour' used especially of Muhammad and his descendants (33–4). Thus, al-Masih seems to be a title of respect. This is also consistent with how the Greek Χρήστος (Christos) was used in the Gentile world outside Christianity's birthplace, where 'the term "Messiah"' had no meaning, since Gentiles were not expecting a Messiah (33).

The Crucifixion

Most problematic of all from a Christian point of view is the Qur'an's denial (some say apparent denial) of the Crucifixion, so central to Christian theology. Q4:157, into which Christians have read Docetic influence, says that the Jews are wrong to claim that they killed Jesus, because he did not die, nor was he crucified; rather 'Allah raised him to himself' (58). Almost all Muslims believe that the crucifixion did not occur or that a substitute was executed in Jesus' place (popularly, Judas of Iscariot fills this role). Jesus, then, did not die. Instead of dying, rising and ascending as in the Christian sequence of events, he was born, lived then was raised to heaven like Enoch and Elijah in the Bible, without dying. However, 4:159 and 19:33 mention Jesus' death, so at some point he must die. 3:55 and 4:159 clearly attributes Jesus a role on the Day of Judgment. A popular Muslim belief is that he will return to earth before the Last Days, marry and have children, help defeat the forces of evil, then die a natural death. This gives us the sequence of birth, ascension, death, as opposed to birth, death, resurrection and ascension. However, based on Q19:33 when Jesus speaks of the day he was born, the day he will die and the day he will be raised up – in this order – some Christians argue that the Qur'an does not deny the Crucifixion, only that it was the Jews who killed him. Translating the word 'mutawaff'ika' (bring thy term to an end) as 'cause thee to die' at 3:55 allows this view, thus 'I caused thee to die then raised you to myself' (Parrinder, 1977: 106). However, 4:195's 'there is none of the People of the Book but must believe in Him before he dies' can also suggest an End-Time death, meaning that Jesus has not yet died; therefore Christians actually believe in a Saviour who has not yet, but who will one day, die. 3:55 ends, referring to the Day of Resurrection, with "I [Allah] will judge between you the matters on which you dispute' which appears to leave resolution of Christian–Muslim disagreement on the Cross to the final judgement. Christians argue that Islam's view of sin and of human nature does not demand a perfect sacrifice, or an atoning death, and thus the Cross is regarded as abhorrent. An *hadith* says that when he returns, Jesus will destroy the Cross, slaughter the pigs (Christians fail to uphold Jesus' teaching regarding what God has declared edible, Q3:49), and defeat Dajjal (Satan's deputy) (*Sahih al-Bukhari*, 3:425). God vindicates His prophets. It was due to plots against Jesus that God had to intervene, and rescue him (3:54). Q5:17, though, says that had Allah wanted to 'destroy Christ', he could have done so, 'for Allah has power over all things'. The syntax of Q4:157 and also the etymology of the phase, *'wa-lakin shubbiha lahum'* (it seemed so to them) invites speculation and manipulation to support the view that Jesus really was crucified.[3] However, even if the text can be made to bear this interpretation, Islam has no place for the sacrificial death of a perfect human in order to atone for human sin. Within the Qur'anic world view, this is unnecessary and alien (see Marshall, 2001:15 and also Zebiri, 1997: 216–217). Rashid Rida (1865–1935), though, thought that Jesus did die and was then raised (see McAuliffe, 1991: 141).

The Qur'an on the Bible

The second set of passages, not unrelated to those that specifically mention Jesus, refer to the earlier scriptures, such as the Torah and Injil, both of which are part of the Christian canon. Indeed, the above discussion mentioned scriptures on several occasions, and how both the Injil and the Qur'an are said to confirm what came earlier, with the difference that it is the Qur'an that confirms the Gospel, not vice-versa. Muslims often refer to the Qur'an as the Last or Final Testament. The Qur'an can be said to confirm the truthfulness of earlier scriptures, which therefore remain valid. This, though, is not how most Muslims regard them. These verses, too, are often in the context of reference to peoples of the books, or to Christians, so relate to the third category of passages. Some of these verses concern Jews and their faithfulness to the Books that they received. Typical here are Q2:83–86 and 2:140 and 3:71. Of these passages, the first two references are set within discussion of God's covenant with the Hebrew people, although Jesus is mentioned in the next verse, 87.

Verse 85 says that the people only believe in 'part of the book', thus they neglect or ignore much of the revelation they received. Such people 'buy the life of this world at the price of the hereafter'. This verse suggests, then, that the Hebrew people were not altogether faithful to their Law. Verse 89 (following the specific reference to Jesus) says that when people receive a Book (which could be taken as a reference to the Gospel) they 'refuse to believe in it', which seems to exempt Christians, who claim to believe in the Gospel. 1:140 refers to Jews and to Christians who 'conceal the testimony they have from Allah'. 3:71 refers to 'people of the book' who 'clothe truth with falsehood' and who 'conceal the truth'. These and other verses that speak of Jews and Christians as 'concealing', 'hiding' or simply ignoring the 'truth' revealed in their books, by their prophets, was formulated classically as the doctrine of *tahrif* (تحريف), that is, the corruption of scripture. The 'verbal form of *tahrif*' occurs, says Michel (1984), four times (Q4:46; 5:13; 5:41 and 42, 75). Some Muslims understand *tahrif* to refer to the textual corruption of the documents of the Bible in order to support Jewish and Christian doctrines (*tahrif- al-lafz*). Some see *tahrif* as misinterpretation, or, as suggested at 2:85, as selective belief in scripture (*tahrif al- ma'na*). In this view, the actual text of the Bible is still revealed truth (see Ibn Taymiyyah, 1984: 89; 225). Yet, given that the Qur'an confirms the content of the earlier Books, and given that there is some degree of suspicion that they have been tampered with, Muslims usually take the view that when you possess the book in which there is no doubt, why waste time reading books about which there is doubt? Some apply the charge of *tahrif* only to the Jews though the verses discussed above appear to include Christians. When critical Biblical scholarship reached Muslims in the nineteenth century, many said that they had been saying all along that the New Testament is really the work of the editors and redactors of the Early Church, who projected their pagan-influenced theology onto the lips of Jesus. Since the four gospels read more like *hadith* (eye witness accounts of what Muhammad said and did) rather than the Qur'an (Allah's direct speech), many speculate that the authentic or original *Injil* is lost, or that the Gospel of Barnabas is the legitimate gospel.

Ibn Taymiyyah, who will be discussed in Chapter 4, saw himself as standing in continuity with the earliest Muslims, the *salaf-al-salihoon*. To introduce new concepts into Islam was anathema. On the gospels, he pointed out that those which Christians possess are not true scriptures, since 'it is not stated that they are the speech of God, nor that Christ received from God; rather they transmit some things from the speech of Christ, some things from his deeds and miracles'. Thus, 'they are of the same nature as the sayings and deeds of the Prophet related about him by the hadith-collectors, the biographers, and the narrators of his campaigns' but 'these latter are not a Qur'an' (235). Much Christian missionary effort has been invested in translating the Bible into those languages, such as Farsi, Urdu, Bengali as well as Arabic, that Muslims speak. Yet this does not take account of the fact that, because of the charge of distortion, most Muslims 'believe . . . the previous scriptures have no contemporary validity', in effect believing 'that the only valid scripture is the Qur'an' (Esack, 2002: 49).

Qur'anic Christians – confrontational interpretations

The third category, verses that specifically refer to Christians, also overlaps with the second genre. For example, the word 'Christian' occurred at 2:140 and in close proximity to 3:71, four verses earlier. Christians are sometimes subsumed into the category of Scriptuary (*ahlu-al-kitab*), sometimes called Nasara (15 times; Parrinder, 1977: 153). This term was probably used for Christians in Arabia and interestingly some Christian scholars think this may have been used by primitive Christians (see Acts 24:5). Parrinder comments, 'there was a Jewish-Christian sect known as Nazaraeans, which used the Gospel according to the Hebrews'. 'However', he continues, 'in Syriac, Christians were called Nasraye and this spread into parts of the eastern empires and was applied exclusively to Christians' (153). Some of the verses that address people of the book as Scriptuaries, or Christians directly, are among those described by McAuliffe as having been 'persistently extracted to serve as proof-texts of Muslim religious tolerance' (1991: 4). Ibn Taymiyyah refuted the Christian interpretations of 3:199, 5:66, 5:82, 28:52–55 and 57:27. These were cited as evidence of a Qur'anic regard, or approval, of Christians by among others Bishop Paul of Antioch (1140–1180). Some scholars refer to certain passages as the verses of friendship, of which Q5:48 and 5:82–3 are examples.

Q2:62 and 5:69 say that those who believe (*mu'minun*), and Jews, and Christians and Sabeans, who believe in Allah and in the Last Day and act righteously have nothing to fear, nor any reason to grieve. Other verses suggesting approval for Christians include 2:139; 42:15; 29:46, 3:199, 49:13 and 57:27. This last verse, like 5:82–83, can appear to praise monasticism, which has generated discussion since Islam does not approve of celibacy. Parrinder cites Razi (d. 1209), who regarded monasticism as a Christian innovation, not commanded by Jesus. However, it did develop from a genuine 'desire for the satisfaction of God' (158). Q9:31–5 accuses some monks of 'wrongly devouring the possessions of others', and of laying up treasures for themselves without 'spending it for the sake of God'.

That 29:46 was taken by some Muslims at an early period as indicative of how they should approach Christians in conversation or argument is instanced by a reference in Abdallah the Hashemite's letter to Al-Kindy (approximately 820–30 CE). Citing the verse, the Hashemite (said to be Caliph al-Ma'mun's cousin) expressed the view that 'it was in full accord with the teachings of the Prophet' for him to 'invite' al-Kindy 'to embrace Islam, and to discuss in a kindly and gracious spirit the merits of their respective creeds' (Muir, 1887: 39; see Chapter 3). In sharp contrast to these 'verses of friendship' (*mawaddah*) are those of Opprobrium, or hostility ('*adawah*) which warn Muslims not to take Christians as friends (5:82), not to trust them (3:75), or to 'fight against them until they agree to pay the *jizya* tax and to accept humiliation' (9:29). *Mu'minum* was the term used for Muhammad's followers before the *hijrah* (622) and the revelation of Islam as the name of the religion (Q5:3). Thus, Paul of Antioch interpreted the verse to mean that Christians, who believe as do Muslims in God and in the Last Day and who live moral lives, are to be counted among the righteous (Ibn Taymiyyah: 90). 'By this statement,' said Ibn Taymiyyah, summarizing Christian claims, 'the Qur'an makes all people . . . equal' (Ibn Taymiyyah, 1984: 246). Two confrontational-inclined Muslim understandings of the relationship between these two genres of verses have been consistently argued. The first uses the doctrine of abrogation. Usually, abrogation is taken to imply a change in circumstances that required a fresh revelation. Muslims point out that many of the verses suggesting that Muslims and Christians worship the same God, and that they should enjoy fraternal relations with each other, occur early in the career of Muhammad. This is subject to debate about when verses were revealed. However, many scholars argue that Q3:85 (or 5:82) abrogated Q2:62 (and thus also 5:69). Argument is complex. Surah 2 is generally taken to be late, not early – although in chapter 5, verse 82 is later than 69. Nonetheless, says Esack, 'This is a very significant opinion attributed to Ibn 'Abbas and a group among the exegetes by al-Tabari' (1997: 162). Its wide acceptance is indicated by inclusion in Hilali et al. (1996: 14; 21). Ibn Taymiyyah, among others, applies the second interpretation. Of 2:62 he writes that Christians and Jews are not praised by this verse, since it 'refers only to those who believe in Muhammad, those Jews who followed Moses, that is, those who followed Moses before its abrogation and corruption, and the Christians who followed Christ, that is, those who followed his religion before its abrogation and corruption' (246). The identity of the Sabeans attracted discussion. Ibn Taymayyah saw them as Arabs who followed a type of Judaism. Ali (2002) describes them as people in the Yemen who 'worshipped the planets and stars' and also as Gnostic Christians who claimed to be Knowers of the Great Light, who dressed in white and often immersed themselves (33). McAuliffe cites Rida that the Sabeans were nearer the spirit of true Christianity than Christians were 'because they practiced asceticism (*alzud*) and self-abasement' (113). Ibn Kathir thought they were a people who lacked a specific religion, living 'according to their Fitrah (instinctual nature)' (2:250). He took it as axiomatic that the *Mu'min* of 2:62 were those who followed Muhammad and that, while before God sent Muhammad, 'every person who followed the guidance of their own Prophet was on the correct path', after Muhammad (citing Ibn Abbas) God only accepts 'any deed or work from anyone' that 'conforms to the Law of Muhammad' (2:249). Anyone persisting in the religion of an earlier prophet can no longer be considered to be following their Prophet, since 'they have disbelieved in the master the mightiest, the last and most perfect prophet'. If they were genuine followers of the earlier prophet, their faith 'would have directed them to believe in Muhammad' (2:405 commenting on Q:29)

Islam as a Superior Religion

McAuliffe's (1991) detailed analysis of classical and modern *tafsir* of these passages concludes that, 'The commentators . . . make a clear distinction between true Christians, a tiny minority, and those who have appropriated and propagated a corrupted form of the religion of Jesus' (286). In this view, this minority of true believers would have embraced Islam, since for such people 'there was not, nor could there be, any incongruity between' the two prophets, Jesus and Muhammad. Rather, 'those who had faithfully followed the former would necessarily be eager to welcome the latter'. Qur'anic Christians are Christians who 'welcomed' Muhammad and 'readily submitted to the final disclosure of which he was the bearer . . . those who did not become *muslimun* . . . did not remain *mu'minun* in this latest manifestation of God's guidance' and ceased to be true followers of Jesus, or true Christians (288). The Christians whose righteousness is acceptable to God, who have no need to fear Judgement Day, whom Muslims can take as friends, are former Christians who embraced Islam during the lifetime of the Prophet. Christianity, as a religious system, cannot remain valid, since 3:85 says that unless you die a Muslim you will not be among the 'saved'. An *hadith* attributed to Muhammad confirms this; referring to his Persian scribe and convert from Christianity, Salman the Farsi, Muhammad said, 'whoever died in the religion of Jesus and dies in submission to God . . . before hearing me will be fine, but whoever hears me today and does not believe in me is already damned' (cited in McAuliffe: 99). Ibn Kathir (1301–1373) followed this line of argument: 'after Muhammad had been sent, nothing that was not in accord with his *shari'ah* was acceptable to God', but before Muhammad's appearance, 'everyone who followed the messenger in his own era, lived a rightly guided life on the way to salvation (*najah*)' (ibid.: 120).

The Charge of *Shirk*

According to the majority Muslim opinion, says McAuliffe, 'Belief in Muhammad' is essential for salvation, since because 'all other religions have been superseded their salvific efficacy' is 'rendered null and void' (7). Acknowledgment of Muhammad as prophet, the second declaration of the *Shahadah*, was, for Ibn Taymiyyah, non-negotiable, and Muhammad had 'declared Christians unbelievers, commanded *jihad* against them' and was 'quit of them and their religion' (105; 250). The idea that the Qur'an has a regard for Christians, or represents them as standing in a right relationship with God, is absurd. Furthermore, the charge of *shirk* remains, despite the Christian claim that the Qur'an exempts them from this (for example, at 98:1, 22:17 and 5:82) (245). Verses apparently exempting them from *shirk* refer to the originally pure, uncorrupted form of Christianity while contemporary Christians are guilty of *shirk*, since they 'do not follow pure *tawhid*' and they venerate 'statues', which Jesus had never commanded. They are included among idolaters at 9:31 (245). Christians, for Ibn Taymiyyah, were 'associators' (*mushrikun*). Q 3:48's 'striving in virtue' between Christians and Muslims found no place in Ibn Taymiyyah's scheme.

Conciliatory View

Muslim and Christian conciliators are much more comfortable with the verses of friendship than with the verses of hostility. However, they have to deal with the latter as well. The abrogation theory, advocated by exclusivists, removes the need for them to regard the verses of friendship as problematical for their view of Islam's superiority. These verses simply reflected Muhammad's hope and expectation, early in his career, that Jews and Christians would accept him as a genuine prophet, and embrace Islam. When this did not happen, Allah responded to the changed context by condemning the people of the books for their disbelief. They should have welcomed Muhammad but failed to do so, just as they had failed to honour prophets in the past. A small number of them were true believers, and became Muslim. Ibn Taymayyah's exegesis allows a greater focus on critical verses, since the verses of friendship in his view do not apply to any living Christian, only to dead ones. Not all Muslims agree. Among recent writers Muhammad Talbi, Farid Esack and M. M. Taha[4] can be cited. Rida parted company from the majority in his interpretation of the relevant passages. He entertained the possibility that some non-Muslims could be counted among the righteous. He did not doubt Islam's superiority as an 'amelioration of Christianity', just 'as Christianity is an amelioration of Judaism' (McAuliffe: 230). Yet Christians have been ill served by their leaders, whose 'thrust for power and temporal domination' blinded them to the reality that Islam improves on Christianity. Similarly, sectarian rivalry between Muslims and Christians has hindered the process by which a genuine friendship should and could evolve. 'The doctrine of Trinity', he suggested, is actually so 'unfathomable and incomprehensible' to most Christians that it does not really distance Christians from Islam. The number of actual Christians who qualify for Qur'anic praise is small but nonetheless salvation does not depend on external identification with any single religious community, 'for Allah does not favor one group while mistreating another' (Rida, 1980: 336). 'Salvation', he wrote, 'is not to be found in religious sectarianism but in true belief and righteous conduct'. Thus, 'Muslim, Jewish or Christian aspirations to religious importance are no consequence to Allah, nor are they the basis upon which judgments are made' (ibid.). Referring to 2:62, he links this verse with 2:38 and includes people of the book as 'believers' (see Esack, 1997: 165). Rida had some harsh criticisms of Christians, too, to whom he referred as 'the worst people of earth, arrogant, greedy and manipulative of the world's destinies' (McAuliffe, 113). Rida was writing in the context of Arab dealings with the impact of European colonialism, which coloured his thought. He was emphatic, however, that people who never heard of Muhammad, for example in the Americas, 'are definitely saved' since God will 'hold those to whom no revelation has been granted accountable on the basis of their thoughts and beliefs about truth and goodness and their opposites' (ibid.: 114–15). Rida began as a disciple of the Egyptian modernist, Muhammad Abduh (1849–1905) but became more traditional, self-identifying as a *salafist*, as had Ibn Taymiyya, whose thought he did much to revive. The *salafists* regard themselves as true to the original, pure Islam of the pious generations closest to Muhammad.

Esack self-identifies as a progressive Muslim and builds on Rida and others to argue in favour of what he calls the 'obvious meaning' of 2:62, that counts Christians and Jews as among those who have no cause to fear, without viewing them as converts to Islam. Initially trained as a traditional Islamic scholar in Pakistan, earning the title 'Maulana' (master), Esack went on to complete his doctorate at Birmingham University, also studying Bible in Germany. He developed his ideas about interfaith collaboration and the priority of liberation during the anti-apartheid struggle in his native South Africa. He thinks that the classical exegetes perform linguistic gymnastics to force the texts to yield an exclusive meaning (1997: 147). Since all Muhammad's followers had converted, why should some Muslims be singled out and placed in a separate category? Thus, if the 'those who believe' refers to Muslims (on which all agree), why would some Muslims then be referred to as if they represented a distinct 'socia-religious category'? There is, he says, no evidence that converts 'existed as a social-religious category apart from the earlier Muslims, which would have warranted their exclusion from the category of "those who have faith"' (164). While Islam as a political system developed a limited system of tolerance towards Christians and other religious, book-possessing peoples, allowing them to maintain separate structures, Islam has 'failed to accept that the faithful adherents of these religions will also attain salvation' (159). Effectively, Islam has dealt with Christians and others as social entities, not as religious communities. 'Notwithstanding the present day use of texts such as Qur'an 3:19 and 39:22 to affirm the superiority of Islam over other faiths', says Esack, 'the universal underpinnings in the term *islam*, lead one to the understanding that the text embraces all of those who submit to the will of God' (133). Here he uses the term '*islam*' in the sense of submission to God, rather than as identification with the social-religious community of Islam, thus the non-capitalization. He is close to an inclusivist Christian view, articulated especially in Roman Catholic writing, that the 'true church' is not identical with any single visible ecclesial community. Esack uses similar language when he speaks of 'reified-islam', that is, the organized, visible community of people who pray five times daily, fast during Ramadan and observe all the external obligations, and of 'non-reified *islam* . . .' to which people who serve truth, believe in God, and live righteous lives (those described at Q2:62) belong, whether they know it or not. As for Rahner, a non-Christian was an anonymous or non-baptized Christian, so for Esack a non-Muslim can be a 'muslim'. Citing from the classical scholar al-Tabari (d. 923), he points out that even in his work, 'it is evident that *din* [religion, the word used in the exclusive text 3:85] is viewed as an active response to the will of God rather than ethno-social membership of a particular group' (Esack, 1997: 133).

The Verses of Hostility: A Conciliatory View ·

Turning to the verses of hostility and also those accusing Christians and Jews of *tahrif*, Esack (2005) points out that many such verses refer to 'a party of them', rather than to all Christians or Jews: 2:109, 'quite a number of the people of the book turn back to infidelity'; 3:75, 'a party of them knowingly perverted the word of Allah', 5:66, 'there is a party on the right course, but many follow an evil path'; 57:26, 'some of them were on the right path but many became rebellious', and that some verses refer to 'a party' positively, such as 'there are currently among the people of the book those who believe in Allah' (3:199). He argues that neither the verses of friendship nor of hostility refer indiscriminately to all peoples of the book. Rather, the former refer to the righteous among them, the latter to the hypocrites, and also to those whose own religious arrogance stands between themselves and doing God's will in the world. Verses such as 3:67, 'Abraham was not a Jew, nor yet a Christian but he was true in faith', and 2:111, 'and they say, "none shall enter Paradise unless he be a Jew or a Christian"' represent a narrow, exclusive religious pride that divides person from person and elevates the wearing of a religious label above conformity with God's will. True faith wears no label, but people who possess this 'spend of their abundance in love for their kin, for orphans, for the needy, for wayfarers, and for the ransom of slaves and practice regular charity' (2:177).

The Qur'an rightly challenges religious arrogance, and castigates those whose religion is divorced from conduct, which runs counter to its own profound and uncompromising concern for righteousness, especially towards the poor and oppressed (*mustad'afun*). Q3:98–101 criticizes those who make the straight path crooked, who cause others to stumble, who refuse to recognize the truth yet who claim to be walking that path. Such people are the *kufr*, unbelievers, against whom the Qur'an is hostile. Numerous verses demand care of the needy. All who orient their lives towards selfless service are 'muslim'. Some hypocrites, claiming to be godly, even urge others to 'refrain from . . . kindness'. Such people fail to feed the needy (Q89:17–18). Pointing to such verses as 5:48, 2:148 and 29:46, all of which can be understood to affirm religious pluralism as intended by God, he rejects the exclusive interpretation of 2:62 as contradictory: 'the Qur'an is explicit in its acceptance of religious pluralism' and, 'having derided the petty attempts to appropriate God' (as in 3:67), 'it is inconceivable that the Qur'an should itself engage in this' (159). Citing 5:48, that God will adjudicate about those matters on which the people of the book differ, he comments: 'If one supposes that this text refers to the pre-Muhammadan communities whose paths are acknowledged as valid, pure and divinely ordained for a specific period, as the doctrine of supercessionism holds, then there is no question of the Muhammadan community differing with them, nor a need for information regarding the differences' (169). The definition of *iman* (faith) at Q8:2–4 sounds generic: 'the believers are those whose hearts tremble with awe when God is mentioned . . . who are constant in prayer, spend on others out of their wealth'. Your 'real friends (*wilayah*)', says Esack (2005), citing Q5:55, are those who pray regularly and give to charity generously, which does not obviously exclude non-Muslims as *wilayah* (181). Allah *could* have made all people one nation, but chose not to. Instead, he revealed different but valid paths (5:48; see also 6:108; 10:99; 42:8). Esack points out that the Qur'an permits Muslims to marry Christian women and also to eat their food, which is inconsistent with the idea that 'enmity' must be 'regarded as the norm in Muslim–Other relations' (160). A verse such as 5:8 summons Muslims to make peace-building and justice-creating their principal aim and not to allow 'hatred of others' to detract them from this course: 'let not hatred of other make you swerve to wrong and depart from justice. Be just: that is next to Piety: and fear Allah.' Another classical scholarly devise used to resolve apparent textual conflict was to identify where the weight of Qur'anic verses lies. Esack refers to the 'weight of Qur'anic' verses when he says that the Qur'an is life-affirming, not warlike (2005: 192).

God, then, can be 'found' in other faiths. Esack still maintains that Islam's message is universal but argues that while pagans and hypocrites are to be 'called' to embrace Islam, Christians and others who have a valid *din* (religion) are to be challenged to be more faithful to the 'revelation' they have received. This is somewhat similar to Newbigin's view of the missionary calling, which leaves the 'result' of proclamation in God's hands, accepting that different people respond differently according to their circumstances. Yet in this view other faiths represent more than an unfulfilled seeking. Non-Muslim faiths are not human constructs but revealed and 'traced out paths'. Whether this is a pluralist theology – salvation is acquired within, or mediated by, each religion – or an inclusivist theology – people whose spiritual journey takes them along a path that approximates or resembles the Muslim path are saved – is debatable. Are Christians, then, saved because of their faith in Jesus – indeed because Jesus died on the Cross – or because they participate in the same religious life as Muslims, praying, giving generously to charity, serving others without wearing the label 'Muslim'? From a Christian perspective, it is not 'work' but 'faith' that saves, while for Muslims it is submission to God's will, which Muslims believe is possible because we are not born sinful. However, most Muslims would agree with Newbigin, indeed with Calvin, that salvation is never a human work but God's free gift of grace, for He is '*arahman arahim*', a God of mercy. Q42:8 reads: 'Allah admits whom he will to His grace.' The criticism that Christians exaggerate Jesus' importance by exceeding the bounds of their religion (5:77), transforming him from a Prophet who pointed people towards God into a deity, remains. So does the Muslim critique of Trinity, a major issue in Christian–Muslim dialogue. Q4:171, perhaps originally revealed during an exchange between Muhammad and a Christian bishop, leaves open the basic question whether Christians and Muslims worship the same 'God'.

Chapter 3

The Traditional Christian Confrontational Approach towards Islam: Classical Contributions

This chapter discusses John of Damascus, Al-Kindy, and concludes with the work of Karl G. Pfander. The historical gap between contributions suggests that this approach to Islam has characterized much Christian–Muslim encounter. It could be debated whether confrontation started before conciliation. Both have long histories. The first historical figure who may be considered conciliatory was probably Mar Timothy, who engaged in dialogue with Caliph al-Mahdi (ruled 775–785), while John probably died in the year 749, which means that confrontation came first. John's tone was not markedly strident, and he primarily wrote for Christians to guide their polemic with Muslims.

John of Damascus Sets the Agenda

John's Background

The precise date of John's birth is unknown. Sahas (1972) discusses possible dates in the context of the story that John was a childhood companion of Caliph Yazid, the second Umayyad and the sixth Sunni caliph. Sahas thinks this unlikely, though not impossible, arguing for 652 CE as John's birth date, which makes him about 15 years younger than Yazid (ruled 680–683). John's family, the Mansurs of Damacus, held high public office as ministers of finance both before and after the Muslim conquest of their city. John's father served under the caliph Abd al-Malik (684–705) as chief advisor in Damascus. This may even have been a more or less hereditary post, because a Mansur (probably John's great-grandfather) held a similar post under the Byzantine Emperor Heraclius (ruled 610–641), Muhammad's own adversary. John is said to have received a 'Saracen' education until he was 12', and according to some sources 'attended school with Prince Yazid I' (Sahas: 40). When he was 12, his father acquired a Sicilian Catholic monk, Father Cosmas, as his tutor. Cosmas, whom the elder Mansur freed, and who later became bishop of Mauma, taught John music, physics, astronomy and theology (Sahas, 1972: 41). After his father's death, John assumed the post of *protosymbulus*, or Chief Counsellor. Some sources refer to him as 'prince of the city'. John's family circumstances were those of the elite. He lived at a very early stage of Muslim rule in Syria when the majority of the population was still Christian. Christians remained a majority until at least the end of the '3rd century of the *hijra*' (circa 922) (12) and comprise 10 per cent of the population today. In these circumstances, the Muslim rulers had little choice but to trust Christians in senior administrative posts: 'the Islamic leadership' had to 'remain on friendly terms with the Christian populations of the lands they conquered', since 'conquered peoples vastly outnumbered their conquerors' and 'only Christians commanded the necessary administrative expertise to make government possible' (Fletcher, 2003: 21). Consequently, what Courbage and Fargues (1997) describe as 'the great tolerance of the early Islamic rulers' emerged (11).

Damascus fell to the Caliph Umar I in 636, and became the Umayyad's capital in 661. The account of its capture is not irrelevant to this survey of Christian–Muslim encounter. Damascus had gates at opposite ends of the city, and the Muslims prepared to attack both of them. Although accounts are conflicting, the traditional story is that one gate resisted while John's grandfather surrendered the other. The Cathedral of St John, in the northwest of the City, was then divided between Muslims and Christians. Later, the great Umayyad Mosque was built on the site and the Church was torn down, but 'the two religions for a long time worshipped alongside each other' (Courbage and Fargues, 1997: 10). At 'Homs/Emesa, a large church provided shelter for the services of the two religions for four centuries', and only ceased to do so as a result of the Crusades (10–11). Greek continued to be the language of administration. Later, caliph 'Abd-al-Malik (684–705) made Arabic the language of government. This has led to speculation about how much Arabic, if any, John knew. Sahas (1972) thinks that as John remained in his important post after the introduction of Arabic, it would have been difficult for him to have functioned without some competency (46). This is supported by his fairly accurate references to Muslim beliefs and to Qur'anic passages. In the end, 'it is difficult to believe that John . . . lived, even after his retirement, in a totally Greek speaking environment' and we know that in the monastery he joined Arabic 'was in . . . common use . . . during the eighth century' (47). We owe what we know of John's life mainly to a legendary Life (*Vita*) written by a John of Jerusalem, possibly Patriarch John who died in 969 (34). The Vatican owns an Arabic copy of this text dated 1226, and there is a Latin version dated 1646.

What is of interest to the concern of this chapter is how John left the Caliph's service. The *Vita* says that he left his post to become a monk at about the time that Emperor Leo III (crowned 717) began to condemn icons, circa 726 CE. John defended icon veneration in several tracts. Possibly because John was otherwise out of his reach, the Emperor, according to the *Vita*, forged a letter allegedly from John in which he plotted treason against the Caliph, which he sent to Damascus. An accompanying letter 'reassured the' Caliph of Leo's personal friendship and of his 'interest to preserve the peace between them' (43). The Caliph believed the accusation and challenged John, who denied it. The Caliph then ordered John's hand amputated as punishment for treason. In the *Vita*, John asks for his hand back, which miraculously heals. Hearing of the miracle, the Caliph assumed John's innocence and offered him an even higher position at court. John, however, had made up his mind to retire to the monastery of St Sabas and begged permission to leave (44). It may have been the case that the Caliph initially believed the accusation then changed his mind, or that once suspicion had been sown John felt unable to continue in his post. Others think that John could have experienced pressure to convert, since 'Abd-al-Malik became less tolerant. Sahas (1972) concludes that John's decision to retire to the monastery was 'primarily personal'. This probably did not take place before Caliph Hisham's reign began in 724 CE. John joined the community of Mar Saba and was ordained by the Patriarch of Jerusalem. He became a renowned scholar, writing hymns, a service book, works of apology, *The Fountain of Wisdom*, or knowledge (Πηγή γνώσεως), *The Orthodox Faith* (*De Fide Orthodoxa*) in which he discussed logic, philosophy, heresies and delineated the contours of the Orthodox faith, and *De Haeresibus* in which he identified one hundred heresies. The final heresy, discussed in an unusually long chapter, 100/101, was that of the Ishmaelites, a somewhat derogatory term for Muslims. In addition to this discussion of Islam he also wrote the *Disputatio*, which was both a discussion between a Christian and a Saracen and a manual to inform Christian polemic. Considered a late Father of the Church, the Vatican declared him a Doctor of the Church in 1883. A Synod in 755 anathematized him but Nicaea II (787) re-instated him. By the time he wrote his works on Islam is it very doubtful if John had any contact with Muslims. On the other hand, he clearly drew on knowledge gained from his Caliphal service and the content, especially of the *Disputatio*, possibly reflects debates that actually did occur. What interests us is the extent of John's knowledge of Islam in terms of its accuracy and his attitude towards Islam. Again, it can be supposed that other Christians shared the same, or a similar view. Sahas thinks that it was John's 'family background' rather than his position on icons that irked the Emperor (31). Two of John's relatives, Sergius I (842–858) and Elias III (878–907), would serve as Patriarchs of Jerusalem and Sahas points out that the chronicler, Dositheous II (1669–1707), who records their deeds did not fail to add that they were sons of 'Mansur, who surrendered Damascus to the Saracens and for this reason has been anathematized by the entire world' (30). What probably irked the Byzantine emperor and his court was that the Mansur family continued to serve Muslim rulers, appearing to collaborate with the enemy.

Islam: According to John of Damascus

The following analysis uses the Greek with English text in Sahas (1972). John Ernest Merrill's 'Of the tractate of John of Damascus on Islam', originally published in *The Muslim World* (1951), gives liberal citations and detailed discussion of the text of Chapter 100/101.[1] In addition to its opening description of the origin of the heresy, the chapter describes discussions between Christians and Muslims, thus 'we respond to them . . .' and 'they also defame us as idolaters'. It proceeds on a 'he said that', 'we said this' basis (137). Merrill's interest, like that of this analysis, is to identify how accurate John's knowledge was. Merrill reacts to James Addison's statement that John knew what he was writing about first-hand, and concludes that John did not have a very intimate acquaintance with his sources, contrary to what has often been argued (Addison, 1942: 26). Either way, John remains of enormous interest. If he did not really know his sources and his information was second or third hand, it is remarkable that a Christian who had such ready access to Muslim officials lacked such knowledge, which suggests that Muslims were not overzealous in attempting to lure senior Christian officials away from Christianity. If John's knowledge of Islam is deemed more intimate, it suggests that the type of candid and perhaps even heated conversations described in both texts could take place, or at least could be imagined, without recrimination. John's view of and approach to Islam set the agenda for many subsequent Christian writers and participants in debate. His negative assessment of Islam contributed especially to Greek views of Islam but in translation his ideas spread further, almost certainly surfacing in Spain in the form of the *Life of Muhammad* that informed the Martyrs of Cordoba.[2] Merrill matches content in John with Qur'anic passages and identifies 22 passages where scriptural material supports what he wrote.

Analysis of the Texts

Muhammad as Islam's Author

Chapter 100/101's opening paragraph contains almost verbatim quotes from surah 4:171, and surah 112 which may well have been revealed at the same time. This section describes the content of 4:157 the Jews, having themselves violated the Law, wanted to crucify Jesus, but 'after they rescued him they crucified His shadow, but Christ himself, they say, was not crucified', which is an interesting mix of what the Qur'an says with popular Muslim belief on the issue. This suggests that John was aware of what Muslims said about the Crucifixion. Most commentators emphasize the fact that John discussed Islam in the context of his polemic against Christian heresy. For John, Islam was, in some sense, a recognizable creed. He describes the 'deceptive superstition' as that of the Ishmaelites, who regard Ishmael as their forebear. The alternative term Saracen, he says, is from Sarah, who was 'sent Hagar empty away'. John's use of the term 'Saracen' does not appear to have had derogatory connotations, although it would be odd for Muslims to associate themselves with Sarah, who was Isaac's mother, not Ishmael's. Others speculate that the term derives from the Arabic word for 'easterners' (*sharqiyyin*). This heretical religion, John argues, was concocted by Mameth who had been 'casually exposed to the New Testament', having met an Arian monk. It is significant in terms of John's supposed intimacy with Muslims that he got Muhammad's name so wrong, Μαμέδ, which also started a trend. Either this was because Christians just could not be bothered to get the name right, or they knew how offensive getting it wrong could be and did it on purpose. Later variations of the Arabic محمد would include Mahoun, Mahun, Mahomet and Mahound, which all became 'synonymous with demon, devil, idol' (Reeves, 2000: 87). Merill thinks that 'Mameth' could have been 'colloquial non-Muslim pronunciation' and suggests that John could not have been familiar with the Arabic, since the m-h-m-d 'would have been unmistakable'. The Spanish *Life* calls Muhammad 'Mahomet' which is more like a clumsy or bad transliteration of the Arabic, especially if the translator was not very familiar with the language. The shorter *Disputatio*, which shows more signs of later editing, uses Mouhamed (Μουχαμέθ). The *Song of Roland* has 'Mahom, God of our race' (Moncrief, 1919: CCLIII/3490). According to John, Mameth then spread rumours that he had received a book from heaven, drafted some ridiculous pronouncements 'worth only of laughter' which he handed down to his followers so 'that they may comply with' them. Throughout, John refers to 'idle tales' and more than hints that Muhammad used his supposed Scripture to justify his own immorality, especially vis-à-vis his marriage to Zaynab. This incident repeatedly surfaces in Christian polemic. The notion that the Qur'an simply does not make sense, pioneered here by John's discussion of the 'She-Camel', also became popular. Christians would develop an almost macabre interest in how Muhammad heard Gabriel's voice, suggesting insanity, epilepsy or pure deceit. John makes much of the possibility that Muhammad was 'asleep', thus leaving open the possibility that he was merely dreaming (135). John may have had Q97:4 in mind, although this does not refer to Muhammad as sleeping when the 'the angels came down' (Sahas, 1972: 79). John finds it anomalous that while witnesses are required for marriage, 'property, assess and everything else', neither Muslim 'faith' nor the 'scripture' requires any. Muhammad thus lacks 'certification from anywhere'.

Islam as a Christian Heresy

John attributes Islam's origin to Muhammad's knowledge of the New Testament, and to the influence of an Arian monk, whom Muhammad 'supposedly encountered'. Merrill (1951) surmises that John may have identified the monk as an Arian because for him Islam was in the main a 'Christological heresy, with teachings resembling those of the Arians'. Arius (d. 336) taught that Jesus was created in time by, and was distinct from, God. The encounter to which John refers is described in the *Sirah* (Guillaume, 1955: 79–82) and took place while Muhammad was visiting Syria with his uncle and guardian, Abu Talib. The tradition says that he met a monk called Bahira (usually identified as a Nestorian) who extended hospitality to the young man, and said that he saw in his features 'traces of his description in the Christian Books' (80). He told Abu Talib to take care of Muhammad, since a 'great future' lay before his nephew. If the 'Jews see him . . . they will do a great evil' (81). Muslims understand the 'description' referred to here as being 'in the sacred books' to refer to such passages as Deuteronomy 18:18 and John 14:16. When John challenges the Muslim to produce evidence that Muhammad was foretold, he does not supply him with any of these convenient biblical verses. Sahas argues that Muslims did not begin 'to use biblical texts in defense of the prophethood of Muhammad' until a later period (81). However, in the standard account, Bahira recognized Muhammad as the promised Prophet like unto Moses, while other Christians would refuse to concede that their scripture foretold Muhammad. Ibn Ishaq, author of the *Sirah*, refers to other 'Jewish Rabbis' and 'Christian monks' who spoke about 'the Apostle of God before his mission' began (90). These included Waraqah, Khadijah's cousin, whom Muhammad consulted immediately after receiving his first revelation (Q96). Waraqah concluded that Muhammad was 'the prophet of his people' (83). Later, the accusation that Muhammad learnt all he knew from the Christian slave, Jabr, resulted in the verse, 'we know indeed they say, "it is a man that teaches him". The tongue of him they wickedly point to is notably foreign, while this is Arabic, pure and clear' (16: 103; Guillaume has 105) (180). These references to contact between Muhammad and Christians meant, for some, that there could not be smoke without fire. John had probably heard these stories, and concluded that Muhammad had concocted Islam from heretical Christian sources.[3] For John, this would explain why Muhammad preached monotheism: 'He says there exists one God, maker of all, who was neither begotten nor has he begotten' (Q112:3). As Merrill points out, John reversed the order; the Qur'an says, 'He begeteth not, Nor is he begoteth'. Merrill suggests that John did not have a direct Muslim source, since this reversal would be unthinkable for any Muslim writer.

Sahas thinks that John had some textual access, commenting that he demonstrates 'wholesome knowledge, experience and understanding . . . of the religion of the Muslims' (122). Merrill concludes that John did not know original sources and had only a basic knowledge of the four Surahs to which he refers by name, one of which he named incorrectly.[4] Interestingly, since this would become a major topic of Christian–Muslim polemic, John makes no explicit reference to the charge, often made by the Qur'an itself, of *tahrif*, or scriptural tampering by Christians, although his statement about men having gone astray because they wrote that Jesus had called himself God is very close. Perhaps Muslims were not emphasizing *Tahrif* at this time, or opinion on this subject was still forming. Merrill also points out that John does not appear to have known verses representing the Qur'an as confirming previous scripture, or those referring to Jesus' death, since awareness of these might have changed his argumentation. John seems unaware of the Muslim claim that the Qur'an confirms previous scriptures, when he asks, 'How is it that your prophet did not come this way, by having others bearing witness to him?', which is actually a dominant theme of the Qur'an. Where the depth of John's knowledge of Islam attracts most criticism is his reference to Muslims worshiping Venus. His identification of the simple Arabic word, أكْبَـر, 'Akbar', used in the call to prayer, and during prayer, الـلـ أكْـبَـر,'Allahu Akbar', with 'Venus' sits oddly with someone who was so close to Muslim society. Of course, it is likely that John knew very well that he was mischaracterizing Islam for the purposes of polemic. Sahas (1972) suggests that John's purpose was to accuse Muslims not of idolatry, but of inconsistency. However, the idea that Muslims worshiped Venus and committed idolatry, hinted at here, would re-emerge in later Christian literature. For example, Marco Polo has Muslims worshiping Muhammad. It was claimed that the Archbishop of Salzburg was executed in 1104 for destroying a Muslim idol, while the *Song of Roland* (circa 1000) has Muslims worshiping three deities, Apollin, Tevaggon and Mohom (Moncrief, 1919: CCLIII/3490). Accordingly, Muslims were polytheists and idolaters.[5]

Islam and the Anti-Christ

Line 10 of Chapter 100/101 identifies Muhammad as a 'pseudo-prophet'. This strongly suggests that the book was intended for Christian, not Muslim, eyes. Primarily a treatise on Christian heresies, it was of little interest to Muslims. We can also assume that calling Muhammad a 'deceiver' and his Book 'laughable' would have stretched the patience of even the most tolerant of Muslims! John was almost certainly aware that in 743, the year he published his *Fountain of Wisdom*, the Bishop of Maiuma had been 'sentenced to death because he condemned Islam publicly, calling Muhammad a 'false prophet' and the 'forerunner of the Antichrist', just as John did (68–69). John's opening paragraph alludes to Matthew 24:24 on 'false Christs and false prophets' as an explanation of Muhammad's career. He refers to the heresy as 'the precursor (*prodromos*) of the anti-Christ'. He also called Nestorius, Leo III and his son, the Patriarch of Constantinople, John VI Grammaticos, precursors of the Anti-Christ. Heretics were those whose doctrines, especially regarding Christ and the Trinity, were in error (Sahas, 1972: 69). For John, Islam qualified. 'Anti-Christ' is usually used in an eschatological context, referring to signs of the End, the coming of the Beast who blasphemes against God and whose number is 666 and to the Battle of Armageddon (see Revelation 13:6; 13:18). The Martyrs of Cordoba would associate Muhammad both with the Beast of Revelation and with the 'Little Horn' of Daniel 7:8, and thought that he had been born in the year 666. They really did believe that Islam prefigured the End, and tried to hasten this by becoming martyrs. John may also have thought that Islam prefigured the End. Merrill refers to literature close to John's time that 'treats of events at the end of the world, including the apparition of the Arabs from Yathrib [Madinah] and . . . the apparition of Anti-Christ'. John may have wanted to warn his readers away from heresy, including the latest version, so that Jesus would find that they had remained faithful and true to *De Fide Orthodoxa*. He may also have believed that Islam was therefore a temporary power, soon to be replaced. He could have understood Islam as raised up by God as a punishment for Christians who had abandoned the true faith, a view suggested by Emperor Heraclius' reported statement 'that the great God had sent this misfortune upon men' (Sweetman, 1955: 9). John also alludes to the Genesis account of Hagar being sent away from Abraham's household, although as Sahas points out, he seems to misquote the text, which does not say that Hagar went away empty but that Abraham 'provided Hagar with bread and water' (133). Nonetheless, he was aware of Muslim conviction that Muhammad's spiritual and genealogical lineage could be traced back to Abraham through Ishmael.

The Qur'an on Jesus

John is an early example of a Christian who selects Qur'anic material about Jesus and regards this as aiding rather than hindering his case, although he is also aware of problematic verses on the Cross and on Christians as associators/polytheists. In the *Disputatio*, he wrote 'Let us make use of your scripture and of my Scripture' then refers to surah 4:42 on Mary as being 'cleansed above all women' and to Luke 1:35 on the power of the Holy Spirit 'overshadowing' Mary, although he identifies neither by chapter and verse (151). This could suggest more than hearsay acquaintance with the Qur'an. At the very least, John appears to have had some exposure to Qur'anic material. He closely follows 4:157 and 4:171 in his discussion of what Muhammad taught: 'He says that Christ is the Word of God, and His spirit, created and a servant, and that he was born without a seed from Mary'. Q4:71 reads 'Jesus . . . was a messenger from Allah and His word . . . and a spirit proceeding from Him.' Here the order is correct, a Word and a Spirit, not a Spirit and His Word. The 'born without a seed' seems to refer to 3: 7, 'how shall I have a son when no man has touched me?', and Jesus as a servant to 4:172, 'Christ disdains not to serve and worship Allah.' It is highly likely that a Muslim referred to these verses in conversation, or debate, with John, raising the very issues that the Qur'an places on the Christian–Muslim agenda: that Jesus was not the Son of God, or the 2nd Person of the Trinity, and did not die on the Cross but rather was a faithful servant of God. John then appears to paraphrase 5:116, just as a Muslim might do in an actual exchange: 'O Jesus, did you say that "I am Son of God?" And Jesus, they say, answered, "Be merciful to me, Lord; you know that I did not say, nor will I boast that I am your servant: but men who have gone astray wrote that I made this statement and they say lies against me and they have been in error". And God, they say, answered to him, "I knew that you would not say this thing".' The Qur'anic verse reads, 'and behold, Allah will say, "O Son of Mary, didst you say unto men,

'Worship me and my mother as God's in derogation to Allah?' He will say, "Glory to Thee. Never could I say what I have no right to say . . ."' The addition of 'men who have gone astray' telling 'lies' against Jesus could be Muslim gloss, reflecting the conviction that Christians tampered with scripture and introduced false ideas into their religion. John was obviously aware of this, as he went on to write, 'some of them maintain that we have added such things, by having allegorized the prophets.' This responded to the specific charge that Christians associate partners with God (137).

The Trinity

John touches, although not in detail, on the Trinity, which he tries to explain or defend by referring to the Qur'an's description of Jesus:

> Since you say that Christ is word and Spirit of God, how do you call us Associators? For the word and the Spirit is inseparable from the one in whom this has the origin; if, therefore, the Word is in God it is obvious that he is God as well. If, on the other hand, this is outside of God, then God, according to you, is without word and without spirit . . . (137)

John returned to the Trinity in the *Disputatio*, where he also shows awareness of parallel debate in Islam about the createdness or uncreatedness of the Qur'an: whether it (like Christ) always existed in the God-ness of God, or was created in time, as Arius' Jesus was. Here we have an early example of Christians and Muslims employing similar language to explain the relationship between God's 'revelation', which for Muslims was a book, for Christians a person and God. Thomas (2001) comments that Christians increasingly adopted terms used in كلام , Muslim theology (*Kalam*), 'to defend the Doctrine of the Trinity in the Muslim context in which they lived' (88). He also comments that John's description of the Trinity followed traditional Greek formulations, and did not adopt Muslim vocabulary (80). However, his discussion of the terms 'word' and 'spirit' appears to have had some awareness of Muslim thinking, since 'the response of the Christian to the accusation of being Associators "is an allusion to the question of the Attributes of God and His nature"' (Sahas, 1972: 101). Again, John invites Muslims to look at the Qur'an to explain the relationship they see there between God and God's Spirit and Word (149). If Christians are Associators, he says, Muslims are 'Mutilators' (*Coptas*) for divorcing God 'from His Word and His Spirit' (82, 137). In the *Disputatio*, he shows some awareness of Muslim debate when his Christian asks the Saracen whether 'the Words of God' are 'created or uncreated?' (151). The Mutazalites, champions of an uncreated Qur'an, emerged a hundred years after John's death, although their pioneer, Wasil b. 'Ata, died the same year as he did (749) (107). John knew that advocates of an uncreated Qur'an were deemed 'heretics' by mainstream Muslims (149). The Mutazalites were dominant during the Muslim *mihna* (Inquistion) between 833 and 848, starting under the caliph al-Ma'mun (813–833).

John's Legacy

The positive aspect of John's legacy is that his text reflects some accurate knowledge of Islam. He pinpointed the main theological issues between Christians and Muslims as the Crucifixion, the relationship between Jesus and God, and Muhammad's claims to be a Prophet. He placed on the agenda the possibility of using Q4:171 to establish some common ground in discussion of the Trinity, God's attributes and the status of the Qur'an itself. He also established some common ground between Christian and Muslim thinking on the question of the created-ness of the Qur'an. Negatively, he depicted Muhammad as an imposter, who concocted Islam from pre-existing sources, and fabricated revelation to justify his own immoral conduct, and he ridiculed the Qur'an and Muslim notions of Paradise.[6] His example of Muhammad's marriage to Zaynab (139) as one of fabricating revelation repeatedly surfaces in later literature. He also strongly hinted that the *hajj* (pilgrimage) smacks of idolatry. Drawing on authentic traditions regarding Muhammad's contact with Christians, he conscripted them as co-authors of Islam as a Christian heresy. Some point out that a heretic should be 'won' back to the true faith, so by categorizing Islam as a 'heresy' John claimed a familial relationship. On the other hand, Christians have always acknowledged a family relationship with Judaism but this has not always resulted in friendship. John did not give much detail of Muhammad's life, nor did he impugn him of converting by the sword, which would later emerge as a major theme, alongside his sexual ethics.[7] Perhaps, since few Christians had yet converted, John knew that Muslims did not generally forcibly convert unbelievers.

Al-Kindy's Risalah

Background

We know less about the author of the *Risalah* (literally a 'Message' but, in this case, 'Apology') than we do about John. The *Risalah* was written in Arabic and shows how many of John's criticisms of Islam and of Muhammad became popular themes. More markedly polemical than John's texts, it purports to have been written in the context of Christian–Muslim encounter at the Court of Caliph al-Ma'mun at Baghdad. Al-Ma'mun (786–833) was intolerant of Muslims who disagreed with his Mutalizalite opinions but was otherwise a Latitudinarian, as Muir describes him (1886: 26). Founding the famous academy the House of Wisdom (*Bayt-al-Hikma*) in his capital, he also made an effort to heal the Sunni-Shi'a divide. The *Risalah* includes a 'letter' by him in which he expresses interest in the inner-intent rather than outward-conformity of Muslims; he knows of many 'who were Christians and embraced Islam unwillingly' who are thus 'neither Muslims nor Christians but imposters', while others had become Muslim 'not from any love of our religion' but 'to gain access to' his court, 'honour, wealth and power'. Nonetheless, he would treat all his courtiers with 'courtesy and forebearence' (29–30). The full text of Muir's abridgement and commentary of Abd al-Masih Ibn Ishaq al-Kindy's *Risalah* is available on the internet.[8] Including introductory segments (prefaces to the 1886 and to the first edition, 1881, and an essay on its age and authorship), the text has 122 pages. Muir believes that the author was a Nestorian Christian but of 'noble, Arab birth . . . and . . . yet an honoured attendant at the court of the caliph' (10). Some suggest that the author was a convert from Islam. This is unlikely if the text is authentic, more likely if the setting is imaginary and it was written at a later date. Identification of the author as the renowned Muslim philosopher, Abu Yusuf Ibn Ishaq al-Kindy (d. 873), is rejected (19). Muir dates the apology to approximately 830 CE. Goddard describes discussion about the date and authenticity of the Apology (2000: 64). What is at issue is not the genuineness of the text as an example of Christian polemic but whether it was written as early as Muir thought, and therefore whether the Hashemite's and the Caliph's letters are authentic. If written at a later date, these letters are likely to be the work of the Apology's author, although he would have represented what *he thought* Muslims *would* have said. The work must predate 1142, however, when Peter the Venerable (1092–1156) arrived in Spain, found a copy and translated it and also commissioned the first Latin translation of the Qur'an. Even if written a century or so later, the text could still reflect the type of encounters that did actually occur, rehearsing arguments commonly employed on both sides. It was almost certainly written in the Muslim world, probably in Iraq as the text itself claims. If a later text, it can be surmised that, while allegedly written as a reply to a Muslim, it was really written for internal Christian consumption, as a manual on how to engage in debate. The supposed context is an invitation by a relative of the Caliph to al-Kindy to become a Muslim. Should he choose not to do so, he should nonetheless reply to his 'epistle without fear or favour, under royal guarantee obtained from the caliph himself, of absolute security' (41). There is no question, given his accurate and extensive Qur'anic references, that al-Kindy knew the Qur'an in its original Arabic (40).

Two aspects of the letter are especially interesting. First, Al-Hashimy greets al-Kindy with the '*asalamu alaikum*' which, Muir notes, is 'unusual', and justifies this by saying that Muhammad greeted both Muslims and *dhimmis* (people of the book) in this way (39).[9] Second, Al-Hashimy cites Q29:46: 'dispute not with the people of the book otherwise than in a most gracious manner' (39). Al-Hashimy pointed out that it had been with the Nestorian branch of the Church that Muhammad had been acquainted. The text has Ma'mun citing 'Allah is the best of all deciders' (Q10:109; Muir has 107). Al-Kindy, acknowledging 'the favour of the caliph' and praying for his 'long life and prosperity' (41), proceeds to defend Christian belief. In no uncertain terms, he also sets down what he perceives as Islam's weaknesses and falsity. His language is much more polemical than John's but the same topics attract his attention. Headings include 'The Trinity', 'Worldly Inducements', 'Contradictory Passages', 'Adoration of the Cross' and 'War as Divine Remedy'. There is also detailed discussion of incidents in Muhammad's life and of the charge of *tahrif*. This only refers to the alleged corruption of the Jewish scriptures, perhaps confirming that Muslims may not have accused Christians of *tahrif* at this period. 'Veneration of the Cross' is also discussed. Muir points out that the only place in the text where the customary salutation, 'peace be upon him', after Muhammad's name is used is in the caliph's letter (30), while al-Kindy 'never speaks of the Prophet by name, but generally as "Thy Master"' (Sâhib) (43). This could have been a device to circumvent the *salallahu alayhi wa salam* as inappropriate for someone who did not honour the Prophet, while still allowing him to remain civil.

Summary of Content

One statement in the text, describing Muhammad's 'chief object and desire' as waging war and marrying beautiful women, sums up al-Kindy's estimate of Muhammad. Similar sentences appear several times (see 53, 90, 100, 107, 120). Like John, he refers to Muhammad as a 'false prophet' who could not produce any evidence to confirm his claims but could only assert them by wielding the sword (100). He wrought no miracles. Unlike John, al-Kindy is aware of miracle stories in the traditions, which he dismisses as fabulous. These sources cannot be trusted; 'the authority is insufficient', and 'the traditionalists themselves' disagree (61). Such stories contradict the Qur'an, which says that Muhammad 'was not gifted with miracles'. (67). Fabulous tales include a shoulder of goat-meat warning Muhammad that it has been poisoned, the production of water for his thirsty men, and the healing of a woman's leg after the battle of Khaybar. The narrators of these fabulous tales could not be compared with the gospel witnesses of Jesus' miracles, about which 'Muhammad himself warned that lies would be told' (61). In the absence of miracles, Muhammad enforced his claims 'by the sword' (61). In contrast, al-Kindy continues, Jesus' miracles are confirmed by the Qur'an (117; Q2:87; 3:49). Reference to Muhammad's sanctioning and using violence occurs throughout the book. Al-Kindy attributes conversion to Islam to worldly motives and inducements, especially Islam's liberal rules on marriage, divorce and concubines (86), as well as the promise of plunder from warfare. Citing 9: 29, al-Kindy characterizes Muslims as intent on world domination: 'the Way of the Lord', he says, 'is to wage war on other religions, to smite with sword, and make slaves of mankind, until they confess that there is no God but the Lord, and that Mahomet is his servant and apostle, or, if they refuse, pay the tribute with their hands and are humbled . . .' (95). He argues that 'dissolute' men, consumed by 'lusts of the flesh', become Muslim, not those who were learned and acquainted with Christian scripture (86). He does not say why women converted. Referring to the promise of immediate entry into Paradise for Muslims slain during Jihad, he wrote; 'they say of him that slayeth or is slain that he shall have inherited paradise' and ridicules why someone guilty of indiscriminate 'plundering, enslaving and ravishing' should go to heaven (106). Ravishing here means that of 'wives and maidens in unlawful embrace'. Jihadists cannot be properly regarded as martyrs, since they die while in the process of imposing Islam on others, while Christian martyrs die for refusing to renounce their faith (105). Al-Kindy did not ask how Muslims understood these incidents or passages and why they did not regard them as impugning Muhammad's integrity.

Al-Kindy does not employ the term anti-Christ but posits a Satanic cause for Islam; there are only three dispensations to which Islam can belong, one divine, one natural, and one satanic (66). It cannot be divine, because that is the religion of Jesus and Muslims know nothing of 'the law of grace and mercy' that characterizes religious truth (67). Nor can it be natural, because that was revealed a long time ago through Moses. Rather, it must be satanic, 'the law . . . of wrong-doing and violence', which, as noted, sums up his view of Islam. The Qur'an is Muhammad's own composition, and was 'freely brought down' to justify his conduct. The example al-Kindy chooses to cite is the Zayd-Zaynab affair (Q33:37), commenting that 'this specimen will suffice for men of understanding' (50). This is followed by a list of Muhammad's marriages (51–53). Since it is difficult enough for a man to please one wife, as St Paul says a husband should, how could Muhammad, busy 'in raids and forays and military expeditions and in ordering his troops for the same, in sending our spies, in planning how to circumvent his enemies, slay their men, take their women captive, and plunder their goods', have pleased 15 (52–53)? In addition to Muhammad's sexual conduct, al-Kindy singles out his treatment of enemies and of critics for censure. His discusses 'assassinations' by Muhammad's 'command' (47–48). People who were 'obnoxious to him' were ordered killed, including Abu Afek, an 'aged man, decrepit and helpless' (47), while a Jewish tribe on the outskirts of Madinah, the Banu Qurazah who had done no wrong were 'besieged and forced to surrender' (48). How consistent is this with Muhammad's claim to be a 'blessing and mercy to mankind' (Q21: 107), he asks (47). He repeatedly describes Islam as spread 'by the sword' and implies that while Christianity teaches universal brotherhood, Islam encourages enmity (112). 'War as a divine remedy' was Muhammad's only option, since he had no other argument (100). Like John, he denies that Muhammad possessed the qualifications of a prophet. In addition to lacking supportive miracles, he had not been predicted, nor was he able to predict the future, as a prophet should (54). Reference to Muhammad's treatment of enemies became a new theme, which Muir also discussed at length in his *Life*, with a footnote reference to the Apology (47). Muir believed that Muhammad encouraged lying and deceit as well as covert military operations (1860: 4: 308–9). The latter has been read into Q9:5's 'lie in wait for them in every stratagem of war' but Muir also attributed this to *taqiyah*, which he said gave 'Muslims divine permission to deny their faith outwardly in situations of danger'.

Nor can the Qur'an be cited as evidence of Muhammad's mission, since it is a jumbled, contradictory, 'confused heap'; 'the sense, moreover, consisteth not with itself, but throughout one passage is contradicted by another' (78–79). He refers to Bahira (105) and to Sergius, whom he describes as an excommunicated monk who travelled to Arabia, met Muhammad and persuaded him to become his disciple (70). Sergius then died and two Jews 'seized the opportunity' to ingratiate themselves with Muhammad (70) who was thus able to draw on Christian and on Jewish sources. Recounting in some detail the story of the collection and recension of the Qur'an, he ascribes a role in this process to Jews and sees the process by which a single version of the Qur'an was compiled under Caliph Uthman as one in which Muslims added to the Qur'an whatever they liked and subtracted what they disliked (78). If an Arabic Qur'an, why does it contain foreign words (Q12:2) (13: 40; 20:111)? 'Thy book is broken in its rhythm, confused in its composition and in its flights of fancy unmeaning' (81). Since a 'monk inspired it' and Rabbis 'interpolated it with Jewish tales and puerilities', it is no credit to Muhammad (26). Sergius's role, too, explains references to Gabriel. Also known as 'Gabriel', Sergius might have been mistaken for the angel of revelation (72). Muhammad only had contact with heretical Christians, who were 'ignorant dogs'. These heretics were responsible for the notion that Christians worship three Gods. He thought that Jews introduced the idea of a feminine 'element' (42; see Q5:116). He thus shares with John the idea of Islam as a composite system, indebted to Christianity and to Judaism but in the main designed to further a personal agenda and to attract others with its promise of plunder and women. Paradise, too, holds out the attraction of 'ladies, like pearls hidden within their shells'. Al-Kindy refers to this as among the inducements offered him to embrace Islam (84, 40). Like John, he stresses that a true prophet would have been foretold, rejecting the contention that the Bible predicted Muhammad. Referring to the Paraclete (119) he does not show awareness that Muslims apply this to Muhammad as a biblical prediction. Al-Kindy argues that pointing to the Qur'an as proof of Muhammad's genuineness fails since such 'witless fables and old wives' tails . . . are no proof whatever of a Divine Mission', again close to John's 'idle tales' (54). The claim that it surpasses all other books in eloquence cannot be verified. What one nation holds to be exquisite others may see as barbarous, since all think their tongue the most beautiful (79, citing Q17:88; Muir has 89). He gives a fairly detailed discussion of what he calls contradictions in the Qur'an. This is especially interesting because he includes here the verses of hostility and of friendship, asking 'which of the two directions am I to follow, the first or the last?' (98).

Tahrif

Unlike John, al-Kindy was aware of the charge of *tahrif* and devoted several passages to defending the Hebrew Bible, indicating that Christians may not have been charged with textual corruption at this time. It would, he says, have been impossible for all the Bibles in existence, scattered throughout the world, to have been altered in exactly the same way (115). Also, if the Bible was corrupted, why would Muhammad have been advised to consult Scripturaries if he was in any doubt (Q2:121; Muir has 122)? The Hashemite had asked al-Kindy to give an account of his own faith; his response is to present the life of Jesus, which he depicts as the opposite of Muhammad's. He prays that his friend will know the 'light and guidance' of the Holy Spirit (114), that he will be guided from darkness to light, from death to life (110). This indicates that he did not think Muslims were saved. What he wrote was a series of polemical contrasts: Jesus was a man of peace, Muhammad was violent; Jesus was foretold by the prophets and attested by miracles, Muhammad lacks such accreditation; the Bible does not predict Muhammad and is uncorrupted; Jesus saves, Muhammad does not.

On the Day of Judgment, Jesus not Muhammad will intercede for humanity (109). His friend had invited him to follow a 'wide and easy path' of rewards and luxury and of 'wives and damsels' but the true religious path is hard and narrow (110). He liberally cites Qur'anic passages on Jesus, commenting that this is the account of him given by the Master himself (116). On Jesus' crucifixion, he cites 3:54–57 as evidence that the Qu'ran testifies to Jesus' death, a verse that John had not known but which would continue to feature in Christian discourse as a rejoinder to Muslim understanding of Q4:157. In his discussion of the comparative claims of Muhammad and Jesus, he refers to the accusation that Christians commit *shirk*: 'that to acknowledge the Trinity and to worship the Cross are . . . blasphemy and error'. He comments that Muslims accuse Christians of *takhlit* (confusion of essence) but says that Muslims do so because they cannot 'comprehend' the Trinity, which is an 'ineffable mystery' (110–111). In his earlier treatment of the Trinity, he stated that the Qur'an misrepresents it (42) and that the Bible attests the Trinity in passages where God speaks in the plural. On adoration of the Cross, he argued that Christians do not venerate the Cross but the 'power' that it symbolizes (111). He also suggests, like John, that the Hajj (pilgrimage at Makkah) is tainted with idolatry, or at the very least is absurd. He compared this with the idolatrous circuits of the Brahmans in India around their idols (92). Nor, al-Kindy concludes, could Muslims claim to be spiritual heirs of Abraham, because his covenant was through Isaac, not Ishmael (42).

Karl Gottlieb Pfander (1803–1865)

This analysis focuses on Pfander's *Mizan-ul-Haq* (Balance of Truth), although he wrote other apologetic works and engaged in public debates with Muslims (see Chapter 5). Pfander attended the Piestist missionary academy at Basel where he studied Arabic, the Qur'an, Bible and Biblical languages as well as a trade. Initially stationed in Shusha in Russian Armenia, he targeted Muslims for conversion. He concentrated on Bible translation, believing that if Muslims read the Bible in their own tongue they will immediately be convinced of Christianity's 'truth and superiority' and abandon Islam as incapable of removing the burden of sin (letter to Basel Mission, 1 September 1831). He then turned to apology, producing the *Mizan* originally in German (1829), followed by Armenian (1831), Persian (1835) and

Turkish (1861). From 1838 he was employed in India by the Church Mission Society, an Anglican agency, where he remained until 1861. He was ordained as an Anglican priest in 1856, the year he received a Lambeth DD. Finally, he worked in Turkey (1861 until 1865). The *Mizan* was rendered into English in 1867. The edition used in this chapter was revised by St-Clair Tisadall in 1910. Available online, hard copy editions are still available.[10] 'We do not hesitate', says the preface to a 1986 reprint, 'to print such a book of fundamental importance . . . Islam is still the same, and needs a definitive answer.' Of the three contributors discussed in this chapter, Pfander has been considered the apologist par excellence. Pfander's mastery of language and knowledge of Islamic sources place him in a different category from John and closer to al-Kindy. The *Mizan* has a lot in common with the *Risalah*. Pfander's language was so eloquent that a rumour had it that an apostate Muslim had written the text (Muir, 1897: 32). Pfander shared attitudes of cultural superiority with colonial officials, such as Muir, who championed his work. It was only by the 'multiplication of such agents that' the church could hope to gain ascendancy 'among the hitherto unreclaimed realms of heathenism' (Muir, 1897: 52) . Powell (1992) comments that Pfander expressed confidence in 'the efficacy of a technologically superior and socially progressive Europe in ensuring the eventual success of the Gospel' and believed that God would not allow India to revert to Muslim rule (155).

An unusual aspect of Pfander's approach to Islam was his reliance on 'reason', rather than on inner renewal and spirituality, Pietism's traditional foci. He wanted to satisfy people's spiritual craving but his writings elevate reason above 'feeling', probably because he was convinced of Christianity's intellectual as well as spiritual superiority, which could be proved at the bar of reason. The 'necessity of revelation' is evident to all 'men of intelligence' (22), given that 'there exist many different religions in the world', each claiming to be true (23). However, all cannot be true and since some contradict each other we need to judge between them. Pfander then claims that the real competition is between the truth claims of Christianity and Islam, since they have the largest following (24). Only one of the two can represent God's authentic revelation. By comparing each against the criteria of what the True Revelation must offer, their respective claims can be adjudicated. Pfander suggests that the criteria (he listed five) are self-evident to reasonable people, and 'can not be *contrary* to the testimony which Nature and Conscience bear to the Creator' (25, original emphasis). His criteria were: one, the true revelation must satisfy the human thirst for knowledge, pardon and purification; two, it must be in accord with the Moral Law that is written on the human conscience; three, it must reveal God as possessing all the qualities of justice and goodness that the human conscience itself affirms as essential; four, it must conform to what reason itself posits about the eternal, immutable, life-sustaining and unitary nature of God; five, it must contain no contradictions. Tisdall (in Pfander, 1910) added six: since 'no book or Prophet can possibly reveal God fully to men' (33) a 'personal manifestation' is necessary (34). This sixth criterion stacks the deck in favour of Christianity.

Discussing each religion's claims against these criteria, Pfander found Islam wanting on all counts, while Christianity passed every test. Section one (41–125) discusses proof that the Bible has not been corrupted, section two (126–221) discusses Christianity's claims, and section three (222–370) Islam's. In the process of applying his criteria to each religion, Pfander covers such traditional issues as the Trinity, Jesus' sonship, Muhammad's moral conduct, the Bible's textual integrity, the claim that the Qur'an was inspired, Muhammad's alleged miracles, how each faith spread in comparison to the other, and whether the Bible predicted Muhammad or not. These are all covered in detail, revealing his knowledge of the Qur'an. Much of the content is similar to Al-Kindy's but as the *Mizan* is longer, it cites more passages. Al-Kindy had only discussed the integrity of the Old Testament; Pfander also defends the New Testament against the charge of corruption. Well aware of Muslim use of the Bible, he examines a total of nineteen Old Testament and twelve New Testament passages (227–252). Since much of what he wrote repeats the arguments of the *Risalah*, this analysis focuses on additional material.

Summary of Pfander's Arguments

On the question of the Bible's integrity, Pfander repeated al-Kindy's argument, also applying this to the New Testament. No one, he said, could have gathered all extant copies of the Bible from across the world to change every text identically. Christians never had an Uthman (111). Even if Christians had lost their scriptures, scripture 'lasts forever' (Isaiah 40:8) and many had learnt large portions by heart. Christians possessed 3,899 manuscripts of the New Testament

either of parts or of the whole which had been carefully examined
(96). When asked to explain when the corruption of scripture took
place, before or after Muhammad's time, Muslims are unable to
reply (106). He cites Q10:49, which advises Muhammad to consult
the Scriptuaries if in doubt about what he had received, which would
not make sense if the Jews and Christians had a corrupt knowledge
of scripture (45–46). However, he admitted that some copyist
errors could be identified, especially within the translation process
(109–10). In each case, the error was not deliberate and has been
detected by others through consulting 'their own manuscripts' (110).
In his public debates, when his opponent, including M. Rahmatullah
Kairanwi, with whom he sustained a lengthy literary correspondence
(see Chapter 4), had copies of German biblical criticism piled up on
the desk in front of him, Pfander conceded more errors.[11] However,
he claimed that no essential Christian teaching or doctrine was
compromised, even if the error could not be explained as a copyist's
mistake. Pfander, unaware of this critical scholarship, later accused
Catholics of supplying Muslims with texts to sabotage the debates.
In contrast to the Bible, the Qur'an's claim to be inspired fails,
because it contains contradictions (291), its contents were largely
'borrowed from other religions' (294) and it does not 'satisfy the
spiritual needs and yearnings of mankind' (299). With reference to
alleged contradictions in the Qur'an, he cites 4:51 which says that
God will not forgive *shirk* (associating a partner with God) while
6:76–78 has Abraham committing this sin: yet Abraham is a Prophet
of God. He also refers to the Satanic Verses (see Q53:21–23).
Muhammad had changed the original words, which recognized the
validity of prayer to the three pagan deities, to those that are now
found in *Surat'un Nahm* (350). The verses of friendship and those
of opprobrium are also contradictory (290), as al-Kindy had argued.
Wine is prohibited on earth but promised in heaven (287). He thinks
it contradictory that Q2:52 calls Jesus a man, while 4:171 says that
he is a 'spirit from God', which is a 'higher title' than that given 'any
other human being' (287). All three writers cite this passage. Biblical
passages that Muslims believe predicted Muhammad have 'in large
measure already been fulfilled in Christ' (116). Verses discussed
include Deuteronomy 18:15–18, Isaiah 54:1, Daniel 2:45, and
from the New Testament, the Paraclete passage (in John) and also
John 14:30, the reference to the 'prince of the world'. Pfander also
discusses contradictions between the Qur'an and the Bible, which, he
argues, if the Qur'an confirmed the Bible, would not exist. Pfander

bypasses the issue of the crucifixion by pointing out that while Muhammad is dead, the Qur'an itself affirms that Jesus was raised up to be with God in heaven (Q4:156; 288). On the Trinity, Pfander points out that unity does not preclude plurality and that Muslims admit that God has many attributes (181). Christians believe in one God, he says, but in three *hypostases*, or persons. On the one hand, the Trinity is a mystery (180) but on the other we know that God is Triune because God has revealed this about God's-self. Pfander claimed that Trinity is supported by scripture but only refers to Genesis as evidence (182). He then points to the world of nature, drawing an analogy between the Trinity and fire, light and heat, which 'are three and yet one' (183).

Pfander regarded the Qur'an as a composite work, in the main composed by Muhammad (254). The Muslim claim that the Qur'an is more eloquent than any other book could not be proved, he said, but is merely the prejudiced opinion of Arabs (264). Muhammad's claim that the Qur'an is a confirming miracle fails. Other miracles recorded in the traditions, such as a tree walking and talking and a wooden column crying out are simply too fantastic to be believed, the stuff of the *Arabian Nights* (322). Had Muhammad really 'wrought them', the Qur'an would undoubtedly 'have mentioned some of them' instead of stating that God did not give Muhammad 'power to work miracles at all' (324; see also 328–29 on miracles). In contrast to the miracles attributed to Muhammad, Jesus' miracles 'are enacted parables, full of spiritual instruction, works of divine mercy as well as divine might' (323). Even the Qur'an attests Jesus' miracles (287–88). Christianity, spread in the face of persecution, offered its converts no sensual gratification or material gain (218). Islam spread by enforcing conversion-sanctioned war and plunder to encourage people to flock to its standard, attracted by the promise of sensual delight both sides of the grave (353). Christians are not permitted to 'use *jihad*' (217) while Muslims are obligated to do so (292). Again sounding like al-Kindy, Pfander says that use of the sword followed failure of peaceful means (352). Once he became the 'prophet of the sword', this became Islam's one and only proof. God's only requirement from Muslims now was that they should 'fight . . . with sword and spear, with bow and arrow and the assassin's knife' (352–53). Pfander suggested that many of the 225 abrogated verses in the Qur'an encouraged 'justice and religious toleration' in favour of those permitting 'oppression and persecution' instead (290). Q4:3, which legalized concubinage and polygamy, rendered 'permanent the evils of which Muslims lands are full' (328–32). Such is the God of Islam. Pfander does admit that the Qur'an contains some valuable content, such as teachings on the nature and attributes of God, reward and punishment, prohibition of murder and encouragement to care for the needy. This content ultimately comes from God but does not confirm Muhammad's prophetic claim, because none of this is original to him (269–70), nor does his moral conduct qualify him as a true prophet. Among other incidents, he singles out Muhammad's marriage to Zaynab (330–32) (cited by all three writers),[12] his dealing with the Jewish tribe of the Quraizah (which al-Kindy had discussed), various assassinations which he is said to have condoned or commanded and Aisha's age on her marriage (329). Traditions on such matters as Muhammad's relations with his wives are 'not pleasant reading' but serve to cast light on 'Muhammad's moral character' (332). The Qur'an, he said, encourages unlimited lust (297) although here too is a contradiction, because Q74:40 to 'some measure condemns lust' (296). Islam satisfies worldly, not spiritual needs (299). The Qur'an aims to substitute Muhammad for Jesus, yet it reserves higher honours for Jesus (288).

Pfander knew more about Muslim use of the Bible than the earlier writers. His knowledge of the Qur'an compares with al-Kindy's and was complemented with greater familiarity with the traditions. Muir, though, thought that Pfander did not draw sufficiently on the 'deduction of modern scholarship' (67). Like al-Kindy, Pfander saw Islam as a religion that attracts people by force or with worldly gain. Like John, he sees Muhammad as the author of the Qur'an. He suggests that Muhammad may have suffered from some sort of malady (348), a view found in many Christian texts from an early period (see Daniel, 1997: 48–9). Pfander pointed out Muhammad's initial doubts, and that he contemplated suicide (344). Pfander does not explore such issues as satanic inspiration – although he comments that some people thought Muhammad possessed (245) – or whether Muhammad was the anti-Christ but rests his case on claiming that Muhammad was not 'in very truth a prophet of God' (348). People must choose between Jesus, who went about doing good and said love your enemies, and Muhammad, the prophet of the sword, who said slay your enemies (368). Early in the text, Pfander established, to his own satisfaction, that the true revelation had to be a person, not a book (203), so Islam fails again. Like al-Kindy, he asserts that on the Day of Judgment Christ, not Muhammad, will intercede for humanity (301). Pfander argued that Islam cannot offer humanity forgiveness from sin, since this is only available through Jesus, the perfect sacrifice. Against the objection that the divine and the human could not be united, he argued that this 'is incomprehensible to our limited human intellect' (167) but possible for God. Jesus' death was necessary to save humanity because only the sacrifice of a sinless life could pay the price of sin (171). What Pfander did not ask was why Muslims, who are familiar with Muhammad's biography, do not regard the incidents he censored as immoral. He claimed that his aim was not controversy but enquiry into the truth (305). Convinced before he began his enquiry that Christianity was the true revelation, he summoned up evidence to confirm this. In his revision, Tisdall said that he tried to maintain a 'conciliatory tone' and to avoid 'needless offence' (4). Generally, Pfander's style was to describe an incident and, after contrasting each point with Jesus' example, to ask whether Muhammad's conduct offered any genuine proof that he was 'a divinely commissioned prophet' (343). Many of the arguments developed by these pioneer polemicists continue to inform contemporary diatribe.

Chapter 4

Classical Christian Conciliatory Appoaches towards Islam

Mar Timothy's Dialogue

This chapter begins with Mar Timothy, then visits the Crusades, arguing that this controversial period of Christian–Muslim encounter also witnessed some examples of *convivencia*. Reference is made to Nicholas of Cusa before concluding with W. H. T. Gairdner and Louis Massignon as more recent examples of conciliation. The chapter includes analyses of Ridley Scott's 2005 film *Kingdom of Heaven*. The earliest example of what this book describes as a conciliatory approach towards Islam is probably Mar Timothy I (728–823), Patriarch, or Catholicos, of the Church of the East, commonly called the Nestorians. In 781, he held a public discourse, often described as a *Muhawarah*, or debate with the ruling Caliph, al-Mahdi (775–785). However, the tone was polite, respectful and irenic, not polemical. Unlike al-Kindy's exchange, which may well be fictitious although representative of actual debates that may have occurred, and in its published form was intended primarily for internal Christian consumption, Timothy's exchange appears to have been genuine and public. Unfortunately, Mar Timothy's arguments did not become standard within Christian–Muslim encounter, because it was only in the early twentieth century that this exchange came to the attention of a wider readership.[1]

Nestorians and Islam

As Catholicos, Mar Timothy I appears to have had easy access to the court. He was recognized as head of a *dhimma* (protected community). There is evidence that the Patriarach or Catholicos of the Nestorians was regarded as head of all Christians within the borders of the caliphate. Having been persecuted by Byzantine Christians, Nestorians may even have welcomed the Islamic conquerors as liberators. It is said that some joined in the enterprise, so that 'at times the first Arab conquests were led – in a noteworthy paradox – under a flag bearing a cross' (Alichoran, 1996: 86). It was perhaps traditions of Muhammad's own dealings with Nestorians that resulted in a special relationship, although one anecdote suggests that not all Timothy's predecessors shared his somewhat positive approach. Alichoran says that a previous Catholicos, Hnanicho, encountered 'Abd-al-Malik (in 691) who asked him, 'What do you think of the Arab religion?' to which the Catholicos replied, 'It is a religion established by the sword, and not a faith confirmed by divine miracles, as with the Christian faith and the divine laws of Moses'. He thus trotted out standard criticisms of Islam, encountered in the previous chapter. The Caliph is said to have ordered the Catholicos' tongue cut off but was persuaded by others not to execute this. Instead, he banned the Catholicos from ever seeing him again (87). Generally, however, 'treatment of the Nestorians up to the seventh century was favorable' (88). Nestorians continued to be active in missions beyond the borders of the caliphate, establishing churches in India and in China. 'Thorough their translations', they also 'transmitted Greek philosophy to the Arabs' exercising 'an important intellectual influence on the Muslim conquerors' (Courbage and Fargues, 1997: 7–8). Nestorian writing on Islam, according to Landron (1994), showed a wide knowledge of such issues as the charge of *tahrif*, 'Muslim incomprehension of a Christian God formed from the Trinity and veneration of the cross as idolatry' (Alichoran, 1994: 89).

Timothy tells us that he often had meetings with the Caliph, sometimes to attend to the business affairs of his community, sometimes to discuss religious subjects. On this occasion, his meeting was a religious discussion. Although described as a debate, the discourse reads much more like a dialogue. Some of the subjects covered are the same as in John of Damascus, Al-Kindy and Pfander but the tone, as well as the style, is different. In fact, the arguments Timothy offered are similar to, if not the same as, those of the confrontationalists. What differs is less content, with one significant exception, than the courtesy with which the discourse proceeds. The exception is that at no point does Timothy say anything critical or disrespectful of the Prophet. Rather, he tries, as a Christian, to locate Muhammad within God's providential purposes without admitting that the logic of this is for Christians to become Muslim. This is the fundamental difference between Timothy and those Christians whose contributions were discussed in Chapter 3. They had no doubt that Muhammad was not a true prophet, whose conduct was immoral, or that Christianity, not Islam, was God's path. There is no evidence that they even tried to understand whether Jesus and Muhammad, Christianity and Islam, might both be from God. This appears to be the challenge that Timothy set himself. If Muhammad was a prophet or a servant of God, his character could not be so deeply flawed that no self-respecting person would follow him. Arguably, this breaks new ground. At the root of any theology that can give space to both Islam and Christianity is willingness to see God at work beyond the visible borders of the Church. A willingness to see God's hand behind Islam does not necessarily attribute Islam equal value with Christianity, as in the pluralist paradigm. An inclusivist would still maintain ultimate loyalty to Jesus while recognizing that a Muslim could also be saved. This review of the conversation or dialogue between the Catholicos and the Caliph focuses on what was said about Muhammad, and what was said about the Unity–Trinity issue.

The Catholicos Honours the Prophet

At a key point in the dialogue, towards the start of day two, the Caliph asks the Catholicos, 'What do you say about Muhammad?' Muslims have often said to me that part of the problem as they perceive it in Christian–Muslim relations is that while they readily answer the question, 'What do they think of Jesus?', with belief in his status as a virgin-born Prophet, Christians either refuse to answer the question 'What do they think of Muhammad?', or reply that he was a charlatan, a false-prophet or a sincere but sincerely misguided man. Timothy's ready and respectful reply suggests that he had already given careful thought to this difficult question. If Jesus is God's way of salvation for all people, offering humanity all that is needed for salvation, what role can Muhammad play? Timothy first of all replied that Muhammad is 'worthy of all praise, by all reasonable men' (61). Already, he has parted radically from the confrontationalists, who never at any point indicate that Muhammad is worth any praise at all, let alone 'all praise'. The Catholicos then explains why he is able to affirm the praiseworthiness of Muhammad. He continues: 'he walked in the path of the prophets, and trod in the track of the lovers of God.' Timothy is moving towards a Muslim view of Muhammad. The Qur'an affirms again and again that Muhammad was the successor of all earlier prophets, including Abraham, Moses, David and Jesus, and complains that Jews and Christians stubbornly refused to recognize him. A Christian explanation of the fact that earlier Qur'anic passages addressing Jews and Christians appear friendly and positive, while later passages appear critical, is that they reflect Muhammad's disappointment that the people of the book failed to recognize him as a legitimate prophet foretold in their scripture. Muir speaks of Muhammad, following the revelation of 9:29, as 'with threats of abasement and cruel words', parting 'from both Jews and Christians, whom he had so long entertained with professions of attachment to their scriptures' (1923: 453–4). Timothy, by describing Muhammad as 'walking in the paths of the Prophet', appears to be offering Muslims what Muhammad may have expected from Christians whom he had encountered: that is, recognition of his prophetic status.

How did Timothy arrive at the decision that, instead of being a false-prophet, Muhammad was actually a prophet of God? He develops his argument in the next few sentences of the apology, in which he describes Muhammad as 'teaching the doctrine of the oneness of God' and as driving 'men away from bad works', 'separating them from idolatry' and 'attaching them to God'. In John of Damascus there was a grudging recognition that Muhammad had preached 'one God' and that previously the Arabs had 'undoubtedly' been 'idolaters', but mixed with this was the charge that he was a 'false prophet' who beguiled men into thinking he was a 'God-fearing fellow'. Also, John was not entirely convinced that Islam was free of idolatry, since he accused Muslims of worshipping the Black Stone. In contrast, Timothy's praise of Muhammad as walking in the path of the prophets, of proclaiming the Oneness of God and as leading men to good works lacks any hint that Muhammad was insincere, or misled people about his true character. Rather, Muhammad had stood firm against persecution, 'fought and opposed' those who 'worshipped idols', 'honoured and worshipped only one God' (62). Timothy went further. Just as Muslims understood Muhammad's eventual victory and the success of Islam's territorial expansion as a sign of God's blessing, so did he: 'God honoured him exceedingly and brought low before his feet two powerful kingdoms' (62). Far from being a charlatan, Muhammad was, like Abraham, a friend of God (*khalil Allah*, a Qur'anic description of Abraham; Q4: 125). As a God-lover himself, Timothy saw no contradiction in uttering what he did of Muhammad, since God had already praised him. Not surprisingly, the Caliph responded by asking why, if he honoured Muhammad as a true prophet, the Catholicos did not also 'accept the words of the Prophet'?

Timothy's reply was cautious. Having, from a Christian point of view, conceded the genuineness of Muhammad's status as a Prophet, was not the logic of his position conversion as a Muslim? Timothy did not regard this as a consequence of what he had said of Muhammad, replying, 'which words' must he accept? Unfortunately, he does not elaborate much on this issue because the Caliph's reply played out nicely for Timothy in terms of the way in which the conversation developed. To the question, 'which words of Muhammad' should he accept, the Caliph offered what amounts to the *shahadah*, 'That God is one and there is no other besides Him'. Timothy did not hesitate to state that he had no difficulty whatsoever in affirming the Unity of God, since his own scriptures (Old and New Testament) also affirmed the Oneness of God. He would 'live and die' by that belief (62). The Caliph may have anticipated that Timothy would affirm his belief in One God but knew full well that Christians speak of One God in Three Persons, which, for Muslims, is problematic. For some, it amounts to polytheism, or *shirk* (associating a partner with God). For others, it falls short of *shirk* but nonetheless compromises Christian monotheism. Thus, the Caliph remarks, 'You believe in One God, as you said, but one in three' (62). From a discussion of Muhammad's character in which none of the usual polemic about his moral character, such as multiple marriages, or the charge that he manufactured revelation featured, the dialogue now moves into discussion of the Trinity. One controversial issue, Muhammad's use of the sword, did feature in the dialogue. As seen in Chapter 3, a standard criticism of Muhammad was that use of the sword was the only argument he could use in favour of Islam, and that Islam spread mainly by the sword but also because it promised sexual and material rewards, at least for men. This argument has re-surfaced recently due to Pope Benedict XVI citation from Byzantine emperor Manuel II Paleologus' conversation with 'an educated Persian on the subject of Christianity and Islam' in Constantinople between 1394 and 1402, in which the Emperor asked, 'show me just what Mohammed brought that was new, and there you will find things only evil and inhuman, such as his command to spread by the sword the faith he preached' (2006). On this issue, the Catholicos departs from the traditional Christian view and states that Muhammad deserved praise because he 'not only fought for God in words, but showed also his zeal for him in the sword' (61). He makes a comparison with Moses, who killed those who had built the Golden Calf. He does not make any comparison with Christian use of the sword. He may not have known of such examples as that of Clovis, chief of the Franks, who was baptized with 3,000 followers on Christmas Day 496 CE then fought both for God and for plunder, claiming that if 'he and his Franks had been there, no one would have crucified Jesus' (Thompson, 1988: 25).

The Unity–Trinity Debate

Responding to the Caliph's question, Timothy states that he does not deny that he believes in 'three in one' and also in 'one in three' but he does deny that he believes in three separate Godheads. He does believe in God, in God's Word and in God's spirit but these three, he says, 'constitute one God, not in their persons but in their nature' (62). Christian belief in the Oneness of God precludes, he continues, the possibility that there are three Gods. The Caliph is unconvinced, asking how 'is it that these three persons whom you mention do not constitute three God's?' (63). Use of the term *prosopon* (person) sounds to Muslims as if Christians believe in three distinct, separate, independently existing entities. How could such three distinct and separate entities be One? Initially, Timothy's explanation attempts to argue from number, proposing that the number one causes the number two which is turn causes number three, and vice-versa, three causes two and two causes one. Thus, 'The Three in Him are the cause of One, and the one that of three' (63). Far from convinced, the Caliph suggests that this argument should result in endless Gods, since three is also the cause of four, four of five. Later, Ibn Taymiyyah argued that for Christians to stop at three is arbitrary and that this effectively limits God's qualities (Michel, 1984: 267). Timothy's response is to claim that any comparison can only be pursued so far and that in this instance there is no need to replicate the process endlessly because three is a 'perfect number'. 'All numbers', he says, 'are included in Three.' Perhaps suggesting that applying any number to God is a human description of God that fails to describe the totality of God, Timothy says that there is 'no number in God' (64). Nonetheless, when Christians describe God as possessing three persons they do not imply any 'multiplication or division of Gods' but are referring to God, Word and Spirit. Still, the Caliph is unconvinced; 'the number three denotes plurality, and since there cannot be plurality in Godhead, this number has no room at all in Godhead'. 'The book', stated the Caliph, attests to the number 'One' (64). Timothy's reply is to assert that, just as scripture attests to the number one vis-à-vis the Godhead, it also refers to God as possessing plurality. He cites as an example Genesis' 'Let is make man in our likeness' and the Great Commission at the end of Matthew, which refers to Father, Son and Spirit. The Qur'an too speaks of God sending down God's spirit, thus, 'the number one refers to nature and to Godhead, the number three to God, His Word and His Spirit' and 'because God has never been, is not and will never be, without Word and Spirit' God is three in one and one in three (65). The Caliph responded that use of 'we' and 'our' in scripture does not imply plurality within God but is a 'mark of Divine majesty and power'. Even human kings, he commented, 'use such a mode of speech'.

Timothy replied that what the Caliph had said is true, and represents the unity between king and a king's people, thus 'if all men are with the king, and the king orders, says and does, all men order, say and do in the king, and he says and does in the name of all'. Yet, just as the king consists of his body and his soul, so God comprises God's Word and God's Spirit. These are living beings and are part of the nature or essence of God, just as the king's 'word and spirit' are part of his 'nature'. Just as there is only one king, so there is only one God. The Word of God and the Spirit of God, he continues, are not made but 'creators and makers' (67). Perhaps the mysterious letters A. L. R., T. S. M and Y. S. M., with which some chapters of the Qur'an begin, denote the Holy Trinity. Timothy may have been consciously moving closer to Muslim belief in the *sifat*, or attributes of God as on the one hand distinct and different qualities but on the other hand as eternally existent within God. The problem for Muslims is that when Christians speak of the Word as Jesus, who was a man on earth, this sounds like a separate person, not like a quality of God, which can be understood as a mode in which God acts, or as a 'way of being'. Nicea condemned a modal theology that described Son and Spirit as temporary, that is, as 'ways of being which God adopted in time' which were not part of God's eternal nature. These modes are 'extrinsic' to God's 'unchanging nature', not eternally and immutably part of God's essence (Michel, 2000). Nonetheless, Timothy steers here towards making a Trinity of modes through which God operates more acceptable to Muslims. Responding to the mysterious letters, the Caliph asks why, if they refer to Trinity, the Prophet would not have said so clearly? Timothy responds that in a society where many people worshipped a multiplicity of idols and false Gods, 'they would have believed that this was polytheism'. That was why Muhammad 'proclaimed openly the doctrine of the one God, but' only spoke of the 'Trinity in a somewhat veiled and mysterious way' (68). One view is that the Qur'an's condemnation of Christians for worshipping Three Gods was directed at Christians who indeed did worship three Gods and was not directed at orthodox Christianity at all. As long as Christians speak of the second person of the Trinity as God's Word, which does correspond closely to Muslim belief in *kalam* as God's eternal speech, Trinity begins to resemble the Muslim *sifat*-doctrine. However, God's Word as incarnate in God's son, who was born as a flesh and blood human, runs foul of the Qur'an's strong affirmation that God neither begets nor is begotten. While Timothy believed, and Christians traditionally believe, in a literal, physical birth, modern Christology does not necessarily endorse this but argues for a spiritual, non-literal understanding of Jesus' divine son-ship, or for Jesus as God's adopted son, whose consciousness of God and complete identification of his will with God's blurred the divine–human distinction. Thus, Jesus is the first human to complete the process of *theosis*, or of divinization.

Discussion continued regarding how the scriptural passages cited above should properly be understood, with Timothy insisting that they indicate God's plurality without compromising God's unity. The *shema* (hear, Israel), the declaration that 'The Lord your God is One Lord', said Timothy, refers to God, to God as Lord, and to One Lord, thus the three words, 'Lord, God and Lord' refer to three persons of that Godhead. This is the same as saying that 'God, His Word and His Spirit were one eternal God' (69). The Caliph repeatedly insisted that God was either One or Three but not both, remaining unconvinced. Timothy then uses an analogy that would gain popularity in Christian–Muslim debate and which probably was not original to him: 'the sun', he said, 'is also one . . . in its spherical globe, its light and heat, and the very same sun, is also three, one sun in three powers'. The fact that the sun comprises of three elements does not 'contradict and annul the fact that they are also one' (69). Exactly the same applies to God: 'the fact that God is one does not annul the other fact that He is in three persons.' The 'eternal nature of God', states the Catholicos, 'consists in Fatherhood, Filiation and Procession, and in three of them He is one God, and in being One God He is the three of them' (70). In his response to Paul of Antioch, Ibn Taymiyyah rebuts a similar argument. The Caliph was still reluctant to concede and asked the Catholicos if, by using such an analogy as that of human nature as composed body, mind and soul and that of the sun as composed of light, heat and sphericity, he was imputing that God's nature is composed of the three persons of the Trinity. The Caliph's point here is that the above are created objects, or parts of human nature. Timothy responds by stating that God is incomparable – 'there is no other God like him' and that any comparison with worldly reality is 'an imperfect comparison', because 'things that are God's are above comparison and likeness'. God's attributes, he says, 'are of the nature of God', and, since 'God has no beginning and end', neither do they (72). The Caliph insists that 'the mind of rational beings will not agree to speak of God who is eternally one in Himself in terms of Trinity', with which Timothy agrees. However, says Timothy, since God has revealed this truth about God's-self, the rational mind, albeit in an 'imperfect and partial manner', can speak of God in this way, which belongs not so much to our 'rational minds' as to 'what God has revealed and taught about Himself' (72).

The next phase of the dialogue revolves around the nature of God's 'perception', that is, if a subject requires an object in order to 'perceive', how could God have been a 'perceiver' before there were any created objects for God to 'perceive'? 'A perceiver', said Timothy, 'perceives a perceived object?' (73). The Caliph agreed. 'How', asked Timothy, 'can God, who is a Spirit without a body, without divisions, without parts . . . perceive Himself' or be 'perceived by others?' (74). Both the Caliph and the Patriarch agree that God does perceive Himself and others and that God's knowledge has no limits. Timothy's solution to the conundrum is that God perceives God's-self through the mirror of the Word and Spirit, which mirror God. God perceives God's Word and Spirit as 'existing divinely and eternally' while God perceives God's creatures 'not as existing but as going to exist in the future'. The Caliph asks if, in order to be perceived, these 'parts' of God must be 'placed at a distance from one another' (74–75). Timothy reverts to the Sun analogy to reply that just as light, heat and the sun's sphere exist within the sun 'without break or confusion', and just as reason, soul and body co-exist without confusion or separateness, so 'The Father is in the Son, and the Son in the Spirit, without any break, distance, and confusion of any kind' (75). Timothy insists again that all comparisons and analogies 'are far below that adorable and ineffable nature of God' (75). There is a real danger in speculating about God's nature, lest we add to God what is wrong, or false. The Caliph agreed. However, said Timothy, with reference to the Trinity, this does not 'add' to God but describes how God actually is and how God has revealed God's-self to humanity (75). Adding 'something' to God is blasphemy but so is diminishing God.

The Caliph then pursed the question of whether God could have perceived 'His creatures before He created them?' Timothy's point had been that while the Word and Spirit were eternal attributes of God, God's creatures are not but that God perceives them in God's knowledge that they will exist. The Caliph presses Timothy here to admit that, if existence is not a necessary condition of 'being perceived', then might there not also be a point at which Word and Spirit did not exist? Timothy responds by arguing that two different types of perception are involved here, that which applies to the perception of what is created, and that which applies to 'the Word and Spirit'. The former are finite, the latter infinite. God perceives Word and Spirit 'in an infinite way' but God perceives God's creatures only 'through His prescience, and not as a substance that is of the same nature as Himself' (77). This does not convince the Caliph, who says that, as far as he can see from what the Catholicos has said, 'the Word and Spirit are also creatures of God, and there is no one who is uncreated except one God' (77). Convinced that Word and Spirit are not only of the essence of God, but God's instruments in creation Timothy suggests that if Word and Spirit were created, God must have created the world 'by means of another word and another spirit'. Such an argument, he said, could go around in circles until all admit that Word and Spirit are 'hidden eternally in God' (78). The Caliph, still unconvinced, tells Timothy that he obviously believes in 'three heads', to which Timothy replies, 'This is certainly not so . . . I believe in one head, the eternal God the Father, from whom the Word shone and the Spirit radiated eternally, together' (78). Word and spirit are from God's single nature. To strip God of God's word and spirit would be like stripping a person of their mind and reason. After this, the Caliph asserted that Timothy's

God is a 'vacuous God, since He has a child'. Timothy replied that he neither believed in a vacuous nor in a solid God because God is an incorporeal Spirit. Fire produces light, just as the soul begets the mind but we 'do not say that either the soul or fire are hollow or solid' (79). The Caliph suggests that bodily comparisons will not take Timothy very far, to which he responds that for people with bodies, such comparisons are the only ones available to us, limited although they are, since we are not spiritual beings. God communicated about God's nature to the Prophets 'not as He is, because they cannot know and hear about Him as He is, but simply in the way that fits in with their own nature' (79). The Caliph agreed that God is 'above all the thoughts and minds of created beings' but suggested that Timothy erred in his analogies because they placed God and God's creatures 'on the same footing' (80). Timothy's reply indicates that the Caliph's reference here was to the Word and Spirit as created; Timothy says that he considered it close to 'unbelief' to reduce Word and Spirit to the status of creatures. In the same way as the Caliph, his lordship and his kingdom comprise one entity, so do the persons of the Trinity. Yet, he says, the Caliph's sons, who are included within the kingdom, possess different personalities from their father. Just so, the persons of the Trinity possess different personalities (81).

The Caliph argued that Jesus, as God's Son, could not be co-eternal and co-equal with God since scriptures describe Jesus as 'God's servant'. A servant is not his or her master's equal. Timothy cites Isaiah's 'for to us a child is born', arguing that this refers to Jesus as 'a son, not a servant and a created being' (83). Just as the Caliph would become angry if his sons were called 'servants', so God would be 'wrathful if anybody called His Word and His Spirit servants'. Why then is Jesus' described as a 'servant' – for example, in Isaiah 53 which Christians apply to Jesus and Philippians 2:7 – asked the Caliph? Timothy argued that just as the Caliph's sons acted in a servant capacity when they carried out duties on behalf of their father yet while doing so do not forfeit their 'royal sonship', so Jesus served God when he came to earth to suffer and die and to rise again and did not 'lose His royal Sonship' or 'become a stranger to Divinity' (84). So, too, the Caliph's sons when he sent them on military missions retain their share in their father's majesty. Ignorant foreigners who do not recognize the Caliph's sons' royal identity may mistake them for mere servants. Those who failed to recognize Jesus' true identity thought that he was merely a man, a servant (85). David, Timothy continued, was God's servant yet through Him all people are promised a blessing. That blessing is Jesus, who will reign over all kingdoms; such a person is no servant but 'a Lord and Master' (86). How then, the Caliph enquires, did Jesus as God 'suffer and die in the flesh'? How can God die? Timothy responded by naming as heresy the belief that God God's-self suffered and died. Rather, it was 'the Son and Jesus Christ' who died (87). Timothy's explanation here, however, is confusing, since he argues that in becoming human in Jesus the Word did not take on the resemblance of mortal flesh but clothed mortal flesh with the resemblance of God: 'it is the painter who paints the picture to his own resemblance . . . not the wood that works and fashions a carpenter in its resemblance' (88). This sounds like an assertion that, since Jesus was immortal, Jesus did not actually die on the Cross. He then appears to suggest that in this world we may never fully understand such matters; we will understand when we die and the 'darkness of mortality passes, and the fog of ignorance dissolves'. Then we will possess the 'pearl'. Yet, something of the lustre of the pearl is visible in this world, because God has not left 'the pure pearl of the faith completely without testimony and evidence' through the prophets and the gospels (89). The Caliph expressed the hope that he might hold the 'pearl in his hands'. Timothy expressed the hope that the Caliph, and his sons, Musa and Harun, would prosper and continue to serve the Sovereign of all 'till the day in which the Kingdom of Heaven is revealed from heaven to earth' (90). The Caliph then entered his audience chamber, while Timothy 'returned in peace' to his 'patriarchal residence'. 'Here ends', says the text, 'the controversy of the Patriarch Mar Timothy I with Mahdi, the Caliph of the Muslims. May eternal praise be to God.' Several issues, including the Qur'an's depiction of the crucifixion of Jesus and how Muhammad could be a true prophet of God if Jesus, as Christians assert, represents the finality of God's revelation, were not discussed. The Caliph was obviously not convinced by Timothy's arguments in support of Trinity, yet the 'controversy' lacked rancour, hostility or anything that could be described as polemical. Throughout, Timothy refers to the Caliph as 'our victorious king', 'O wise sovereign' or as 'your Majesty' and the Caliph speaks with respect to the Catholicos as 'O Catholicos'. The dialogue shows how difficult it is for Christians, even in such an irenic and open context in which both sides appear to have genuinely listened to the other, to progress on these problematic issues. Perhaps what this much more conciliatory approach points towards is the possibility that Christians and

Muslims are both right, that both theologies are true but that God is indeed ultimately beyond any human description, and, in communicating to us, does so at a lower level of truth. Nowhere did Timothy imply that God does not communicate through the Qur'an. Indeed, when speaking of Jesus as Word and as Spirit he referred to the Qur'an's description of Jesus as 'the Word and Spirit' (83; Q4: 171). Timothy was, though, wrong when he asserted that the Qur'an does not describe Jesus as a servant, since it does so in such passages as 4:172 and 19:30. Timothy does not cite actual verses but refers to the content of verses, suggesting that he may not have had the same textual familiarity as al-Kindy, who gives complete passages. Here, he is closer to John of Damascus. Muslims themselves at that time would not reference the Qur'an in the modern manner; they would first cite the chapter by name and then recite the relevant verse. At bottom, Timothy implies that he and the Caliph stand on the same, not different ground. While his conviction that to speak of God as non-Triune diminishes God and is blasphemous sounds like a parallel charge to the Muslim accusation that associating partners with God is a sin, he does not explicitly say this. Rather, he implies that Muhammad stressed the Unity of God, in which Christians also emphatically believe because of the circumstances of his time. He also argues that Trinity is implicit in the Qur'an's references to sending down God's spirit, to God's saying 'we did' or 'we made' (Q19: 17; 2: 133). Christians and Muslims may therefore both be right. Sadly, this issue remains one of the most widely debated, alongside that of Muhammad's moral character. The latter, for Timothy, was not an issue.

The Crusades and Exceptions to the Demonizing View of Muslims

Timothy lived at a time when Christians fared well in the world of Islam. Muslims only formed the majority of the population shortly before the first Crusade, and even when the Crusaders arrived in the Holy Land, many people were recent converts. Treating non-Muslims respectfully may have been pragmatic. Nonetheless, Jews and Christians occupied significant posts. For example, Caliph al-Mutasim (833–42) had two Christian ministers, although his successor, al-Mutawakkil dismissed all Christians from their jobs

(Courbage and Fargues, 1997: 25). The Fatimds in Egypt (910–1171 CE) were generally well disposed towards Christians and Jews and even appointed them as *wazirs* (Michel, 1984: 79). Many new churches were built. The 'descendants of the Fatimids – the Ismailis, Nusayris, and Druzes of Syria' – continued to 'cooperate with Christians in assisting Mongols to fight Muslims'. The reigns of al-Hakim (996–1021) and of al-Mustansir (1036–94) were exceptions. Under Saladin, who defeated the Fatimids (1169), Christians and Jews were 'humiliated in their daily lives' but were 'not persecuted' (17). Saladin initially treated Copts harshly because he associated their religion with the enemy's but the Copts remained neutral towards the Crusading Franks. However, when the Mamlukes seized control of Egypt (1250), they reversed the policy of tolerance, dismissed Christians from their posts, forbade the building of new churches or the repairing of existing ones and required Christians to wear distinctive clothes. Courbage and Fargues suggest that this change of attitude was partly due to the fact that as non-Egyptians, the Mamlukes only shared religion with their subjects and were 'therefore intolerant towards Christians' (19). While the Muslim conquest of much of Spain and memory of the Battle of Tours (732) infuriated Christians in Europe, fuelling animosity towards the Saracen as the Godless enemy, relations were not always negative. In Spain itself, Christians, Jews and Muslims studied together at the great academies. Some inter-marriage occurred, as between Alfonso IV of Castille (1065–1109) and Princess Zaida, 'whose father was the most powerful among the rulers of the *taifa* states', the remaining Muslim territories in Spain (Fletcher, 2003: 116). Christian scholars visiting Spain from France and from England eagerly translated Arabic versions of Greek classics as well as the works of Muslim philosophers into Latin, so that Muslims such as Ibn Rushd and Ibn Sina not only acquired Latin names (Averroes) and (Avicenna) but would be cited by such eminent Christian thinkers as Aquinas (1225–1274) with respect. Scholasticism in Europe is generally said to have been heavily influenced by Muslim philosophy, so much so that one of the main schools was known as Averroism. It drew heavily on Averroes' commentaries on Aristotle. Aquinas explored the same issues as had the Muslim philosophers and, open to hearing God's voice through a variety of sources, saw himself and Muslims as occupying the same intellectual world of rational discourse. Muslims, he believed, could be won for Christ through reasoned argument, even with love. Such men as Peter the Venerable

(1092–1156), Ramon Lull (1234–1316) and Roger Bacon (1220–92) all believed that 'reason' not force was the correct *modus operandi* for Christians in relationship with Islam. Such legends as the Story of Roland and El Cid's chronicle still depicted Muslims as idolaters but more accurate information was becoming available.[2]

As well as a translation of Al-Kindy, Peter commissioned the first Latin rendition of the Qur'an, which, completed in 1143 has been described as 'a landmark . . . for the first time', Europeans had 'an instrument for the serious study of Islam' (Southern, 1962: 37). It remained the standard rendering until the sixteenth century. The translator was an Englishman, Robert of Ketton (1110–60), who had travelled in Palestine and appears to have settled in Spain in order to work as a translator. He was also an Archdeacon. Ketton's Qur'an was glossed with hostile footnotes (Fletcher, 2003: 128–9) but it at least gave Christians access to the complete scripture, rather than to selected sections. Lull, Bacon and others called for Arabic chairs at Paris and Oxford. Lull's own conviction that Muslims should be reasoned with did not preclude him from using some harsh language when addressing Muslims. A tertiary Franciscan, Lull was twice deported from Tunisia. On a third visit to the Muslim world he ended up defending the Trinity by publicly abusing Islam: 'the law of the Christians is holy and true', he said, 'and the sect of the Moors is false and wrong' (Daniel, 1997: 141). Stoned by the crowd, he died on ship before reaching his native Majorca. Yet the method he bequeathed, *ars inveniendi veritatis,* the art of finding the truth, was dialogical not confrontational and greatly influenced missionary thought. The Crusaders did not consider evangelism, the attempt to win the hearts of Muslims, as even worth trying, since Muslims were culpable and their death glorified Christ. The essence of crusading was 'to slay for God's love'. Muslims, said one Christian, were not worth disputing with but 'were to be extirpated by fire and the sword' (Daniel, 1997: 136). Lull suggested that instead of conquering the Holy Land by force, Christians ought to do so 'by love and prayer and the pouring out of tears and blood' (cited by Gairdner, 1920: 179; for Gairdner on Lull, see 178–86).

Commerce and trade was also carried out between Europe and the Muslim world. Famously, Charlemagne and Caliph Harun al-Rashid (763–809) exchanged ambassadors and the Caliph appointed the Emperor as guardian of Christian holy places. Charlemagne was granted 'permission to send regular aid to the Christians of Palestine and to finance various ecclesiastical institutions' (24). Christians were able to make the pilgrimage to Jerusalem without let or hindrance. This changed, though, when the Fatimids seized Palestine in 1009 and Hakim the Mad desecrated the Church of the Holy Sepulchre. Hakim's behaviour was eccentric. He imposed harsh restriction on Christians one day, reversed them the next, ordered their conversion one day, then rescinded it the next. He proclaimed himself the Mahdi (expected one thousand years after Jesus), although some claim that he converted to Christianity (Courbage and Fargues, 1997: 25). Hakim banned Christians from Jerusalem. His own successor rebuilt the church with assistance from the Byzantine Emperor. Pilgrimage was allowed again but Jerusalem was now a football between the rival dynasties, falling to the Seljuks in 1071 and again to the Fatimids in 1098, making pilgrimage risky. Both the Seljuks and the Fatimids were Shi'a. The first Crusade, launched in 1095, proclaimed by Pope Urban II, took advantage of this rivalry to seize the city from both and reassert its Christian ownership. Capturing Jerusalem in 1099, the crusaders helped to weaken Fatimid power. Saladin's rise to power in Egypt, at exactly the same time that the Crusaders reigned over Jerusalem, removed one of the Shi'a dynasties. His goal as a Sunni was now to defeat the Seljuks, to reunify the Sunni world. As it happened, the Crusaders states represented a buffer between Saladin and his northern enemies which, at times, was quite convenient. This is why Saladiin entered several treaties: in 1175 and 1180 with King Baldwin; and in 1192 with Richard the Lionheart, since his purposes were best served by the Crusaders remaining in place until he was ready to defeat the real enemy.

Saladin believed that the Crusaders would not be able to maintain their foothold, as indeed they could not. They had to rely on help from Europe, which either arrived too late or not at all. They needed to expand their loyal population through settlement but failed to attract enough European migrants (Courbage and Fargues, 1997: 49). They distrusted Eastern Christians so much that even when they offered help, they refused it (51). Eastern Christians, such as the Copts in Egypt, remained neutral. Even though many Muslims 'were descended from families who had only converted a few generations earlier' the Crusaders actually succeeded in making conversion to Christianity unattractive. Converts either had to 'remain in servitude or enlist as an auxiliary in the Frankish army' (51–2). Jews, many of whom had returned to Jerusalem, were banned; when Saladin retook the city, possibly assisted by Arab Christians, he lifted the ban against Jews and 'encouraged them to resettle in the Holy Land'

(53). Saladin, it is said, died 'at peace with his people, his enemies and with God', and was 'remembered by Muslims with love and by the Franks with respect' (Howarth, 1982: 178). However, at times some Christians and some Muslims allied themselves against the common enemy, the Mongols. There was even a truce between the Knights Templar and the Assassins (see Howarth, 1982: 128).

Later, in 1229 under Frederick II (1194–1250), Jerusalem was regained for ten years due to another peace treaty, identical in terms to one that St Francis of Assisi had negotiated exactly ten years earlier, which had been turned down by the papal legate to the fourth crusade, Cardinal Pelagius. The only condition was that the Crusaders left Egypt alone (Howarth, 1982: 200–02): 'The Holy City . . . Nazareth and Bethlehem and all the lands between them were there on a plate . . . but they turned it down because no Christian should treat with an infidel.' Francis is said to have regarded the Sultan as more humane and inclined towards peace than the Cardinal. The Sultan, Melek-el-Kamil (d. 1238), gave Francis the keys to his own mosque so that he would have a place to pray, reminiscent of Muhammad allowing the Christians of Najran to pray in his mosque. Pope Innocent III, who launched the fifth crusade, believed that Islam would flourish for 666 years – the number of the beast in Revelation – and then be defeated which, according to his calculations, would occur in 1226. This precluded the need for any treaties. Frederick II had been excommunicated and had no objections. In 1239, the Templars entered a Treaty with Damascus against Egypt.

St Francis represents a conciliatory approach to Islam. His willingness to negotiate peace with the Sultan of Egypt, and his rubric that while his Friars could pursue 'disputes and controversy', another method was to 'preach the word of God', qualify him as a conciliator. Some Friars did enter disputation and, as had the martyrs of Cordoba, deliberately insulted Muhammad to attract the death penalty. Several Friars were expelled from Seville for abusing Muhammad outside the royal palace and deported at their own request to Morocco, where they continued with this tactic. Arrested, they still acted in the same way. The Muslim authorities moved them from prison to prison in what appears to have been an effort to prevent them from so annoying the public that a death sentence would be unavoidable. This proved to be the case, and they were executed (Daniel, 1997: 144). Apocalyptic predictions that around about the year 1000, the end-time events, involving conflict with the representatives of Satan, would start to unfold lie behind the Crusades. Some success in defeating the Moors in Spain, such as the taking of Toledo (1085), raised Christian hopes that Muslims could be defeated. As the religious and cultural Other, Muslims were easily demonized. If Christians worshipped the true God, Muslims must worship a false God. The Crusaders did not merely set out to defeat Muslims but to kill[3] them as an act of merit that would result in the crusader's own salvation. It was as much spiritual as physical warfare. Crusaders, who took a vow, were also pilgrims: 'its exact terms are not known but it must have involved a promise to pilgrimage to Jerusalem combined with a pledge to liberate it by force' (Riley-Smith, 1987: 15) so that its pagan defilement could be wiped out (ibid.: 12). Most Muslims today point to the Crusades as an example of Christian aggression, and see this repeated in modern times by the West's support of Israel, which they regard as a contemporary Crusader state in the middle of the Muslim world. They also regard the invasion of Afghanistan (2001) and of Iraq (2003) as well as the 'war on terror' as anti-Muslim Crusades. Fletcher (2003) points out that there is no 'Islamic historiography of the Crusades' since even though they are currently perceived as having permanently damaged Christian–Muslim relations, at the time Muslims saw them as border skirmishes that only inflicted pinpricks on the fringe of the Muslim world (84).

The Kingdom of Heaven and Christian–Muslim Relations

Even in the Crusader states, friendships did develop between Christians and Muslims. Howarth and Fletcher both refer to Prince Usama of Shaizar, who 'liked and respected the Templars', admired Frankish justice but found their medicine primitive (Howarth, 1982: 122). Usama, says Fletcher, was a frequent visitor to the royal court in Jerusalem (91). King Baldwin IV (1161–85), supported by such barons as Balian of Ibelin, favoured establishing peaceful relations with his Muslim neighbours but others, such as Reynold of Chatillon, opposed this. Balian, after bravely defending Jerusalem, negotiated its surrender to Saladin. In the film *The Kingdom of Heaven*, this role falls to his fictitious son. Saladin entered Jerusalem, ransomed off 7,000 of the remaining 20,000 Franks, released 1,200 and enslaved the few who could not pay for freedom 'but no one was killed' (Howarth, 1982: 155). 'I am not those men', said Saladin, when reminded how much Muslim blood the Crusaders shed when they had taken the city. In the film, we see him picking up, with respect, a fallen cross. When Balian is on his way to the port of Messina, he passes a supporter of the Crusades, who cries out 'to kill an infidel is not murder; it's the path to heaven'. However, when Balian arrives in Jerusalem he is surprised to see Muslims at prayer, and comments that it 'sounds like our prayer'. 'At the end of the world you are not what you were born but what you have it in yourself to be . . . there is peace between Christians and Muslims . . . we live here together', he is told. Muslims tried to be 'one, one heart, one morality'. Were they, indeed, his brothers? Tiberius, the king's commander, however, is pessimistic that this *convivencia* will outlive the ailing king: 'when the king is dead, Jerusalem will be no place for friends of Muslims.' Tiberius is weary because he had thought that he was 'fighting for God' but realized that many Crusaders were fighting for 'wealth and land'. He no longer put any 'stock in religion' which was the 'lunacy of fanatics'. What mattered, he said, what made for holiness was 'right action' and 'courage on behalf of those who cannot defend themselves'. Balian found himself thinking that no one and yet everyone had a claim to Jerusalem; Jews, Christians and Muslims had their holy places yet what was most important of all was not its stones but its people. The kingdom of heaven was on earth, where people had the opportunity to realize their common humanity; he would rather live with men than kill them. The true kingdom could never be surrendered. Raymond himself, says Fletcher (2003), spent 15 years in Aleppo as a prisoner of the Muslims. He hated Muslims and was eventually executed for 'war crimes' by Saladin yet he also 'adopted much of the manner of life of the Arab world' (88). Raymond's pro-war stance, his breach of the treaty with Saladin and his execution all feature in Ridley Scott's film. The film also shows Saladin as a gracious and humane leader, who genuinely respected Baldwin, offering to send him physicians to treat his leprosy.

Medieval Conciliators

Paul of Antioch (1140–80) was a Melkite or Greek Catholic bishop in communion with Rome when Antioch was a Crusader state (1098–1268). On the one hand, his Letter to a Muslim argued that

Islam offers Christians nothing that can save them. On the other, it accepts that Muhammad may 'well have been sent with the Qur'an to the pagan Arabs' but says that he is not to be regarded as a universal prophet (Michel, 1984: 88). The bishop cited the verses of friendship as evidence that Islam is not hostile to Christianity and such a passage as 5: 8 to refute the charge of *tahrif*. Since Ibn Taymiyyah's refutation of Christianity includes a rebuttal of Paul, I summarize the details of Paul's argument in Chapter 5. However, as well as Paul, Bishops William of Tripoli (1130–86) and William of Tyre (1120–73) emphasized points of similarity between Christianity and Islam and thought that Muslims were 'not far from the path of salvation' (Southern, 1962: 62). William of Tripoli saw Islam as truth mixed with error but chose to dwell 'more upon the brightness of the "borrowed plumage" than upon the blackness of the crow that it wore' (Daniel, 1997: 190). Tripoli did think that Islam's end was imminent, when Muslims would embrace the Christian faith. Like Paul of Antioch, he thought that Islam could be valid for Arabs, a national but not a universal faith (Daniel, 1997: 40). He also suggested that Christians and Jews had, as the Qur'an claims, failed to properly preserve their revelations and thus God revealed 'their own law, the Qur'an, in its excellence and purity' to the Arabs. Such language as this would never have passed John's or Al-Kindy's lips. Another conciliator from this classical period was Nicholas of Cusa (1401–64), a German scholar, bishop and Cardinal whom Pope Pius II asked to write in support of his crusading plans. Already influenced by Lull, Nicholas instead produced a work called *Cribratio Alcorani* ('The Sieving of the Qur'an'), which suggested that although it mixed truth with error, when properly understood the Qur'an is compatible with Christian teaching (Fletcher, 2003: 148).[4] Nicholas used Ketton's translation, so his citations do not correspond to standard references. He also travelled to Constantinople to interview Christians there at the Church of the Holy Cross, where he found an Arabic Qur'an. The brothers 'explained' this 'to him as best they could in regard to certain of its points' (Hopkins, 1994: 965). When he asked whether Greeks had 'written against these foolish errors' he was told that John of Damascus had. In addition to Ketton, he made wide use of Ricoldo's *Confutatio*. Ricoldo (1243–1320), a Dominican missionary in Baghdad, was more of a polemicist than an apologist yet grudgingly wrote of Muslim virtues, good manners, hospitality and 'love for each other' (Daniel, 1997: 231). Ricoldo knew al-Kindy but he could also cite some *hadith* and, says Sweetman (1955), despite inability to transcend the limitation of his time, we 'can discern' here 'a competent mind, a high degree of proficiency in Arabic' and 'a fairly wide knowledge of literature dealing with Islamic tradition' (159).

Nicholas cited Ricoldo's attribution of much of Muhammad's teaching to his meeting with Sergius (Hopkins, 1994: 969). However, since Nestorians were heretics, Muhammad never enjoyed contact with Orthodox Christians. On the one hand, his errors can be explained by his ignorance; on the other, they are also due to Muhammad's 'malevolence' (968). Muhammad also desired to glorify himself, not God (969). Yet Muhammad did not write anything against 'the most holy trinity' except that he condemned the doctrine of a plurality of Gods (971). 'Even though Muhammad himself was very far removed from a true understanding of the Gospel', the 'truth of the gospel' can easily be found in the Qur'an (971). 'To the wise', wrote Nicholas, 'the splendour of the Gospel shines forth in the Qur'an' (984). In discussing the Trinity, Nicholas uses the same arguments as Timothy; thus, just as when Muhammad used 'we' of God, he 'did not mean to affirm more than one God', neither does the Trinity (1018). A detailed argument for the Trinity follows which does not interact very closely with Muslim argumentation. He does not attempt to use an analogy with *Sifat*. He suggests that the Qur'an deliberately obscured Christ's death, since this would have seemed like failure to the Arab mind (1031). Nicholas, like earlier polemicists, did refer to inconsistencies in the Qur'an. However, he does not ridicule Muhammad's fabrication of verses to further his personal, immoral agenda but suggests that Muhammad prevaricated on some issues, such as on who would be saved, because he did not know the truth. He did, though, take up the sword when he saw that people would not recognize that he was God's prophet without such persuasion (1060; here he cites from the *Confutatio*, Chapter 7l; see Hopkins, 1994: 1099, n. 36). The tone of the book is not polemical. Most of the text consists of reasoned argument. Fletcher surmises that Nicholas thought that 'ways to God existed independent of confessional allegiance', leaving open the possibility that 'if a Christian mystic could find God, could not a Muslim Sufi also?' (148).[5]

Gairdner and Massignon

More recently, the Anglican W. H. T. Gairdner (1872–1928) and the Catholic Louis Massignon, the former tentatively, the latter explicitly, have entertained the possibility that Muslims can find God. Others think that they while they may sincerely seek for God they cannot complete the journey within Islam. Gairdner, an Anglican missionary in Egypt, translated *Al-Ghazali's Niche of Lights* (1924) and wrote such books as *The Rebuke of Islam* (1920), previously called *The Reproach of Islam* (1909), and the *Muslim Idea of God* (1925). Published by the Royal Asiatic Society, the *Niche* does not offer any Christian critique but is a penetrating and appreciative analysis of Al-Ghazali's text. Al-Ghazali (1058–1111), says Gairdner, offers as convincing a 'place for the Universe, philosophically, with or in Allah' as has any Western philosopher (74). Kerr (2002) says that it was as a result of this work that Gairdner 'turned . . . from a polemical to a spiritually searching approach to Islam' (13). In his missionary-oriented *Rebuke*, he argued that the only way by which Christianity had reached the Arabian prophet was through false gospels and the other literature of some heretical sects, which denied the divine sonship and the redeeming death of Christ (1920: 39). In this view, Q4: 157 is derived from Docetic belief in a Jesus who only seemed to be human, who therefore did not die or suffer on the Cross. Islam, for Gairdner (1920: 19), represented a rebuke to Christians, because had Christians of Muhammad's time borne him authentic witness, he would have been a Christian! Christians owed Muslims authentic witness. Building on the notion that Greek philosophy might be a schoolmaster pointing the Greeks towards Christ, Gairdner also spoke of Islam as a *preparatio evangelica* although he did not see Christianity as the completion of Islam so much as satisfying Muslims' spiritual aspirations (see Vander Werff, 1977: 217–19; Kerr, 2002: 13). Yet like Nicholas of Cusa, Gairdner believed that, read correctly, the Qur'an points towards, not away from Christ. Gairdner offers many of the standard criticisms of Muhammad and of the Qur'an. Muhammad set out to become a Moses-type prophet-leader of his people (53). Initially sincere, later, the 'fitness of the revelations to the circumstances increased, and ever increased until they seemed to degenerate into sanctions for his personal needs, notions and polices' (36). Yet Gairdner develops what he himself calls a 'non-controversial' style (205), which, he says, requires a thorough knowledge of Islam. He did not elaborate in great detail on the above reference to the fit between the Qur'an and Muhammad's agenda. He believed that simply being *present* as a Christian among Muslims witnesses the gospel by manifesting the 'spirit of Jesus' (243), an idea that would influence Kenneth Cragg. It also has much in common with Massignon's missiology.

Massignon's work, despite its continued influence and significance, is not easily accessed. His four-volume study of Al-Hallaj,[6] his 1922 doctoral thesis, is a work of outstanding scholarship but does not reveal his own convictions about Islam and its relationship with Christianity. Massignon lost his Catholic faith when he was 20, and embraced agnosticism and, as he put it, his own passions. A 1901 trip to sub-Saharan Africa attracted him to its lifestyle. In 1904, he went to Morocco to study classical and colloquial Arabic so that he could complete his degree at the College of France with a thesis on the geography of Morocco. In 1906, visiting Cairo, he first encountered the thought of Al-Hallaj, the Sufi mystic executed in 922 for declaring himself to be حـق, 'truth'. In 1907, the French government commissioned him to lead an archaeological expedition in Mesopotamia. While in Baghdad, he was arrested on suspicion of espionage. Taken in by the Alusi family, who were Muslims, it was their hospitality that changed his life. They also helped him acquire material for his work on al-Hallaj. During an illness precipitated by a failed suicide attempt, Massignon believed that he was visited by a 'stranger without a face'. He was so overwhelmed spiritually by this experience that he repented of his unbelief and found himself at peace with God. Later, he ascribed his re-conversion to the prayers and intercession of friends, or witnesses, including Al-Hallaj, his mother and Charles de Foucauld (1858–1916): Foucauld was then living as a hermit in Algeria, offering hospitality and adoration of God. In 1908, Massignon founded the Badaliyya, 'an association of Christians who lived among Muslims and, rather than proselytizing, expressed their Christian presence of witness by offering prayers of intercession and fasting on their behalf' (Zebiri, 1997: 185). Later, as executor of Charles de Foucauld's will, he helped establish the Little Brothers of Jesus who settle, work, pray and offer hospitality in Muslim lands but who do not talk about their faith unless they are invited to do so. During World War I, as an officer in the French army, Massignon befriended T. E. Lawrence. He was also a member of the French delegation to the Sykes–Picot negotiations that divided the Ottoman Empire among the allies, leading to the British Mandate of Palestine. After the war, he became Professor of

Muslim Sociology at the College of France, continuing to visit the Muslim world. On one of many visits, in 1933, at the old Franciscan church in Damietta, which St Francis had visited, he and a friend pledged themselves to live for the sake of Muslims, not so that they would be converted but so that God's will would work through them in Muslim lives.

A tertiary Franciscan since 1931, Massignon became a Greek Catholic in 1949. In 1950, he was ordained as a priest which, baptized as a Western Catholic, required special permission.[7] His theology was that some of us can offer our lives in substitution (*badaliya*) for others through prayer and fasting. Hospitality was central to his missiology; he never forgot that the Alusi had saved him. He stressed the common spiritual tie of Christians and Muslims to Abraham, taking the religious name of Ibrahim. He suggested that through Islam God was gathering in those who had been excluded from previous covenants, and that Islam fulfilled God's promise to bless Ishmael (Zebiri, 1997: 192). Muslims need not embrace Christianity; our faith can substitute for theirs. Al-Hallaj, he believed, had enjoyed a real relationship with God. As a Melkite priest, he worshiped in Arabic; he wanted to penetrate Islam's inner reality, to 'know' Islam from the inside-out. His writing demonstrates a profound knowledge of and empathy with Islam. Massignon, who is never polemical but always conciliatory, is an acknowledged influence behind Vatican II's *Nostra Aetate*. He may have entered the Muslim thought and linguistic world more completely than any previous Christian. Perhaps only Cragg has fully followed him on this journey. Nasr regards Massignon as having had a 'genuine if not always total and complete' love and knowledge of Islam (1990: 253). Talbi refers to him as 'my eminent master . . . whose whole life was a living dialogue' (1990: 86). Massignon admired Gandhi, adopted non-violence, and, in later life, worked for peace and reconciliation between Jews, Muslims and Christians in Israel–Palestine. He believed that harmonious co-existence is a real possibility. Jesus, he observed, had forgiven his enemies on the Cross. Said (1978) praises Massignon's endeavours in 'support of Palestinian refugees, in the defence of Arab Muslim and Christian rights' and of 'Muslim civilization' in general (270). 'One would be foolish', said Said, 'not to respect the sheer genius and novelty of Massignon's mind' (269). However, he also points out that Massignon was often consulted by governments (210) and that, while critical of the West's colonial project and its 'relentless attacks on Islam' (270), he nonetheless saw

East and West as *essentially different*. For Massignon, 'the essence of the difference between East and West is between modernity and ancient tradition' (269). Said suggests that Massignon rooted his understanding of Islam in 'ancient texts' and so, in his effort to understand the Israeli–Palestinian conflict, 'never really got past the quarrel between Isaac and Ishmael', which brings us back to foundational biblical texts once again.

Chapter 5

The Traditional Muslim Confrontational Appoach to Christianity

This chapter examines traditional Muslim appraisal of Christianity, beginning with early examples of negativity towards Christians represented by their expulsion from Arabia under Caliph Umar II and with early examples of persecution and intolerance. Friedmann (2003), who provides useful data on the interpretation of Qur'anic material and of relevant *hadith* on the status of non-Muslims in classical Islamic *fiqh* (law), points out that Muslims have in practice determined their relationship with Others in terms of either 'tolerance or intolerance' according to the particular 'historical circumstances in which the encounter took place' (1). They could choose to stress the verses of friendship alongside such texts as 5:48 and 109:6, or they could choose to stress the verses of hostility alongside the sword verses (9:5; 9:29). Certain *hadith* could be affirmed or rejected. The Hanbali jurist al-Khallal (d. 923 CE) rejected a *hadith* that stated that Christians and Jews belonged to Muhammad's community. Ibn Hanbal, he reported, was so 'furious' when he heard this *hadith* that he declared the idea so 'filthy' that it 'should not be discussed'. He dismissed it as too low to regard anyone who transmitted the *hadith* to be a true Muslim (Friedmann, 2003: 32). Ibn Taymiyyah, rejected the commonly cited *hadith* 'he who harms a *dhimmi* harms me', arguing that this *hadith* amounted to 'absolute protection to unbelievers; moreover, it would make it a travesty of justice, for, just as in the case of Muslims, there are times when they deserve punishment and physical harm' (Michel, 1984: 81). Christians should, in this view, 'feel themselves subdued' when they pay the *jizya* (Q9:29). Khadduri (1955) comments how jurists interpreted this verse to justify humiliating non-Muslims as punishment for 'persistence in disbelief' (200). When Muslims were themselves either a minority or a small majority, leniency was often practised and non-Muslims occupied significant posts. At such times, certain restrictions applied, such as not performing rituals in public, ringing church bells or sometimes riding a horse. Christians were often required to wear distinctive clothes, yet as Friedmann says, 'Muslims can take comfort in the commonly held view that the living conditions of non-Muslims under Muslim rulers were significantly better than those imposed on Jews and the religious minorities by their Christian counterparts' (4). Nonetheless, considerable discussion did take place on the status of Christians and Jews and some influential Muslim voices argued that they should be humiliated and subjected to systematic oppression until they embraced Islam.

The words of Q9:29 'until they are brought low' are thus interpreted to mean that 'humiliation should be inflicted on the People of the Book as a punishment for their obduracy' (34). Zamakhshari (1074–1144) ruled that non-Muslims must kneel before the tax collector, who is to seize them by the neck, demand payment, then slap them on the face as a reward for payment. However, Umar I ordered that *dhimmis* not be taxed beyond their capacity to pay (Bukhari, Vol. 4 Bk 52 Ch. 74 *hadith* 174). Khadduri lists disabilities attributed to Umar I's so-called Pact;[1] non-Muslims must not ride horses, must wear a yellow patch or girdle or a tall hat, must not consume pork or alcohol in public, must not assist the enemy, must show respect towards Muhammad and the Qur'an, and must not build houses higher than Muslim houses or weep loudly at funerals (196–8). In addition, non-Muslims must not attempt to convert Muslims or attempt to prevent anyone from becoming Muslim; they should stand up in a Muslim's presence if the Muslim sits down, must not use Arabic on their seals or imitate Muslims in any way. This means that the traditional Muslim greeting of 'peace be on you' should not be exchanged. Non-Muslims must not carry any weapons. There was discussion, though, on whether non-Muslims could assist in *jihad*; most scholars said that they could not but some *fuqara* said that if they were already subordinate to Muslims (presumably as slaves) they could help, since 'this was like seeking help from dogs' (Friedmann, 2003: 36). Christian and Jewish cemeteries must not be close to Muslim burial grounds, neither Crosses nor their Holy Books must be publicly visible. People of the Book could not give evidence against a Muslim, although a Muslim could against them (Friedmann, 2003: 35). If accidentally killed, Ibn Hazm maintained that no blood-money, or compensation to the victim's family, is payable; but the Maliki and Hanbali schools of jurisprudence allow a payment of one third of what a Muslim would receive (48). Marriage of a *dhimmi* man to a Muslim woman was an offence that carried corporal punishment as a penalty. Muslim men could marry Jewish and Christian women, who had the right to continue to practise their faith. Some *fuqara* argued that the husband could order his non-Muslim wife not to drink wine or eat pork. Some said he could order but could not enforce these restrictions (188). A false accusation of adultery against a non-Muslim wife resulted in a less severe, discretionary penalty than one against a Muslim wife (60 lashes) (188). A discretionary penalty must not exceed a *hudud* (statutory penalty). A non-Muslim wife who converted would automatically be legally divorced from her Christian or Jewish husband and 'ordered to marry a Muslim' (164, 166). Friedmann does point out that in the earliest period some scholars were 'willing to countenance the preservation of a Muslim woman's marriage to an unbeliever' but says that annulment became the 'established law' (172, 182). The People of the Book could choose their own leader, at least in theory. However, the Caliph had to validate the candidate and in practice often chose whoever pledged to collect the highest amount of taxes (Ye'or, 1996: 126).

Ye'or (1996), a vehement critic of what she calls *dhimmitude*, describes it as ultimately deliberately destructive of Jewish and Christian culture and religious identity. It aimed to Islamize the Scriptuaries. Although the *jizya* tax was only meant to be levied from able-bodied men, it was, she says 'extracted by torture' from 'children, women, widows, orphans, even the dead' (78). The system, she says, was designed to subjugate, oppress, exploit and humiliate whole communities (247). She thinks it specious to claim that in comparison to Europe, non-Muslims in the Muslim world were well treated, since comparison requires defining 'areas of comparison' and the 'segment of history' and to debate the 'degrees and subtleties of tolerance'. Friedmann differs, commenting that 'undisputed facts' support the claim of relative tolerance but that this should not mistakenly be identified with what tolerance means 'in the modern sense'. Rather, current discussion should focus on how Muslims today understand their tradition. They, like previous Muslims, are free to 'choose from their tradition elements that are compatible with their values and to disregard those that contradict them'. Thus, a contemporary Muslim might choose to 'adopt the broadest interpretation of Qur'an 2:256' (4–5). Friedmann (2000) cites Q3:110, which says that Muslims are the 'best community' as explicitly exalting Muslims above other people (34; cited by Taymiyya, Michel, 1984: 243). People of the book may be tolerated but it 'becomes only natural' to inflict 'misery on the unbelievers', which actually parallels much historical Christian attitude towards the Jews, who were seen as a stubborn people who refused to accept the truth about Jesus. As Chapter 2 argued, the 'people of the book' to whom the verses of friendship refer are taken almost universally to refer only to those who were contemporary with Muhammad, who recognized his divine mission, that is, who became Muslim. Umar I, citing varies *hadith* to the effect that Muslims should not co-inhabit the *hizaz* with any other people, permanently expelled Jews and Christian from the Saudi peninsula. It remains illegal for Christian working there to worship, in public or in private.

Ibn Hazm (994–1064) on *tahrif*

Ibn Hazm was born in Cordoba during Umayyad rule. His grandfather and father served at the Umayyad's court, as did Ibn Hazm under various rulers. He also spent some time in prison due to his ongoing support for the Umayyad dynasty during its years of decline in Spain. He developed what became known as the Zahiri (literalist) school of law which, although not as popular as the four schools of Sunni jurisprudence, is still recognized as a valid school. He did not accept use of analogy to deduce legal opinions but restricted himself to the Qur'an, *hadith* and to the plain, literal or clear meaning of the text, which he believed anyone could understand. He is best known for his *Kitab-al-Fasl*, or *The Book of Distinction*, in which he examined the claims of different religions, including Christianity, against what he saw as the superior claims of Islam. Fletcher says that he 'demonstrated a remarkably detailed knowledge of Christian sacred texts, presumably acquired by reading the Arabic translations of the Bible used by Mozarabic Christians'. He read the Bible, as many Christians read the Qur'an, 'solely for the end of refuting it'. He achieved this, says Fletcher, 'by pedantic exposure of textual inconsistency' (127). He may well be credited with the full-blown development of applying *tahrif* to Christian as well as Jewish scripture, which would explain why Al-Kindy did not respond to the charge that the gospels are corrupt but defended the authenticity of the Hebrew Bible. On the other hand, Al-Kindy's defence that it would have been impossible for all the Bibles in existence, scattered throughout the world, to have been altered in exactly the same way may have been familiar to Ibn Hazm. He argued that there was a time when a single copy of the Bible existed in the custody of the High Priest in Jerusalem, and claimed that Ezra altered the text during the construction of the Second Temple. Ezra, in Ibn Hazm's opinion, could not have been a true prophet or he would not have falsified scripture (Michel, 1984: 114). Examples of *tahrif* in the Hebrew Bible are descriptions of Prophets committing major sins, such as David's adultery with Beersheba, which is not included in the Qur'anic account. Ibn Hazm did not merely depict the Bible as a book containing a few errors or mistakes but as what he called 'anti-scripture'; it is an ' "accursed book", the product of satanic inspiration' (Michel, 1984: 90). No few Christians have suggested a Satanic source for Muhammad's inspiration and thus for the Qur'an. Ibn Hazm's writing is not easily available but Constable (1997) has an extract from *Kitab-al-Fasl* called 'On the Inconsistencies of the Four Gospels' on which the following analyses is based.

This is a short extract of only four pages but it gives the flavour and tone of Ibn Hazm's approach and, as the editor says, 'exemplifies his method' (81). First Ibn Hazm cites Matthew 10: 34–36, then Luke 12: 49–53, which appear to be parallel passages implying a common source. Jesus describes himself as coming with a sword, not peace. Dividing husband from wife and children from their parents, he will create division among the nations. Then, Ibn Hazm cites Luke 9:52 and John 10:34. (He actually makes a mistake here by identifying the second passage as from the twelfth chapter of John.) In these two passages, Jesus describes himself as a peace-maker. Thus, says Ibn Hazam, 'the last two passages contradict' the first two passages. Since the Messiah (peace be on him) cannot lie, the 'four iniquitous men who wrote these corrupted, altered gospels' must have lied (82). Ibn Hazm did not refer to Christian interpretation of the first set of passages as applying only to the destruction of those who did not believe in Jesus, not to 'the destruction of souls who believed in him', but argued that Jesus' was speaking 'in general' without singling out 'any particular group'. Next, Ibn Hazm turned to a passage in Matthew about John the Baptist, who 'did not eat or drink', then when Jesus came and ate and drank the people called him a 'glutton and an imbiber of wine, a wanton friend of tax collectors and sinners' (Matthew 11:18–19). This passage lies, says Ibn Hazm, because we are told in Mark 1:6 that John ate 'locusts and wild honey'. Also, if John the Baptist was really able to 'do without food and drink' he would be more exalted than Jesus, who 'cannot do without food and drink' (83). This is false, because Christians exalt Jesus more highly than John! Ibn Hazm then takes the opportunity to argue that Christians should not in fact picture Jesus as eating and drinking because this does not sit logically with their conviction that Jesus is God: 'how could this God eat and drink?', he asks. If Christians reply that Jesus' human, not divine nature, eats and drinks, Ibn Hazm reminds them that Orthodox Christian doctrine is that these two natures co-exist in one person: there are not two Christs, one who drinks, one who doesn't. Or, he jokes, 'did half the Messiah eat and half the Messiah drink' (83). If only half of him ate, the report is still false because it says that 'the Messiah ate', whereas actually 'only half of Him ate'. All this shows, he says, that 'the Christian community is altogether vile'. This is strong language, calculated to antagonize not to befriend. Ibn Hazm had an extensive knowledge of the Bible and clearly some awareness of Christian theology, which he did not acquire in order to build a bridge of understanding with Christians but to refute their beliefs. Michel comments that while some subsequent Muslim writers thought Ibn Hazm's position on the almost total corruption of Jewish and Christian scripture too extreme, 'the question of *tahrif* . . . was one that no polemicist – Christian, Muslims or Jewish – could leave untreated' (90). Ibn Hazm did not claim that Torah and *Injil* contain no truth at all, or else verses that Muslims believe point to Muhammad would also have to be false. Truth could be distinguished from falsehood, he said.

Ibn Taymiyyah's refutation of Christianity

Ibn Taymiyyah's treatise on Christianity, partly a response to the writings of Paul of Antioch, was published in 1320. Tom Michel's annotated translation is not easily available. However, in 2000 he presented the D'Arcy Lectures in the University of Oxford on 'Paul of Antioch and Ibn Taymiyya: The Modern Relevance of a Medieval Debate' and these are electronically available at www.sjweb.info/dialogo. This is a very good summary of the main points of Ibn Taymiyyah's refutation. Ibn Taymiyyah remains an influential scholar, especially amongst salafist Muslims. Ibn Abd-al-Wahhab

(1703–92), founder of the *al-Muwahhiddun* (Unitarians, usually called Wahhabis), cited him, although not as extensively as has sometimes been implied. Today, such men as Osama bin Laden defer to his opinions. Ibn Taymiyyah was also largely responsible for reviving the Hanbalite tradition of law, which is the only school recognized in Saudi Arabia. Ahmad Ibn Hanbal (780–855), like Ibn Hazm, was suspicious of using anything other than Qur'an, *hadith* and *ijma* (consensus) to formulate Islamic law. Taymiyyah, who detested any innovation or foreign import into Islam, wanted to return to the original, pure, uncorrupted Islam of the *salafa*, that is, Muhammad, his *sahaba* (companions), their children and grandchildren. Such more recent reformers as Ibn Abd-al-Wahhab and Rashid Rida shared this agenda. Taymiyyah was both a popular and a controversial figure in his own day; at times he was employed by the political authorities, at other times he was imprisoned by the same authorities. Born in what is now Turkey, his family moved to Damascus, then under Mamluk rule, in 1268. Baghdad, the Abbasid capital, had fallen to the Mongols in 1258. His father preached regularly in the Umayyad Mosque, where once Christians and Muslims had worshipped side by side. Taymayyah succeeded his father as professor of Hanbali law in 1282. Taymiyyah studied with some of the leading scholars of the day, including Zaynab bint Makki, a female expert on *hadith*. Crusaders were still in possession of certain cities but Christians were not the only people against whom Taymiyyah thundered. He denounced the Mongols, whose conversion to Islam he did not regard as genuine, and the Sufis, who were growing in popularity as the Muslim world itself fragmented into smaller political units. By following their *Yasa* code instead of the *Shar'iah*, Mongols were actually living in ignorance (*jahilia*), which made *jihad* against them a duty.

Taymiyyah's solution for the problems of fourteenth-century Islam was to return to the ideals of the first Islamic century. In 1299, following a *fatwa* that annoyed other jurists, he was dismissed from his post but the following year was appointed official preacher of an anti-Mongol *jihad*. He was dispatched to recruit support in Cairo but once there he soon fell foul of the authorities over his views about the anthropomorphic verses of the Qur'an, and was imprisoned. Released in 1308, he was quickly re-imprisoned, this time for denouncing prayers to Sufi saints. He then spent time in jails in Cairo and Alexandria. In 1313, he was allowed to resume teaching in Damascus. In 1318, the Sultan forbade him from issuing any opinions regarding divorce, since he differed from the majority of scholars on allowing one repudiation (I divorce you) to substitute for three. When he continued to issue *fatwas*, he was again imprisoned. Released in 1321, he was re-imprisoned in 1326 but carried on writing until pen and paper were denied him. On the latter occasion it was his condemnation of Shi'a dogmas at a time when the Sultan was attempting to build bridges with Shi'a Muslims that attracted censure. The Shi'a, he said, wrongly claimed infallibility for their 12 Imams, just as Christians were wrong to claim this for the apostles and Sufis for their Shaykhs (218). Paul of Antioch actually referred to the apostles as 'prophets' (*rasul*), thus claiming infallibility for the texts they wrote. Ibn Taymiyyah denied them this title. He died, in prison, in 1328 but was so popular that between 60,000 and 100,000 people attended his funeral, including many women. Ibn Taymiyyah was an activist as well as a scholar: in 1300 he was part of the resistance against the Mongol attack on Damascus and personally went to the camp of the Mongol general to negotiate release of captives, insisting that Christians as 'protected people' as well as Muslims be released. In 1305, he took part in the anti-Mongol Battle of Shakhab and fought various Shi'a groups in Syria.

While stimulated by Paul of Antioch's writing, Ibn Taymayyah's book did more than reply to the bishop's 24-page *Letter to a Muslim*. An expanded version of Paul's letter appears to have been written by Christians in Cyprus, and it was this version to which Ibn Taymiyyah responded (Michel: 94). His response, says Michel, was also 'incorporated into a comprehensive view of mankind's response to revelation' and comprised 'over a thousand printed pages' (98–9). Much of the content rehearsed well-known Muslim arguments against the Trinity, the integrity of scripture and Christian belief about Jesus, but Taymiyyah took 'these elements of polemic' and explored them more fully than had previous writers. He repeated arguments that were common to other polemicists but 'reworked and integrated' these 'into a consistent, unified theological outlook' (94). First, this analysis summarizes Paul's apology, then outlines Ibn Taymiyyah's refutation. Paul cites among other Qur'anic verses 5:82 to support his contention that Muslims and Christians should enjoy cordial relations, and 5:48 to deny the possibility of *tahrif*, which says that God 'guarded in safety' the previous scriptures. Paul of Antioch interpreted Q5:112–15, a passage alluded to by John of Damascus, as praising the Christian Eucharist and also pointed out that the Qur'an 'praises Christian monks and priests' (Michel, 1984: 90). He understood 4:159 as guaranteeing Christian faithfulness until Judgment Day. He cited passages that speak highly of Jesus and Mary, including Jesus' 'assumption into heaven' (88). Paul, like Timothy, endorsed the legitimacy of Muhammad's prophethood but not of his universal claims; rather, God had sent him as a prophet to the 'Arabs of the *jahiliyya*'. Hence, references in the Qur'an to its Arabic character (107). Christians had never been guilty of worshipping idols as have pagans, who unlike Christians 'deserve to have *jihad* waged against them'. Massignon, centuries later, offered a similar view. Displaying knowledge of Muslim theology as well as of the Qur'an, Paul compared Christian belief in three hypostases, of God as Father, Son and Spirit with Muslim attributes. In fact, Paul avoided using the Arabic term *'uqnam* for hypostasis (plural *aqanim*) and instead used *ism* (name). The former sounds like three separate, distinct 'beings', the latter like different 'names' for a single 'being'. Christians use three different names to describe the one God as 'an existing being (*shay'*), living (*hayy*) and speaking (*natiq*)'; these 'names' represent the three 'substantive attributes (*al-sifat al-jawhariyya*) of existence, speech and life' (91). Like Timothy, he uses the analogy of the Sun. He also addressed incarnation, drawing on a range of Bible passages that 'speak of individuals such as David as sons of God, or which refer to the indwelling of the divine spirit in men'. God, he argued, 'has taught men these names', so there is no reason why they should 'stop using them'; but again as did Timothy he suggests that any language that we use to describe God is ultimately inadequate (92). Here, he parallels the difficulty that Muslims have with the anthropomorphic verses of the Qur'an, known as *tashbih*, as opposed to verses that prohibit comparing God with anything human or created (the verses of *ta'til*). The extended version, however, was not so careful with its language. Taymiyya's own position on this issue had already earned him a jail sentence. Jesus as God's son implies for many Muslims that some sort of sexual union took place between God and Mary, as in the reference to the Trinity as God, Jesus and Mary at Q5:116, which they find obnoxious. Q5:116's reference to a Trinity of God, Jesus and Mary can be interpreted in this way.

Taymiyyah's Reply

Michel points out that while Taymiyyah aimed to produce a definitive refutation of Christianity, and so certainly had Christian readers in mind, he was also writing for Muslims, comparing Sufi with Christian practices, for example, to stress the falsity of both. Just as some Christians argued that God had preserved Judaism as a warning to Christians of what befalls a people who abandon their God, so Christianity is as an example of what Muslims should not imitate. This was a major theme in Ibn Taymiyyah's writing. Muslims should separate and distance themselves from other communities; dissimilitude should exist in every aspect of life, practice, dress, prayer and worship. He cited an *hadith* that said, 'whoever cultivates resemblance with a people is one of them' (82). Some Muslims, it seems, were actually joining in certain Christian festivals, at least to the extent of walking with them in their processions and 'colouring Easter eggs, fixing a special meal, wearing new clothes, decorating houses and lighting fires' on feast days (82). Not only must Muslims not participate in any way in Christian festivals, he said, but they must not even sell them 'anything needed for the feast' or 'give them presents' (82). He supported the dress regulations that prohibited Christians from wearing the same style of dress as Muslims. He also supported collecting the *jizya* from monks who were engaged in agriculture or business, whereas some jurists exempted all monks and priests (81). When the dress code was re-introduced in 1301, Christians complained to the Sultan. Some Christians lost their posts at the same time. Ibn Taymiyyah ruled that they must 'return to the prescribed code' (81). He was emphatic that Muslims must not enter alliances with Christians, as some Muslims had during the wars against the Mongols. Anything which might contaminate Islam's strict monotheism must be repudiated. Christians also complained that the closure of churches was a breach of the Pact of Umar, but Ibn Taymiyyah ruled that if the Sultan 'decided to destroy every Church' within the Muslim territory he would be entitled to do so (79). Much blame fell on the Fatimids, who had been far too lenient in their treatment of Christians. They had 'ruled outside the *Shari'ah*' (79). It was not a surprise, he said, that the Fatimids failed against the Crusaders (79). It was better, Taymiyyah advised, to employ a less able Muslim than a more able Christian, although the opposite had been practised by many Caliphs. Muslims did not need Christians and should 'make themselves independent of them'

(80). Practices such as visiting the tombs of saints, praying to them, preparing 'banners', and forming processions for the leaders of Sufi orders all represented innovation (*bida*) possibly in imitation of Christians. His rejection of prayer to the saints earned him a jail term. This analysis will focus on what Ibn Taymiyyah wrote about *tahrif*, the Trinity and the verses of friendship.

Ibn Taymiyyah on Tahrif

Ibn Taymiyyah, like Ibn Hazm, thought that Ezra had altered the text of the Hebrew Bible when, as the Second Temple was under construction, there was only one copy available. Paul of Antioch argued that the Qur'an affirmed the legitimacy of the earlier scriptures, so any alleged alteration would have to be subsequent to Muhammad's time when Christians were scattered 'throughout the globe', so textual corruption would be impossible. Unlike Ibn Hazm, Taymiyyah held that Ezra may have been a Prophet, in which case he would have copied the book accurately; or he may not have been a prophet, in which case 'errors could have crept in' (114). Thus, the Hebrew Bible may or may not be corrupt. On this issue, Ibn Taymiyyah was less emphatic than a writer such as al-Kairanwi, for whom the Bible is a catalogue of errors. On the one hand, the consequence for Muslims is that doubt exists about the authenticity of the Bible while there is no doubt about the Qur'an. On the other hand, this still allows Muslims to claim that some Biblical passages predict Muhammad, which presumably would not have remained in a totally corrupted text. Taymiyyah thought the New Testament much more suspect. He pointed out that in form it resembles *hadith* rather than Scripture (235). Christians, unlike Muslims, cannot authenticate their scripture with reference to a chain (*isnad*) 'of reliable, trustworthy' transmitters (232). Regarding innovation, Ibn Hazm identified anything that introduced notions not found in previous Scripture but especially in the Qur'an. Use of the word 'Father' for God is an innovation; *hulul* and *ittihad* (fatherhood and sonship) may exist as concepts in the Bible but Christians apply these terms to Jesus 'in a radically different sense' (116), which cannot be justified. Jesus never said, 'Go into all the world and baptize in the name of the Father, the Son and the Holy Spirit' (260). The Crucifixion, says Ibn Taymiyyah, did not happen. He did not accuse the disciples of deliberate falsification, since they had not personally witnessed whatever did happen, keeping 'at a distance through fear' (305). Rather, they 'believed what they were handing on about Jesus' (236). Christians, in fact, are divided about what happened to Jesus and there are some who hold that the Jews crucified someone else by mistake (307) which is closer to the Qur'anic statement that they did not crucify Jesus but it 'appeared so' (307; 225). The Qur'an clearly states that God raised Jesus up in order to prevent his death (306). Throughout, Ibn Taymiyyah demonstrates detailed knowledge of different Christian groups, such as the Nestorians, Melkites and Jacobites (see 309). 'If you have ten Christians', he wrote, 'they would split into eleven opinions' (309). In addition to belief in the crucifixion, belief in the incarnation and Trinity are innovations, as are most common Christian practices such as praying to the east, glorifying the cross, omitting circumcision, monasticism and eating pork. Jesus did not command any of these any more than he commanded Christians to worship himself (253, 356). Christians have permitted what is prohibited and prohibited what is permitted (241) while Muslims command what is right and prohibit what is forbidden (243). On the atonement, he rejected the need for a sacrificial death of a uniquely sinless individual on the basis that God had forgiven Adam (120, 222).

Far from God's Holy Spirit dwelling in the disciples, as Christians claim, and thus preventing them from error, it was perhaps some demon instead who imitated the risen Jesus and deluded them: 'Since Jesus was not crucified . . . it could not have been the resurrected Christ who appeared to the apostles' (110). Demons 'turn people away from the true *tawhid* preached by the prophets by insinuating false information and practice of *shirk*'. Christians, though, fall somewhere between upholding God's unity and associating partners with him: 'They do not follow pure *tawhid*, but neither are they like the idolaters who worshipped idols . . . God therefore sometimes categorized them separately from the idolaters, and elsewhere cursed them for the *shirk* which they innovated' (246). Until the time of Constantine, Christians had been persecuted and 'continually conquered'; Constantine used the sword to establish Christianity but 'the religion he made victorious was changed and not the religion of Jesus' (362). Here, Ibn Taymiyyah turns on its head the Christian criticism that Islam only gained adherents by using force, that before Muhammad resorted to the sword he attracted few followers. Christianity, said Taymiyyah, struggled before Constantine threw the weight of imperial Rome behind the Church. In contrast, Islam's success can only be interpreted as a sign of God's favour (135). Islam flourished as has no previous religion (362). On idols, Ibn Taymiyyah suggests that Christians replaced worship of statues with that of 'icons', replaced prayers to them for prayers to the 'sun, moon and stars, and fasting in the spring in order to combine revealed religion and the natural order' (346). Christianity was a construct from 'two religions', genuine revelation and idolatry. Ibn Taymiyyah's pupil, Ibn Kathir (1301–73), author of the popular commentary on the Qur'an, argues that Biblical material can only be used 'as supporting evidence, not as evidence in themselves', that is, when Qur'anic verses testify to the truth of the Biblical narrative, otherwise Biblical sources should not be used (2000: 1: 31). Constantine's role in establishing a corrupted, false Christianity remains a popular theme in contemporary Muslim writing of the polemical genre.[2]

Incarnation, Trinity and Divine Indwelling

Not surprisingly, a refutation of the Trinity featured prominently in Ibn Taymiyyah's response to Paul of Antioch. Unfortunately, since he responded to the longer edited version which was not so careful to avoid use of the problematic term *uqman*, we do not know whether Ibn Taymiyyah would have found such a formulation of the Trinity less objectionable. That would probably have been unlikely, since he had a thorough knowledge of Christian thought and was well aware that Christians traditionally speak of three hypostases, not three names. He was also aware that Christian belief in Trinity differed from Muslim belief in the 99 Names of God. Incarnation, Trinity and Divine Indwelling were, he argued, all innovations. He rejected the claim that these are all supported by Scripture. Here, he sounds a little like the Caliph al-Mahdi, suggesting for example that Christians are irrational to stop at three, 'since the names of God are many, such as the Loving, the Powerful, to limit to three without the others is wrong' (267). Rather, the 'names of God are extremely numerous'.

Ibn Taymiyyah argues throughout this discussion that Trinity is both irrational and Scripturally unfounded. Any Biblical reference to God as Father means that he is the creator of all people, while references to God supporting people through the Holy Spirit (Q2:87; 2:253; 5:110) do not mean that God dwells within people, that is, comes down to earth, but refers to 'the holy angel such as Jibril, or it may mean the revelation, guidance and support which God sends down either by mediation of the angel or without it' (262). References to the Holy Spirit in Scripture do not imply that God 'subsists' within human individuals. God's Spirit does not 'subsist' anywhere outside of God (272). Thus, God could not have 'subsisted' in Jesus. Christians themselves have problems explaining how a man could be both human and God at the same time and had to develop the doctrine of two natures, one divine and one human (328–9). For God to become human requires a diminishment of God's divinity (329). Some Christians regard Jesus as a 'son' by adoption, or special favour, that is, as a friend (*khalil*) of God (310). Others say that the divine and the human natures 'inhabited' Jesus 'without any contact' or that 'union' was somehow imprinted on Jesus 'like a seal on wax' (312). There is a great deal of debate on this issue. The term 'son' in Scripture is only applied to a 'created son', not to something divine (275). The term merely implies God's 'lordship over creation' (122). The names Father, Son and Spirit applied to God are names which Christians have innovated; they 'were not revealed by God on His authority' (277). He rejects comparison of Father, Son and Spirit with *sifat* or attributes of God, pointing out that no Muslim has ever claimed that any of God's attributes, such as Power or Life, are separate substances or persons from God, while the Father, Son and Spirit exist as distinct realities. Discussing Paul's analogy of the sun, its rays and its light, Ibn Taymiyyah dismisses this, pointing out that 'the rays subsisting in the air, on earth, on mountains, trees, and walls are not subsisting in the sun itself' (280). The heat and light of the sun are accidents, subsisting outside of the sun (273). Muslims – that is, Shi'a – who speak of members of the family of Ali, or of their Shaykhs – Sufis – as divine and who describe this with reference to 'attributes not stated in the Book' are just as wrong and Christians (131).

The Salafi, if asked whether an attribute of God were different from God or the same, would desist from replying, since if they affirmed that they are the same they would identify God totally with a single attribute while if they denied sameness they would make God's attribute dissimilar to God (281). The statement that there is One God but three attributes is disingenuous, since the Creed states that Jesus is equal to the Father in substance, which means that Jesus exists as a 'substance' in addition to the 'substance' of the Father (271). The Trinity, he declares, is 'opposed to sound reason' (285). Taymiyyah refutes the argument, suggested by Timothy I, that ultimately all descriptions of God are inadequate on the basis that 'revelation must be in accord with what is reasonable', which sounds like Pfander (122). Christians weaken their claim that Trinity is derived from Scripture when they rely instead on 'natural philosophy or ontology' (121). Christians borrowed too much from philosophy. Any theology that depends on philosophy is inadequate. He descibes Al-Farabi, Ibn Sina, Ibn Rushd and others as infidel for teaching that the world is eternal and therefore making God redundant (16). God may well be at one and the same time Creating, Living and Communicating but this does not mean that three distinct 'persons' subsist in God. Christians cannot themselves agree whether the hypostasis are 'substances', 'characteristics', 'attributes' or 'persons' (311–12). Comparison of Jesus as God's Word with the Qur'an fails, since Muslims do not restrict God's speech to the Qur'an: God has other utterances nor do Muslims call any of these words 'creator, lord or God' (124). Sufi Shaykhs and others who claim union with God or that God dwells in them are also mistaken; they may be demon possessed (296) or, referring to al-Hallaj, what they describe is actually the presence within them of profound 'faith in God, knowledge of Him, His guidance, light, and mental image' (343). Union between man and God is 'inconceivable and logically contradictory' (125). He implies a biological coupling of God and Mary, which he finds abhorrent (122).

Even if Christians do not call Mary God's wife, Ibn Taymiyyah writes, 'this is the consequence for the generality of Christians for he who gives birth must have a spouse' (260). He rejected Paul's claim that there is a parallel between Trinity and the anthropomorphic descriptions of God in the Qur'an as spurious, since, he said, while the former is 'incompatible with prophetic teaching', the latter is not. Anthropomorphic language is found in the Hebrew Bible but 'the Trinitarian formula appearing in the Nicene creed . . . it is an innovation both in terminology and in the description of God towards which it points' (131). Following Hanbal, Ibn Taymiyyah's view was that it was better to suspend judgement on such questions as whether God possessed a body, 'if not, how does He hear, speak, etc.', on the basis that there is danger in denial and in affirmation: denial makes God 'inoperable in human life', affirmation become a less than useful 'negative formulation' (*salb*) (43). Taymiyyah upheld the existence of attributes which he took to be the consensus of the community and criticized the Mutazalites for denying these (49). Speaking of God's attributes does not contradict Scripture but where, he asks, does Scripture say that Jesus is 'true God from true God . . . that he is equal in substance to God . . . that he is the creator who created everything', or 'that he sits at the right hand of God?' Which prophet, he says, ever called God's wisdom or speech or knowledge God's 'offspring' or spoke of God's son as 'generated and at the same time eternal?' (340). 'Where', he continued, 'in their message is it that God has a third hypostasis which is His Life, called the Holy Spirit, who is also the living, life-giving Lord?' (340). There is actually evidence that Taymiyyah was a Sufi; what he condemned was the excesses of Sufi claims (25). Terms such as 'union' are not found in Scripture, 'neither in the case of Christ or anyone else' (343). Sufis who claim union with God, however, are worse than Christians, who at least make this claim on behalf of a true Prophet (344).

The Verses of Friendship

Discussing verses cited by Paul of Antioch as evidence of Qur'anic praise for Christians, Taymiyyah refutes this claim. The verses of friendship refer to those Christians who, during Muhammad's life-time, duly recognized him as God's Prophet and embraced Islam. These verses do not refer to Christians or to Jews who have lived subsequent to Muhammad's life-time; 2:162 does not praise Christians but 'refers only to those who followed' Jesus' 'religion before its abrogation and corruption'. Christians contradict themselves, too, for the verse to which they refer, if it praises them also praises Jews, whom they regard as unbelievers (246). People of the Book 'after the abrogation and corruption of their religion' are not counted among those of whom the verse says have faith in God (247). Even if the Qur'an does affirm that Christians have faith in God this does not mean that they will not be punished (244). The statement that Christians are 'nearer in friendship' to Muslims means just that; it does not imply that 'they are deserving of a reward'. Christians, the Qur'an says, are too easily misled by their leaders, whom they turn into infallible guides, blindly imitating them (*taqlid*): but these men distort and corrupt the religion of Jesus (252). In contrast, whenever some error or innovation creeps into Islam, there are always faithful men, true to the teachings of the *salaf*, who correct the error; 'God has . . . raised up in every age people of knowledge . . . who guard His religion and keep it safe from the *tahrif* of the extremists, the syncretism of the wayward, and the groundless interpretation of the ignorant' (238). Unlike some writers, Ibn Taymiyyah did not apply *naksh* (abrogation) to make the later verses of hostility cancel out earlier, friendly verses but denied that the verses of friendship could be applied to Christians after the coming of the complete and perfect revelation. 'The people of the book after the abrogation and corruption of their religion were not among those who put their faith in God, the Last Day, and good works – as God has said' (9:29) (247). Christians are 'unbelievers', he says (353).

He also refuted Paul's claim that Muhammad was only a prophet for the Arabs; his mission was universal and his message was for Christians just as much as for anyone else. Indeed, Christians need the Qur'an and its messenger, because both teach much better ethical guidance. Muslims are better followers of Christ than Christians are, since by altering Jesus' religion Christians 'quit of the faith of Christ' while Muslims 'glorify Christ better and follow him more truly' (249). Ibn Taymiyyah cites the Qur'an's description of Jesus, pointing out that Jesus only commanded people to worship God, not himself (303–08). He also cites *hadith* that before the End of Time, Christ will return, 'break the Cross, slaughter the pig and defeat the Dajjal, the anti-Christi' (78). Michel remarks that 'the imagery of the return of Christ . . . appears surprisingly often in Ibn Taymiyyah's writing' (78). The Gospel is inadequate, he contended, since 'there is no independent *shari'ah* in it', as Nasr has argued more recently. Neither the Gospel nor the Torah contains anything that is not found in the Qur'an, which, in contrast, contains 'guidance and true religion in beneficial knowledge and upright deeds which are not found in the other two books' (355). As for Paul's argument that Judaism was the religion of law but that as the religion of grace, Christianity superseded Judaism and requires no supplement, Ibn Taymiyyah asserted that Christianity in fact does need supplementing and that Islam, which harmonizes law and grace, is God's final and perfect revelation (135). Christians need Islam's clear, unambiguous ethical guidance, which the Gospels lack. Jesus' commands that we 'love our enemies, do good to those who wrong you' need to be 'balanced by the Qur'anic judgments against wrongdoers' if social anarchy is not to prevail (133). Addressing whether Muhammad might have sincerely mistaken himself to be a universal messenger when he was really only a prophet for the Arabs, he concluded that 'such an interpretation might be possible for any one other than a prophet, but that it is impossible for any claimant to messengership' (111). While Paul accepted that Muhammad was a prophet, although not a universal prophet, Ibn Taymiyyah referred to Christian argumentation that Muhammad 'was no prophet at all'. In reply, he testified to Muhammad's 'knowledge of unknown matters in . . . the past and the future, his miracles' and to 'the Qur'an, which is the greatest miracle', and to 'the fine qualities of his community', which is 'the best' (111). The question of whether or not Muhammad's messengership had been attested by miracles was a common Christian argument, with Christians typically dismissing stories of Muhammad's miracles as fabricated. Islam is both necessary, and superior, says Ibn Taymiyyah, and the Qur'an contains 'the perfect legislation' (133).

Rahmatullah Ibn Khalil al-'Uthmanu al-Kairanawi's response to Pfander

Some Christians regard Pfander's *Mizan-al-Huq* as a definitive refutation of Islam; some Muslims regard al-Kairanawi's rebuttal as a definitive refutation of Christianity. It can be considered to be in the top ten of Muslim works of anti-Christian polemic, gaining a very wide circulation and population throughout the Muslim world (see Schirrmacher, 1997). Although the author was Shi'a, his Shi'a identity rarely intrudes into the text, hence Sunnis have embraced it enthusiastically. Pfander and al-Kairanawi (1818–91) did not only debate in print but face to face as, unlike Paul and Ibn Taymiyyah, they were contemporaries. Zebiri (1997) describes Al-Karairanwi's *Izhar-al-Haq* as 'a seminal work for modern Muslim refutations of Christianity' (47). The Muslim rebuttal is not a point-by-point rejoinder but focuses on the charge of *tahrif*, perceiving this to be a weakness in Pfander's arguments. Trinity, however, is also addressed. Pfander and his Muslim respondent initially debated in newspapers and it was after a decade of literary exchanges that the two agreed to meet in public debate, which took place at Agra in 1854. Each principal was supported by seconds; Pfander's were Thomas Valpy French (1825–91), later Bishop of Lahore, and William Kay (1820–86), later principal of Bishop's College, Calcutta. Al-Kairanawi's were Dr Wazir Khan and Imad-ud-Din, whose later conversion to Christianity would be claimed as a victory for Pfander. Khan had studied medicine in London, where he obtained copies of books by such Biblical scholars as T. H. Horne, J. G. Eichhorn and N. Lardher as well as D. F Strauss's *Das Leben Jesus*. Pfander was totally unfamiliar with their approach to the critical study of the text of the Bible, and unprepared for his opponents' reliance on their scholarship. During the debate, he admitted that there were more textual discrepancies between the four gospels than can be explained with reference to copyist error but argued that this did not detract from the essential doctrines of the Christian faith, including the Trinity. Al-Kairanawi pressed his advantage home, arguing that just as the New Testament had fulfilled the Old Testament, so it in its turn was fulfilled in the Qur'an. In the end, both sides claimed victory but whereas Pfander's earlier, literary exchanges with Muslims attracted wide publicity, silence followed this debate on the Christian side. Muslim accounts rolled off the presses. Al-Kairanawi's *Izhar-ul-Haq*, which appeared in 1864, was written as a systematic presentation of the arguments used during the 1854 debate and makes extensive use of critical European scholarship. Pfander regarded this as infidel and accused Catholics of sabotaging the debate by supplying these books to his Muslim opponents. According to *Izhar-ul-Huq*, Pfander admitted 'that there were alterations in the Bible in seven or eight places' (xi). Al-Kairanawi responded that if this was true, then how could the missionary 'claim that' the Bible 'is true and how could' he 'believe in it'? Establishing, in his estimation, that the Bible is rife with error, Kairanawi went on to present 'by contrast the indisputable and absolute authority of the Qur'an and the Prophethood of Muhammad' (xvi). The following analysis is based on the 2003 translation by Muhammad Wali Raazi. This is a very large book, consisting of 474 pages. Most of the book discusses *tahrif*. Given the size of the book, this discussion will identify the main points of al-Kairanawai's refutation of the Bible as authentic scripture, his argument against Trinity and his claims on behalf of Islam.

Al-Kairanawi on Tahrif

In over 400 pages of English text, the author identifies discrepancy after discrepancy in the books of the Bible. He first reviews the process by which the Church codified and determined the canon. His purpose here is to highlight difference of opinion on what should be included, including more than 70 books that were excluded (18).

Referring to the Hebrew Bible, he claims that the extant Torah is different from the Book that Moses received from God, since there is no evidence of a Torah existing until the reign of King Josiah (20). It was later re-written by Ezra. That copy, however, was 'destroyed and burnt by Antiochus' when he sacked Jerusalem in *circa* 165 (21). However, neither Ezra nor the two prophets, Haggai and Zechariah, who assisted him could have erred, thus the extant Torah is not the text that they wrote but an even later compilation of 'stories and traditions . . . current among the Jews, and written down by their scholars without a critical view to their sources' (22). He identifies numerous errors. For example, the Pentateuch (Deut 5:9) says that the sins of the fathers will be visited upon their sons, which is denied by Ezekiel 18:20. He questions the accuracy of references to numbers and of genealogies. For example, Numbers 31:7 says that all the men of Midian were killed, yet in Judges 6 they are described as a numerous and powerful people. Leviticus 4:14 says that the congregation shall offer a bullock for their sins; Numbers 14 stipulates that a goat should be sacrificed (406). Moses sanctioned divorce (388); Jesus prohibited divorce. 2 Kings 16:2 says that Ahaz was 20 years old when he started to reign, 2 Chronicles 28:1 says that he was 25. More significantly, incidents such as Lot's and David's adultery and Solomon's worship of idols could not have occurred, since prophets do not sin (382). He identifies 119 contradictions and 110 errors, 43 additions and 18 omissions. All these errors crept into the text before, not after, the time of Muhammad (218). Any passage, however, that is confirmed by the Qur'an can be identified as genuine (219). Among the many errors in the Gospels, he identifies John 3:13, which says that no man has ascended to heaven, which is contradicted by Enoch's and Elijah's ascent. On Matthew's account of the Temple curtain being torn and graves opened when Jesus died (27:51–53) he says that this is a concocted account, possibly based on stories prevalent in Jerusalem at the time of the Temple's destruction. Contradiction Number 72 repeats Ibn Hazm's choice of John's alleged diet: Mark has John eating locusts and wild honey; Matthew has him neither eating nor drinking (85).

Matthew and Luke have Jesus forbidding his disciples from carrying staffs with them when they went out to preach; Mark has Jesus allowing them to carry these (87). At Luke 14:26 Jesus says that those who follow him must hate their parents; at Matthew 15:4 he says that God commands us to honour our parents (179). In an interesting passage with a direct reference to Pfander, he dismisses the Virgin Birth, upheld by many Muslims, on the basis that contrary to Pfander's assertion that *'alamah'* can only mean 'virgin', this word from Isaiah 7:14 can also mean 'young woman' (145–6). Matthew has Judas betraying Jesus with a kiss; John has Jesus volunteering that he is the one for whom the guards were looking (91). Contradictions 84 to 87 are discrepancies in the Crucifixion narrative, strongly suggesting that Jesus was not executed. Matthew has the angel rolling the stone away from Jesus' tomb as Mary Magdalene approached it; Luke has it that the stone had already been rolled away (95). Based on his identification of so many errors and additions, al-Kairanwi asserts that the four gospels and the *Injil* that Jesus received from God are not identical. An original Hebrew version of Matthew appears to have been lost, while the lateness of the Gospels calls their accuracy into question. Their authors, too, were not prophets and so they were capable of error, thus aligning himself with Ibn Taymiyyah on this issue (218). Apostles of Jesus did not write Matthew, Mark, Luke and John (41–4). Although he does not assert this in *Izhar-ul-Haq*, Al-Kairanwi probably took the Gospel of Barnabas, to which he does refer and of which he possessed a copy (330), as the authentic Gospel. Schirrmacher (1997) suggests that it may have been al-Kairanwi who first brought this book to the notice of the Muslim world. It was possibly from al-Karawanwi that Rashid Rida was directed to Barnarbas, publishing an Arabic edition in 1908. Both scholars saw this as an authentic gospel from close to the time of Jesus that unambiguously predicted Muhammad.

Against the Trinity

What emerges from the combined work of the German and other biblical scholars was a stripping away of the miraculous elements from Jesus' story, including his virgin birth, his miracles and his resurrection, leaving behind a man, not a man-God. In an interesting passage, al-Kairanwi quotes George Sale (1670–1736), whose translation of the Qur'an was, he said 'quite popular' (448). In fact, Sale was accused by some of being a closet Muslim. Sale advised, al-Karawani wrote, that Christians should not 'preach doctrines that are openly irrational' because Muslims 'cannot be overcome in these matters'. Such doctrines included the Eucharist as well as the Trinity. Al-Karawani's rejection of the Trinity is based on his view that this is an un-biblical doctrine invented after Jesus' life on earth. Trinity is contrary to the teaching of the Qur'an. In his view, the Old Testament unambiguously affirms that 'God (Allah) is one, the Everlasting, the Undying' who 'has no equal'. 'None', according to the Old Testament, is similar to God 'in essence or in attributes' (410). Jesus, too, refuted the Trinity when he referred to God as the 'only true God' (448; John 17:3). A 'weak mortal' such as Jesus, whom Christians claim died on the Cross, could not possibly be God, who is 'immune to death' (454). While a Christian priest explained to him that in becoming human, it was necessary for Jesus to 'bear all human sufferings' (455), Al-Karawani rejects this as a 'rational impossibility'. He dismisses the doctrine of original sin as inherited by all people as absurd: 'it is logically inconceivable that all of a man's progeny should suffer for the sin of their father' (457). Jesus had stressed his 'humanity', that he was a 'like others' (459) and, until the Nicene Creed, Christians had been Unitarian (455). References in the Bible to Jesus as 'Son of God' are no more meant to be understood literally than are references to Adam as God's son, 'since he was created by God without biological parents, metaphorically he has been ascribed to God' (464). Jesus also had no biological father. Jesus' own description of his unity with God, when he says 'I am my Father are one' (John 10:30) is not a literal unity but reflects the fact that Jesus was obedient to God, and righteous in his deeds (468).

Al-Karawani's Continued Popularity

Al-Karawani's writing was circulated widely and achieved considerable popularity in the Muslim world, especially as a refutation of Pfander's book, equally popular within the Christian world. Compared with some later Muslim polemic, al-Karawani wrote in a tempered, academic style, drawing on a great deal of Christian Biblical scholarship to support his arguments. His use of Jesus' own words suggest that he did not consider the whole of the New Testament to have been corrupted, a view that this writer has often encountered among Muslims. Interestingly, his reliance on several passages in John's Gospel would not attract the support of many contemporary New Testament scholars, for whom very little of what Jesus says in John is accepted as authentic. Al-Karawani opposed British rule in India and supported the rebels during the revolt of 1857–8, which the British traditionally describe as the Indian Mutiny, and now more commonly known as the first Indian war of independence. After the revolt was crushed, al-Karawani fled India with a price on his head, fleeing to what is now Saudi Arabia. In 1861, Pfander was transferred from India to Istanbul to establish a new mission. His strategy there was similar to the one he had employed in India, and before that in Russian Armenia: outdoor preaching and distributing literature, this time in the precincts of the Hagai Sophia, then a mosque. In India, he had the support of Christian officials who, although officially banned from aiding missionary activities, did so in their private capacities. Also, British troops were always close at hand. In 1861, Pfander published the Turkish edition of the *Mizan* and it appears that copies of the *Izhar-al-Haq* were also in circulation. The Ottoman Sultan, or Caliph, invited al-Karawani to Istanbul, apparently to instruct the *Ulama* there in anti-Christian polemic. It is not known if he and Pfander encountered each other again. However, in 1864, the *Mizan* was banned by the Sultan, who closed down Pfander's preaching hall in the market and imprisoned any Muslim who had become Christian. The mission was relocated to Egypt. Pfander himself went to England on home leave, where he died shortly after, somewhat disillusioned with the prospect of converting Muslims to Christian faith (Bennett, 1996: 78). Had death not intervened, however, he would almost certainly have continued his efforts elsewhere. Al-Karawani influenced one of the twentieth century's most active and prolific Muslim polemicists against Christianity, Deedat (1918–2005), who, like al-Karawani, debated with Christian scholars, almost all of them from the more conservative wing. His contribution is discussed in Chapter 7.

Schirrmacher (1997) points out how al-Karawani started a trend in Muslim writing on Christianity, that is, using biblical scholarship to support their critique of Christian beliefs. The salafist thinker Rashid Rida (1865–1935), in his *tafsir* on the Qur'an, drew on European sources to argue that Paul had introduced heathen ideas into Christianity, which had been Unitarian until the Council of Nicea in 325. The form, source and redaction criticism that European scholarship has applied to the Old and New Testaments confirms, from a Muslim point of view, that the Bible is 'full of errors, misconceptions, contradictions, absurdities if not willful distortions' (Schirrmacher). Schirrmacher comments that while Muslims had always known this, it now seemed that Christians were admitting the inconsistency of their beliefs. From a Christian perspective, the Bible as an inspired book is also a profoundly human book. Christian fundamentalists, such as those against whom Deedat debated, may believe that it is infallible and without error, but many Christians accept that the Bible represents human response to the divine and that sometimes people remembered, or experienced, revelation differently. The Bible witnesses to revelation but it is not considered to be itself revelation, unlike the Qur'an. In refuting the Bible, al-Karawani and others treat it as if it were the same type of scripture as the Qur'an. Christian reflection on who Jesus was and on his relationship with God may be derived from, rather than rooted in, the biblical record. Al-Kawarani may be right to argue that the Trinity cannot be explicitly found in the Gospels. However, Christians believe that they continued to communicate with Jesus through the Holy Spirit after his death and that their theological deliberations were guided by Jesus, who promised them continued inspiration: 'I am with you always', he said (Matt 28:20). The early Christians were Jews, for whom any compromise with monotheism was unthinkable: yet God's Spirit and God's wisdom, and notions of God's Word, were already available to them. Trinity as a rigid dogma may well be incompatible with the biblical record. Trinity as the expression of what Christians experienced to be spiritually true may be biblically sound. It seemed to the first Christians that Jesus had enjoyed such an intimate relationship with God that the divine–human distinction became blurred. It also seemed that the Spirit that came upon them at Pentecost linked them powerfully to both God and Jesus, so that, although Jesus no longer walked with them on earth in physical form, he was with them in spirit. This experience resulted in the Trinity. Al-Karawani was not interested in understanding the experiential process that resulted in the formulation of Trinitarian theology, only in refuting it as non-biblical. He is not altogether to be blamed for this. Pfander presented the Trinity as if it were self-evidently true and could be proved by pure reason, while Christians often, as Ibn Taymiyyah pointed out, drew on allegory and on parallels in the natural world, rather than on scripture, to justify Trinity. From my own perspective, this approach to Trinity reduces it to some sort of mathematical formula, when it is actually an expression of the mystery of how God has revealed God-self to and within human experience. Our experience of the reality of God can no more be reduced to a formula than can the essence and nature of God.

Chapter 6

Classical Muslim Conciliatory Appoaches towards Christianity

This chapter begins with examples of irenic Muslim encounter with Christians from the earliest period, including Muhammad's meeting with the Christian delegation from Najran, then continues to look at conciliatory approaches in such mediaeval writers as Al-Ghazali (1058–1111) and Ibn Arabi (1165–1240) and at positive Christian–Muslim interaction during the Moorish period in Spain. It concludes with Sayyid Ahmed Khan (1817–98) from the colonial period. As with previous chapters, the context in which contributors wrote will be explored. Muslims look first of all to the Qur'an for guidance on any subject, then to the *sunnah* or example of the Prophet. Since Muhammad's example is understood to be the best guide to the Qur'an, and since the Qur'an cannot easily be interpreted without reference to Muhammad's biography, book and messenger can almost be regarded as a single entity. Muslims who adopt a negative, polemical approach to Christians and to Christianity cite the verses of opprobrium to support their views. They also point to examples of Muhammad speaking about Christianity as superseded by Islam and as a less than ideal or perfect religion. They dismiss the verses of friendship as having been abrogated by those of opprobrium, while examples of Muhammad treating Christians with respect is assigned to an earlier phase of his career, in contrast to his end-position, which sharply criticizes Christianity. Ibn Taymiyyah could dismiss the *hadith*, 'he who harms a *dhimmi* harms me', while others can cite Muhammad's reply to Al-Jarud, a Christian who asked him for 'surety of salvation' should he convert to Islam from Christianity. Muhammad said, 'I am thy surety that God hath guided thee to a better faith' (Ibn Hisham as cited by Muir, 1923: 461). A popular interpretation of both the Qur'anic material and of Muhammad's attitudes towards Christians is that earlier scriptural verses and sayings of Muhammad reflected the conviction that Christians would embrace Islam and endorse Muhammad's prophetic status, then, when this did not happen, later verses and sayings criticize Christian blindness, exclusivity and misinterpretation or corruption of their own scriptures. On the other hand, the *dhimmi* provision for Christians, Jews and for other recognized people of the book remained in force even at the end of Muhammad's career and continued to be regulated by Islamic law as an undeniable right throughout Islamic history, certainly until the end of the Ottoman Empire. The *dhimmi* system cannot be said to fulfil modern requirements for freedom of religion and for human rights under contemporary international conventions but represents a limited toleration only. On the other hand, when compared with the legal status of minorities elsewhere in the world at the time, it can be argued that Islamic law was lenient and enlightened.

It would be anachronistic to read too much into classical and medieval Muslim or indeed Christian writing. While some Muslims today embrace broadly pluralist theologies, classical positions are closer to what would be considered inclusivist positions. Representatives of the conciliatory tradition in Islam are almost exclusively from the Sufi strand of Islam, although at least one contributor, al-Ghazali (1058–1111) was also a distinguished legal scholar and is widely credited with having helped to reconcile Sufi Islam with the more legalistic tradition. Ibn Taymiyyah was vehemently critical of Sufi Islam although he may also have been a member of a Sufi order, the Qadiri *tariqah*, which makes his attitude towards Sufi Islam enigmatic (Michel, 1984: 28). Polemicists can dismiss the Andalusian experience of positive interaction between Christians, Jews and Muslims on the basis that Moorish Islam was heterodox. Polemicists view many of the famous Muslim philosophers whose works became popular in Christian Europe as infidels. Sayyid Qutb (1906–66) argued that no true Islamic concepts could be found in the work of Ibn Sina (980–1037), Ibn Rushd (1126–98) or al-Farabi (870–950), whose 'philosophy is no more than a shadow of the Greek philosophy which in its essence is foreign to the spirit of Islam' (1999: 118). The argument offered by some that European science stood on the shoulder of Islamic thought is thus rejected by those who claim that the Muslims who influenced European thinkers were heretics who had abandoned Islamic truths for a false reliance on reason without the need for revelation, or for God. On the other hand, not all Muslims reject the Islamic *bona fides* of the thinkers who interacted with Christians in Andalusia, and some regard *convivencia* as the best paradigm, not as an aberration. This chapter argues that Andalusia's *convivencia* is not unique but has or has had other parallels, including examples where Muslims were in the majority.

Muhammad's Encounters with Christians

Muhammad's earliest encounter with Christians was positive. As a child, while accompanying his uncle, Abu Talib, on a trade mission in Syria, he famously encountered the Christian monk Bahira, probably a Nestorian, who, on seeing Muhammad, predicted that the boy 'had a great future' (Ibn Ishaq, 1955: 79). Shortly before Muhammad's marriage with Khadijah, the wealthy widow who employed him, another incident occurred involving a monk. According to the *sirah* (biographical accounts of Muhammad's life) Muhammad was resting under a tree near a monk's cell, also in Syria. The monk saw Muhammad and asked Maysara, a young member of the party, who it was who was resting there. When Maysara replied that he was 'of the Quraysh', the monk 'exclaimed, "none but a prophet ever sat beneath this tree"' (82). Maysara then saw two angels 'shading the apostle from the sun's rays'. When Khadijah told her cousin, Waraqah, a Christian renowned for his knowledge of the Bible, about this incident he responded, 'If this is true, Khadijah, verily he is the prophet of this people' (83). Following Muhammad's first revelatory experience, which he confided to Khadijah while still unsure about the meaning of what had happened, she went immediately to Waraqah and related the account of how Muhammad had received Surah 96 from an Angel. Waraqah replied:

> Holy! Holy! Verily by Him in whose hand is Waraga's soul, if thou hast spoken to me the truth, Oh Khadija, there have come unto him the great Mamus [meaning Gabriel] who came to Moses aforetime, and lo, he is the prophet of this people. Bid him be of good heart. (107)

These three incidents depict Christians recognizing and affirming Muhammad's status as prophet of his people. While Khadija is universally recognized as the first to believe in Muhammad's mission, the *sirah* thus has Christians as the first to affirm Muhammad's status, although unlike Khadijah they did not follow him. It is interesting that they called Muhammad 'prophet of this people', which is similar to Paul of Antioch's description of Muhammad as having been 'sent with the Qur'an to the pagan Arabs' (Michel, 1984: 88). This, of course, contradicts Muslims' conviction, as expressed by Ibn Ishaq, that God sent Muhammad as 'an evangelist to all men' (10; see Q2:143). Ibn Ishaq, Muhammad's earliest biographer, added to the account of Muhammad's prophetic calling in his fortieth year that:

> Among the things which have reached me about what Jesus the Son of Mary stated in the Gospels which he received from God for the followers of the Gospel, in applying a term to describe the apostle of God, is the following. It is extracted from what John the Apostle set down . . . When the Comforter has come whom God will send to you from the Lord's presence, and the spirit of truth which will have gone forth from the Lord's presence, he [shall bear) witness of me . . . the *Munahhemana* (God bless and preserve him!) in Syriac is Muhammad, in Greek he is the Paraclete. (103–4)

Here is a very early example of Muslim belief that the Bible, at John 15:26, prophesied the coming of Muhammad. Deuteronomy 18:18–22 became a popular text to support this depiction of the Christian Waraqah recognizing and affirming Muhammad as a prophet in succession to Moses. The point here is that Christians did affirm Muhammad's status, which was consistent with his own conviction, once he understood his prophetic role, that the earlier prophets and scriptures had anticipated his mission. The Book that Muhammad received, Muslims believe, confirmed the content of previous revelation (Q3:3), which suggests that the message of all these scriptures is the same. Thus, the Children of Israel part company from their covenant with God if they fail to recognize Muhammad; 'believe in what I reveal, confirming what you already possess . . . depart not from my revelations . . . and keep your duty towards Me' (Q2:41).

Another example of positive relations between Muhammad and a Christian involved the ruler of Ethiopia, who welcomed and gave refuge to those of his followers whom Muhammad sent there to escape persecution at in Makkah. In Ethiopia, the believers (not described as Muslim until after 622) could 'serve God without fear' and were hospitably received by the Negus (Ibn Ishaq, 1955: 148).

According to the Negus, what Muhammad's followers related to him about their religion, and what Jesus had taught, 'came from the same' source. 'Of a truth', he said, 'this and what Jesus brought have come from the same niche' and he would never surrender one of Muhammad's followers to their enemies (152). Even when, following the defeat of the Muslim armies at Tours (732) during their northerly advance towards Europe, they notionally divided the world into *Dar-al-Islam*, territory under God's law, and *Dar-al-Harb*, territory yet to be brought into submission, Muslims placed Ethiopia in a third, exclusive category of its own, that of *dar-al-hiyad* (neutral territory). Muhammad is reported to have said that Muslims should leave Ethiopia in peace as long as the Ethiopians left them in peace. This tradition outlived the idea that Muhammad's attitude towards Christians changed towards the end of his live, becoming more critical and condemnatory.

Muhammad's attitude, even late in his career, can be seen as open and dialogical. When a delegation of 60 Christians led by Bishop Abu Haritha visited him from Najran in the Yemen, he received them courteously. This was less than two years before the Prophet's death. Initially, his reception was cool; they wore sumptuous robes, which he found offensive and wasteful, commenting that 'Satan accompanied their finery and jewel'. After they changed attire, a *Mubahila* (debate) ensued. Q 3:59–60 and Surah 112, emphasizing God's unity and denying that he begets children, may have been revealed at this time and possibly 5:14, charging Christians with abandoning their covenant. The account says that the debate was tripartite, with Jews joining in as well. The verse at 17:90 saying that even the *jinns* could not produce a single Surah to match the Qur'an was revealed shortly before this debate, during a dialogue between Muhammad and Jews. In response to his claim that the Torah spoke of him, they challenged him to call down a Book from heaven. In this episode, the Christians did not convince Muhammad nor did he convince them. However, when it was time for their worship, Muhammad allowed them to pray in a corner of his own mosque. Finally, noticing the nobility of the Prophet's family when they saw Fatimah, Ali, Hassan and Husayn together with him, the Bishop said, 'do not indulge in debate with this family, for I am observing such pious faces that if they would order the mountain to come to them this mountain should move towards them'. In less respectful usage, this gets reversed, though few people know they are citing a *hadith*. He continued, 'it is therefore prudent to make treaty with them, rather than confrontation' (see Guillaume,

1955: 270–1; Muir, 1923: 549–60 and Subhani, 1984: 729–34). The subsequent treaty included the words, 'their lives and property, lands and places of worship shall be under the protection of Allah and his property . . . Muslims shall assist them against oppression' and the tribute was remitted for two years. Many Muslims regard this as typifying the attitude they should have towards Christians. Tradition even records that when Muhammad, after the fall of Mecca in 630, cleansed the Ka'bah of all idols and images, he left an icon of Mary and Child intact, suggesting that he did not regard this as a form of idolatry (Ibn Ishaq, 1955: 774).

While Muir remarks that at about this time, Muhammad finally parted company from Christians with 'threats of abasement and cruel words', casting 'contemptuously aside' the 'means by which' he had achieved his success, which for Muir was what he had 'borrowed' from the Bible (454), Christians continued to enjoy protection on condition that they 'paid the tribute'. After Muhammad's death, the second caliph, Umar, gave instructions that *dhimmis* must be protected and not taxed too harshly (Bukhari, V4, Bk 52, *hadith* 287).[1] Another *hadith* links the amount of tribute payable to individual wealth (V4: 383). The pact of Umar did place greater restrictions on Christians and Jews but this can be identified as 'the work of later generations', since it departed from the instructions of tolerance and protection which are attributed to Umar (Khadduri, 1955: 193–4). A large number of *hadith* guarantee Christians the right to worship and to govern their civil affairs, provided they did not try to convert Muslims or rebel against the state. In return for protection by the state, the tribute or tax had to be paid. It has been argued that both Qur'an and the *sunnah* provides material to support either a more or a less tolerant attitude towards *dhimmis*, depending on the social-political context with which a ruler had to deal. This explains periods when Christians were employed in key positions, and also when they were dismissed, only to be re-appointed by a future ruler. Even in Andalusia, the intolerant Almohads (who seized power in 1145) threatened Jews with death or expulsion if they did not convert but later entered into alliances with Christian rulers and even encouraged Christian to settle in Fez. Maimonides (1135–1204) fled Andalusia yet found refuge in Muslim Egypt, where he became court physician. Muslims who wish to live in peace with Others will choose traditions that support *convivencia*. Muslim conciliators also point to the Constitution of Madina, the treaty between Muhammad and the different communities of Madina, including some Jewish tribes, recognizing his leadership. This, they say, was essentially a pluralist arrangement. Nor was there any requirement for non-Muslims to become Muslim.

Other Examples of Christian Life Flourishing under Islam

During much of Ottoman history, Christians did not fare badly. Martin Luther described the Turks as the 'devil incarnate' and did not expect his tract to earn him a 'gracious reception' if Suleiman the Magnificent read it. However, the Sultan himself is reported to have said that were he and Luther to meet, the latter would find him a 'gracious Lord' (Schultz, 1967: 170; 205[2]). According to Courbage and Fargues (1997), after having decreased during the Mamluk period in Egypt, the Christian population began to grow again under Ottoman rule (from 1517). In fact, under the Ottomans Christianity was 'revived and flourished' (xi). In the Fertile Crescent, after 'four centuries of Ottoman rule', the Jewish population 'doubled and the Christian tripled: more than twenty percent of the population' was 'by that time Christian and two percent Jewish'. At the beginning of this period, the population was 92 per cent Muslim, seven per cent Christian and only one per cent Jewish (61). Interested in controlling society rather than 'taking over and changing it', the Ottomans allowed different communities a large degree of 'autonomy in matters related to religion, law, culture and health' (xi). In the Shi'a world, too, Christians enjoyed considerable freedom during the reign of Shah Abas (1571–1629), the Safavid ruler who united Iran. He was probably more tolerant of non-Muslims than of Sunnis; he allowed Christians to wear what they chose and to ride on horseback, whereas the various restrictive codes practised at different times prescribed rigid rules of dress and prohibited Christians from riding. Writing about Bosnia before the Balkan War, with its 51 per cent Muslim population, Sells (1998) describes Sarajevo as the 'center of a pluralist culture' where 'mosques, synagogues, Catholic and Orthodox churches' stood side by side, and where people were 'skilled at languages and navigating the concourses of differing traditions', a bridge 'between the increasingly polarized spheres of the East and the West' which could play 'an important role in preventing a war between the majority Christian world and the majority Islamic world' (148).

Abu Hamid Al-Ghazali

Al-Ghazali is one of the recognized masters of Islamic thought. He has his critics, not least of all for his preference for Sufi Islam, but citing him as a conciliator carries undeniable authority, perhaps as a counter-balance to Ibn Taymiyyah, although they do stand on some common ground. They share, for example, a critique of the Muslim philosophers, the *falsafa*. According to Ibn Taymiyyah, the philosophers employed 'vague and general terms not taken from the sacred books' (Michel, 1984: 21). Al-Ghazali offered a similar critique in his classic *The Incoherence of the Philosophers*, where he argued that the cosmological system of the philosophers did not need God to sustain it, and they only quoted the Qur'an to appear pious! Ibn Taymiyyah criticized al-Ghazali for appearing to believe that by following the mystic path, Muslims could actually experience fresh revelations from the Divine:

> Abu Hamid [al-Ghazali] and those like him who command this Way do not think that it leads to unbelief . . . they command the disciple (*murid*) to empty his heart of everything . . . They believe that if his heart becomes empty, he is then ready and the sought-for knowledge descends upon his heart. (Michel, 1984: 38)

Ibn Taymiyyah condemns this as *bida* (innovation).

William Montgomery Watt's *The Faith and Practice of Al-Ghazali* (1952) is available online at www.ghazali.org/works/watt3.htm. Watt describes al-Ghazali as 'the greatest Muslim after Muhammad' (13). While mainly reliant on secondary sources, an accessible discussion of al-Ghazali on Christianity can be found in van Gorder's *No God but God* (2003: 81–6). Van Gorder cites Duncan Black Macdonald's opinion that al-Ghazali was the 'most original thinker Islam has produced and its greatest theologian' (81), which reflects the fact that Christian writers have often been attracted to al-Ghazali, including Aquinas, who cites him 31 times. Even Zwemer wrote that a study of al-Ghazali's life might awaken in non-Muslims an appreciation of 'what is highest and strongest in . . . Islam' since his books 'are full of reverence for Christ' (1920: 12). Zwemer's book on al-Ghazali is available online at www.ghazali.org/books/zwem1.pdf. The following analysis draws on Watt for relevant biographical details, on van Gorder for Ghazali's conciliatory approach to Christianity and on a variety of sources for additional material. What al-Ghazali wrote about Jesus and Christianity was informed by his preference for Sufi Islam, as well as by his inclination towards harmony rather than polarization. What earned al-Ghazali's reputation was his attempt to bridge the divide between the legalistic Islam, and Islam's then much maligned Sufi school. The charge of heresy against Sufi Islam was mainly the result of al-Hallaj's execution, in 922, for crying out that he was 'truth', which was interpreted as blasphemy, since 'truth' is known only to God and is indeed an attribute of God. The difference between al-Ghazali and Ibn Taymiyyah on Christianity is less *what* they believed than *how* they presented their ideas and arguments. While Ibn Taymiyyah brought to bear on Christianity his preference for total dissimilitude between Islam and all other faiths, al-Ghazali brought to bear his harmonizing tendency.

Al-Ghazali's Spiritual Interpretation of Islam

Al-Ghazali was born in 1058 in Tus, in what is now Iran. His father died while he was still a child but left a legacy behind so that al-Ghazali and his brother would receive an education. He studied under Abul Maali al-Juwayni (d. 1085), a renowned professor of Shafi jurisprudence. Ghazali was trained in Shafi law and in Asharite theology at Nishapur academy. Al-Ashari (d. 945), an opponent of the Mutalaalites, had defended the uncreated Qur'an and the existence of divine attributes. In 1091, al-Ghazali was appointed professor at Baghdad's Nizamiyah academy under the caliph's sponsorship. He excelled as a teacher, attracting a large number of students. His book on the incoherency of the philosophers only added to his scholarly reputation. Suddenly, during the year 1095, he started to experience profound doubts about the direction his life was taking, despite his prestigious post and not inconsiderable personal wealth. He began to question his motives, which he found wanting; he taught not from a desire to serve God but for influence and recognition (Watt, 1952: 136). He was 'deeply involved in affairs' but thought that much of his time was spent dealing with 'branches of knowledge which were unimportant and worthless'. What would today be described as a psychotic episode or a breakdown followed. One day, in his lecture room, he was simply unable to speak, later writing that 'God caused' his 'tongue to dry up so that' he 'was prevented from lecturing', an 'impediment' that 'produced grief' in his 'soul'. When his physicians proved unable to help, Ghazali decided that he needed to seek for inner peace through travel and spiritual inquiry. Resigning his post – which was assumed by his brother, Ahmad – he made provision for his family and left for the *hajj*, which he performed in 1096. He spent time in Damascus, in Jerusalem shortly before the city fell to the Crusaders, in Hebron where he prayed at Abraham's tomb and in Egypt, where he visited the tombs of Daniel and Alexander the Great. Searching for truth, he investigated different schools of thought but found them all wanting. Increasingly, he became convinced that knowledge of God results only from spiritual, inner illumination, from the soul's journey to its source. He finally decided that the Sufis of Islam were walking the right path: 'I learnt with certainly that it is above all the mystics who walk on the road to God; their life is the best life, their methods the soundest method' (Watt, 1952: 63). Returning to Tus, he took over the running of a *khanka* (Sufi hospice and study house). There, he produced his most famous work, the *Ihya ulum-al-din* (Revivication of the Religious Science). His renown led people to refer to him as *Hujjut-il-Islam* (the proof of Islam) and as a *mujaddid* sent at the start of a new millennium to revive and purify Islam. In 1106 he returned to public teaching in Baghdad, feeling a compulsion to teach again before he died.

Ghazali's reputation as a Shafi lawyer meant that no one could accuse him of disloyalty to legal Islam. Many Sufis were lax in their external compliance with the rituals of Islam, convinced that they enjoyed spiritual communion with the divine. Ghazali urged his fellow Sufis to observe the outer rituals of Islam and other Muslims to accompany external compliance with inner purity, since outer worship without inner sincerity is worthless. Prayer or performing the *hajj* has no value unless the worshipper and the pilgrim also journey within their own souls. However, al-Hallaj had overstepped the mark when he cried out اخا الحـق, *ana-al-Haq*' (I am Truth), confusing nearness to God with identification, that is, the wine with the wine glass. Instead of saying that the 'wine is as it were the wine glass', he cried out that 'the wine is the wine glass' (Peters, 1994: 343–4). Sufis, intoxicated with a sense of Oneness with God, who declare that they and God are the same, speak about that which should not be spoken, just as 'words of passionate lovers . . . should be hidden away and not spoken'. Sufi Islam seeks to journey inwardly towards God, along a *tariqah* (path) towards a conscious merging of the self with the divine. In the process, the *nafs* (self) dies to selfishness. The teacher–pupil relationship is an important aspect of Sufi Islam. The path also involves stages and states: stages are steps taken by the *salik* (traveller) such as renouncing wealth and serving others; states are God-gifted chances in spiritual perception, including knowledge (*ma? rifah*) and awareness of 'unity' with the divine (*wujud*). Sufi Islam stresses the qualities of love, peace-with-all, tranquillity, humility, generosity, selflessness and inner joy. Ghazali is generally credited with reconciling Sufi Islam and legal Islam by explaining al-Hallaj's ecstatic cry as not really blasphemy at all, and by encouraging Sufi Muslims to also keep their *fard* (obligatory) duties.

Ghazali and Christianity

In one passage, Ghazali writes about *jihad* against non-Muslims as an annual duty, saying that Christian and Jewish books should be destroyed, their trees cut down and their food appropriated (see 1979: 186–90). However, this passage occurs in his manual on Shafi law, so he was describing Shafi opinion rather than stating his own. Similarly, when commenting on Q9:29 he says that when paying the tax, *dhimmis* must hang their heads while the official grasps them by their beard (presumably this only applied to males), he was stating the Shafi position (1979: 186f.). Muhammad al-Talbi refers to Ghazali, whom he describes as 'a completely orthodox theologian' considered by Sunnis 'without exception to be the authentic spokesman for Islam' as holding that there are some circumstances in which non-Muslims can be considered 'saved' (Talbi, 1990: 92). In various writing, Ghazali discussed such issues as the reliability of Christian scriptures, the status of Jesus and the historicity of the Cross. When writing on these issues, he 'approaches the Bible with respect' (van Gorder, 2003: 85) and cites from the Bible in a way that suggests an apparent willingness to accept Biblical material (84). This places him in a different category from ibn Hazm, for whom the Bible was 'an accursed book' (Michel, 1984: 90). Ghazali does speak of corruption of the text at, for example, John 17:22, which implies that God gave divinity to Jesus when in his opinion divinity can not be 'given'; but he also cites passages in support of his own argument. Arguing that Jesus, although intimate with God, was human and not divine, he cites Mark 11:12–13 when Jesus cursed a fig-tree, expressing anger, a human not a divine emotion. 'Growing', too, in stature and wisdom (Luke 1:40) is a human, not a divine, attribute

(Van Gorder: 83). 'How could Jesus be God yet also pray to God?' Ghazali asked. A passage such as 'he who has seen me has seen the Father' refers to Jesus' intimacy with God, not to identification with God. Here, Ghazali uses the same argument he had developed to explain al-Hallaj's cries of ecstasy. Jesus, said Ghazali, was a perfected man, who possessed a 'boundless love of God' and whose life was so united with God's will that it represents a 'pattern that others should seek to emulate' (von Gorder, 2003: 82). For Ghazali, Jesus was a Sufi, a *'faqir* who is to be imitated in his world-renouncing zeal'. Jesus' ascetic lifestyle made him a true Sufi:

> Consider Jesus Christ, for it is related of him that he owned nothing save one garment of wool[3] which he wore for twenty years and that he took nothing with him on all his wanderings save a cruse and a rosary and a comb. One day he saw a man drinking from a stream with his hands, so he cast away the cruse. (Ghazali cited in Zwemer, 1920: 269)

Later, says Ghazali, Jesus gave away the comb as well when he realized that he could use his fingers instead.

Christians actually diminish Jesus by insisting on his divinity, while Muslims do him the greater honour by insisting on his humanity. As a human prophet, we can emulate him. As a divine person, we cannot. Ghazali does not reject such language as 'father' and 'son' but allegorizes these terms. 'For the esteemed Imam', says van Gorder, 'much of the bible should be read as metaphoric poetry' (83). Jesus' intimacy with God can be regarded as a type of theophany, but only in a metaphorical, not in a literal, sense (84). Ghazali emphasized that Jesus taught an ethic of love. Jesus is the 'prophet of the heart'. Jesus is to be 'emulated, not worshipped'. For Sufi, love of God (*mahabbah*} is the highest virtue. This is a standard Muslim view of Jesus, with which Ibn Taymiyyah would agree. Arguably, Ghazali on Jesus is no closer to a Christian on Jesus than Taymiyyah, but he writes in a conciliatory, irenic style. Ghazali, though, does establish some common ground between Muslims and Christians; both maintain that the spiritual goal is 'a degree of intimacy with the Almighty' and agree that this 'is both desirable and possible' (von Gorder, 2003: 85). Ghazali also believed that in performing miracles, Jesus sometimes worked 'through the divine spirit' (83). In expressing their beliefs about Jesus, Christians exceed the bounds of acceptable vocabulary, just as some Sufis do.

Al-Ghazali describes the Trinity as a 'delusion' and accepts the traditional Muslim view that Jesus was not crucified. He cites the crucifixion narrative as proof that Jesus could not have been divine, since God could not die (van Gorder, 2003: 84). Christian doctrine about Jesus' incarnation and divinity blur his real identity as a Prophet and the distinction between the human and the divine, two natures which 'must be mutually exclusive' (84). Ghazali was also troubled by Christian 'denial of the prophetic status of Muhammad' (83). He appears to have responded specifically to points of debate with Christians and in doing so opened up the possibility of Muslims holding Jesus in very high esteem as the 'prophet of the heart', as a guide to a life in conformity with God's will in the inner, spiritual realm, with Muhammad perhaps serving as the guide par excellence to a life of conformity with God's will in the external, physical realm. For Ghazali, understanding is a divine gift. Reason can observe the relative but unaided by revelation it cannot comprehend the infinite. Ghazali's ideas and teaching appear to have had a positive impact on treatment of minorities within Islam, reinforcing tolerance. Where anti-Sufi interpretations of Islam dominate, such as in Afghanistan during the rule of the Taliban, distinguishing dress codes have been imposed on non-Muslims, and ancient Buddha images were destroyed, while in Somalia under the Islamic Courts' government non-Muslims were declared apostate Muslims subject to the death penalty.

Ibn Arabi on Jesus as 'Spirit of God'

Muhyi al-din ibn al-Arabi was born in 1165 CE in Murcia, Spain, into the world of *convivencia* that serves, for some Muslims, as the best model of how Muslims should relate to Christians, Jews and followers of other religions. His father may have been a minister under the local Muslim ruler. He studied jurisprudence, the traditions (*hadith*), philosophy and metaphysics in Seville, where his mentors included two women, Shams and Fatima of Cordoba. The move to Seville was partly to escape from the rule of the Almohads, who swept into Andalusia in the twelfth century and, stressing the unity and uniqueness of God, set out to purify Islam of corruption, which for them included Sufism and the *falsafa*. They also reversed their predecessor's toleration of Christians and Jews, expelling Jews (including the famous Maimonides). Yet even the Almohads changed their tactics and entered alliances with Christian rulers towards the end of their rule (1229), and actually encouraged Christians to settle in Fez. Ibn al-Arabi encountered Sufis on visits to Tunisia, where he later said that he met with the Pole of the Age, that is, the recognized spiritual adept who ranks above all other Sufi masters. Later, ibn al-Arabi was recognized as the Pole, or Seal, for his age. He also met Ibn Rushd, whose funeral he attended but was 'skeptical of the value of philosophical speculation' (Austin: 7). He was reluctant to allow reason to arbitrate all knowledge. He was initiated as a *salik* at the age of 20 but soon attracted his own disciples. Teaching followed, as did a great deal of travel. He served several mosques as *khatib* (preacher) before leaving Spain in 1200, visiting Makkah, where he quickly gained a reputation as a spiritual guide and was dubbed by some as the Seal of the Age, earning the title '*al-Shaikh al-akbar*', the Greatest Sheikh. van Gorder says that he was 'also called an 'animator of the faith' because of his influence' (173). In addition to his reputation as a Sufi master, Ibn al-Arabi was also known for his knowledge of *hadith*, for his generosity and ascetic lifestyle. He did not enjoy the type of reputation that al-Ghazali had as a legal scholar but his standing as a student of the traditions did give him a certain status among traditional or legally inclined Muslims. He spent time in Baghdad, Mosul, Cairo, Aleppo and Konya before settling in Damascus, where he died in 1240. The Ayyubids remained in power in Damascus until 1260. Under their rule, Christians were allowed to pilgrimage to Jerusalem and to reside in the city, as were Jews. It is said that at the beginning of their rule only one Jew lived in Jerusalem while at its end there were several thousand. Ibn al-Arabi's spiritual interpretation of Islam did not always please the political authorities and on several occasions he moved on due to opposition to his views, such as when he left Cairo (1206). In Damascus he encountered some opposition but also enjoyed the protection of the Ayyubids, the dynasty established by Saladin, which took control of Damascus in 1174. A prolific writer, Ibn al-Arabi produced some 300 publications (some sources say over 800) of which over 100 have survived. He became a friend of Jalal al-Din Rumi and other leading Sufi masters. His *The Bessels of Wisdom*, or *Wisdom of the Prophets*, written in Egypt (1206), on which the following discussion is based, is available in various English renderings. He is said to have received the contents of this text in a 'single dream'. The text used in this chapter is the 1980 translation by R. W. J. Austin. His influence spread beyond the Muslim world, percolating into the 'mystical and poetical imagery of Europe' (15). There is considerable similarity between what Ibn al-Arabi wrote about Jesus, and what Ghazali wrote. While Ghazali appears to have responded to Christian belief about Jesus, tackling such Christian doctrines as incarnation, Trinity and Jesus' divinity and addressing Christians on these points, Ibn al-Arabi's writing on Jesus is set in the context of his exploration of the phenomenon of prophecy. Each of the 27 chapters of *The Bessels* discusses a different prophet, beginning with Adam and ending with Muhammad. Jesus is the subject of Chapter 15. Ibn al-Arabi is often described as the most influential exponent of the doctrine of oneness of being (*wahdat al-wujud*). Like Ghazali, he is primarily interested in how people can achieve their fullest spiritual potential, which is a life lived in total conformity with the will of God. Like many Sufis, he used the term 'Perfect Man' (*al-insan al kamil*) to describe such a fully realized, spiritually mature individual. The goal of Oneness is best understood in terms of 'perception' and implies a tension between 'perception and being, subject and object, the knower and the object of knowledge' (26) which Austin summarizes thus:

His doctrine of the Oneness of Being/Perception means that the sole, whole Reality is far more than the sum of its parts or aspects and that, however things may seem from the standpoint of the differentiated being or perception, all being is nothing other than Its being, and all perception, however limited, is nothing other than *the* Perception in a particular mode. (27)

Like most Sufi writers, Ibn al-Arabi used metaphors to express his views, one of which was that of the divine pen and Tablet. The pen represents universal intellect (ibn al-Arabi was influenced by Platonic thought), or God as creating subject, the Tablet the natural world, or the created, objective Cosmos:

'so that the relationship between the Cosmos as created object and God as creating subject is envisaged within the context of the patriarchal perspective in which woman, as the human image of Universal nature, is always seen as being derivative from and dependant on man, as the human agent of the Spirit. (30)

The pen is a Qur'anic metaphor; Q96 v 4 says that God teaches 'by means of the pen' (*Allazi 'allama bil qalam* Against this background, what did Ibn al-Arabi say about Jesus? His chapter on Jesus consists of thirteen pages (174–86). There is no attempt to respond to Christian beliefs or to deal with biblical material, so the charge of *tahrif* is not addressed. He does refer to 'certain people who speak of incarnation' (177) as 'unbelievers' but he does not explicitly identify these people as Christians. The view of Jesus that develops is based on Qur'anic verses. It could be argued that Ibn al-Arabi does not represent a contribution to Christian–Muslim encounter since he is writing for Muslims about a Muslim prophet. However, what he wrote about Jesus is available for Christians and Muslims to read and so can inform encounter. There is also a synthetic aspect to Ibn al-Arabi in that he appears to have fused ideas that influenced him from a multiplicity of sources, both Muslim and non-Muslim, thus 'Ibn al-Arabi's thought . . . more than any other in the world of Islam, brings together in a wonderful synthesis a multitude of spiritual traditions and esoteric lore, both Islamic and non-Islamic . . . the influences of which have permeated deeply, not only into all subsequent Sufi thinking, but also into the fabric of Christian mysticism' (xviii). In other words, his legacy has become part of Christian–Muslim encounter, even if he did not necessarily write in the immediate context of an encounter. On the other hand, there is some evidence that Ibn al-Arabi supported restrictive codes vis-à-vis Christians, since when asked by the ruler of Konya 'regarding the proper treatment of his Christian subjects', he replied that he should impose on them the 'full rigor of Islamic Law regarding the restriction of their public worship' (Austin, 1975/1980: 10). Ibn al-Arabi may have wanted to impress the sultan with his external conformity to the Law.

Q4:171 serves as Ibn al-Arabi's key to exploring the unique significance of Jesus. In each chapter, he draws on the Qur'an's references to the Prophet under discussion to identify what was distinctive about their experience so that the pious can learn from them. He understood all prophets as corresponding to a prototype and as receiving divine wisdom which becomes an essential part of their humanity. There is thus an intimate relationship 'between divine revelation and its human recipient'. In each instance of prophecy, it is the 'receptive form which invites and compels divine revelation to reveal itself in one way and not another' (Burckhardt, 1975/1980: xiv). In discussing Jesus, Ibn al-Arabi stresses the role of God's spirit in creating Jesus and also in Jesus' actions, especially raising the dead. When Gabriel appeared to Mary (Q19:17) he 'blew Jesus into her', says Ibn al-Arabi (175; see Q21:91, 66:12). Referring to 5:171, he comments that this blowing, in fact, transmitted 'God's word to Mary, just as an apostle transmits His word to his community'. 'God', he continued, 'says, He is His word deposited with Mary, and a spirit from Himself' (175). 19:17 says that Gabriel appeared before Mary 'as a man'. From this, Ibn al-Arabi surmises that Jesus' body was 'created from the actual water of Mary and the notional water of Gabriel inherent in the moisture of that blowing, since breath from the vital body is moist owing to the element of water in it'. Gabriel had taken on a 'human form' (176). Jesus was therefore a 'divine spirit' and as such could raise the dead (Q3:49). However, this can only notionally be attributed to Jesus, because it is 'by God's leave' or 'permission' that he heals the sick, cures leprosy and raises the dead. Just as, according to Ibn al-Arabi, Jesus was created by the act of 'blowing', so 'blowing' or 'breathing' allows Jesus to perform miracles. 3:49 describes Jesus 'blowing' into a figure of a bird that then 'became a bird'. Had Jesus lacked God's permission, nothing would have resulted from his 'blowing'. Like al-Ghazali, Ibn Arabi stresses Jesus' humility and links this with Q9:29, the requirement that Christians humble themselves when they pay the poll-tax. Jesus taught that when struck on one cheek, you should 'offer also the other' (177). Ibn al-Arabi saw something of the feminine in Jesus' example of humility, which may have sprung from 'the fact that Christ was born from his mother without a father' (van Gorder, 2003: 174). Had Gabriel 'not come in human form, but in some other, whether animal, plant or mineral, Jesus would have been able to quicken the dead by taking' that form himself. However, since it was in human form that Gabriel blew life into Jesus, Jesus was able, with God's permission, to breathe life into the dead. Where people are led astray is when they confuse the vessel with what it contains, that is, they confuse Jesus as a receptacle of God's spirit with God, thus 'This matter has led certain people to speak of incarnation and to say that, in reviving the dead, he is God.' He describes this as a form of concealment, since 'they conceal God, Who in reality revives the dead, in the human form of Jesus' (177).

Yet, says Ibn al-Arabi, we can identify three 'sensible forms' within Jesus, namely, Word of God, Spirit of God and Slave of God (178). 'Considered in his mortal form', he is Mary's son, 'considered in his form of humanity', he can be regarded as Gabriel's son, while as reviver of the dead, 'he is of God as Spirit' (178). Ibn al-Arabi refers to this as a 'triple manifestation'. The 'Divine Breath is receptive to cosmic forms, in relation to which it is like the primordial Substance being very Nature Herself' (180). He thus links this breath of life with the act of creation itself, so that 'all is essentially in the Breath' (181). Ibn al-Arabi pointed out that when God created Adam, he also breathed His spirit into him but that this was after God had first moulded Adam's body from clay (Q15:29), thus perfecting His creation. The case of Jesus, however, is 'otherwise, since the perfection of his body and human form was included in the blowing of the spirit, which is not so of other men'. There is therefore a unique aspect to Jesus' creation. On the other hand, all humans are essentially spiritual beings. God can be described as 'Merciful Breath' (179), which can be equated with the Cosmos itself (180). Jesus, however, has a special relationship with the spirit because the 'blowing' described above made him a channel that transmitted 'the divine Command in all its modes' (Austin, 1975/1980: 174) Whoever wants to know the Divine Breath, says Ibn al-Arabi, 'let him know the Cosmos', for 'Who knows himself, knows his Lord' (181). Ibn al-Arabi described Jesus as the 'seal of all the saints' (van Gorder, 2003: 174, citing Burikhardt, 1975/1980: 71) and stressed his role as a 'sign' (Q23:4). In addition to the spiritual aspect of Jesus, Ibn al-Arabi emphasized Jesus' role as God's servant, or slave, emphasizing that Jesus only acted and spoke as he was commanded to do so by God, saying 'I told them only what you commanded me to say' (182; 5:117). Nor did Jesus tell anyone to take himself and his mother as 'gods' (5:116). Nor did Jesus claim absolute knowledge of God; God knew what was in Jesus' heart but he did not know what was in God's, except when speaking in God's name. Jesus fully acknowledged God as his Lord and as the object of his worship: 'Worship Allah, my Lord and your Lord', yet, says Ibn al-Arabi, God's relationship with each of his creatures is different and unique, which is why Jesus said, 'My Lord and your Lord' (183). Ibn al-Arabi states on the one hand that Jesus was not God, but a creature within which God's word and spirit dwelt. Yet, on the other hand, he argues that Jesus' whole life was an event through which God acted in human history. Thus, when Jesus described himself as a 'witness over them' he referred to the 'witness of God in' his own 'substance', as God's 'tongue, hearing and sight' (184). Jesus was not God yet when Jesus spoke and acted: it was God who spoke and acted through him. Ibn al-Arabi's Jesus was 'one with God' in terms of a complete coincidence of his will with God's will, not in terms of an ontological identification. This at-one-ness with God is identical to the relationship that a true Muslim enjoys with God. Jesus therefore provides an example that is to be emulated. Like Muhammad and all the prophets, he represents a perfect being and a true friend (*walil*) of God. The life that Jesus lived, though, was an 'outworking of the truths that were later to be revealed in the Qur'an' (van Gorder, 2003: 174). Those who follow Jesus can achieve the same status, not through faith in his death or resurrection but by sharing his humility, his turning away from lust and material possessions to walk the spiritual path. Van Gorder argues that, for Sufis such as al-Ghazali and Ibn al-Arabi, Jesus could be regarded as a 'theophany (*mazhar*) of the all-comprehensive name of God . . . a truest devotee of God . . . able to perform miracles' but says that he is 'never perceived as a "savior" but is confined to being honored as an ascetic capable of emulation, but not deserving of worship' (178). Nonetheless, he continues, here is fruitful material for Christian–Muslim discourse; 'Sufism's largely positive portrait of Christ may . . . predispose Sufis from dismissing the prospect of dialogue in which Christ is the central concern'. Their emphasis on Jesus as 'synonymous with love' could, he says, provide a 'starting point'.

Sayyid Ahmed Khan (1817–98): Christians and Muslims as Friends

Sayyid Ahmed Khan is credited with being a pioneer Muslim modernist and reformer. He is widely regarded as the father of modern Islam in India. Born into a family descended from the Prophet Muhammad, he was raised by his grandfather following his father's early death. As a youth he studied Arabic and Persian although he did not attend a traditional Islamic school. He also studied science and medicine with various private tutors. His maternal grandfather was Principal of the Calcutta Madrasa but also entered British service as a political officer in Burma. Ahmed Khan followed his grandfather into the civil service in 1838, joining the judicial branch. Over the years, he worked his way up to occupy the highest position then open to Indians, judge of the small causes court (1867), also serving from 1878 on the Legislative Council and from 1878 until 1882 on the Education Commission. From 1887 he served on the Civil Service Commission. He was knighted in 1888 and was awarded an honorary doctorate by Edinburgh University in 1889. A prolific writer, he first ventured into print at the age of 23, with a series of tracts on religious matters. He established several schools and learned societies but is best known as the founder of what became Aligarh Muslim University, originally the Anglo-Mohammedan Oriental College, known as MAO (1877). Ahmed Khan remained loyal to the British throughout the rebellion of 1857–8 advocating that friendship and cooperation with the British was the best option for Indian Muslims. In this, he took the opposite approach of some Muslims, who advocated either non-cooperation, or revolt. In their view, India under British rule was within the house of war, and it was their duty to restore Muslim rule. He countered the contention that Muslims were bound by their religion to rebel against non-Muslim rule by arguing that Muslims had no justification to compromise the 'security' they enjoyed under British rule. Instead of calling India *dar-al-harb*, Ahmed Khan described India under the British as '*dar-al-aman*' (place of security). Thus, 'as long as Musalmans can preach the unity of God in perfect peace, no Musalman can, according to his religion, wage war against the rulers of that country' (Khan, 1871: 81). When Sir William W. Hunter published his report *Indian Musalmans* (1871), arguing that the British government should not expect Muslim loyalty because the duty of *jihad* compelled them to rebel, Ahmed Khan again argued that Indian Muslims could under no circumstances 'renounce the *aman* of the English', citing in support a tradition that whenever Muhammad 'marched against any infidel people . . . he stopped the commencement of hostilities until morning . . . to find out whether the *azan* (call for prayer) was being called in the adjacent country' and if it was, 'he never fought with its inhabitants' (Khan, 1871: 81–2).

What concerns us in this chapter is not so much what Ahmed Khan wrote about Islam but about its relationship with Christianity. The former, though, is more accessible: Kurzman (2002) reproduces Ahmed Khan's 'Lecture on Islam' (291–303), while his review of Hunter is available at https://dart.columbia.edu/library/DART-0045/DART-0045.html. His approach to Islam was to argue for reinterpreting the tradition instead of blindly imitating past interpretations, and for the primacy of reason in religious matters. He did not think that an alliance of the political and religious was binding on all Muslims. Rather, this depended on circumstances. He wanted to harmonize religion and science and depicted Islam as a positive catalyst for social progress. He identified with the pioneer rationalists of Islam, the Mutazalites. In writing on Islam, though, he often had Christian criticism in mind. His 1870 *Essays on the Life of Muhammad and Subjects Subsidiary Thereto* was a response to Sir William Muir's *Life of Mahomet* (1857–61) as well as to the public debates between Pfander and al-Kairanwi. He wrote his essays while visiting England and had to finance publication himself, since no publisher was willing to publish a defence of Islam, which, according to Muir, was 'the most stubborn' enemy of 'Civilization, Liberty and the Truth which the world has yet know' (1894: 506).[4] Islam, wherever it held sway, held back social and moral progress, said Muir. Ahmed Khan enjoyed a professional and a personal friendship with Muir, whom he appointed official Visitor to Aligarh; but he disagreed with his estimate of Islam, commenting that Muir's own pro-missionary sympathies prevented him from seeing anything beautiful in Islam (1870: xvii). Unlike many non-Muslim writers, Muir has used original sources, though, and his *Life* was 'the best . . . from the pen of foreign authors' (1870: xvii). Unfortunately, Muir had not used the best sources and too often 'selected for discussion those . . . which' Muslims 'consider . . . the least entitled to credit' (*Essay of the Holy Koran*: 42[5]). Khan singled out Edward Gibbon, Godfrey Higgins and John Davenport (1870: xxi) as having 'taken a correct view' of the Prophet but these men were marginal to mainstream Christianity, or even opposed to it. Of Khan's extensive writing, most relevant to Christian–Muslim relations is perhaps his *Commentary on the Bible* (1862; 1865), in which he discussed Genesis and Matthew but which, sadly, is difficult to access. Ridgeon's summary of Khan's 'vision of Christianity' (1999: 2–13) probably provides the best access to Khan's contribution, although this is not a primary text and relies mainly on secondary references. Three aspects of Khan's 'vision of Christianity' are highlighted below, chosen because they relate to previous discussion in this book, namely, the corruption of scripture, the trinity and the nature of Jesus. We shall also note how Khan used the Qur'an to support his contention that Muslims and Christians should regard each other as friends. He even appears to have believed that the British ruled India as a result of divine providence (Ridgeon, 2001: 4).

Khan on the Corruption of Scripture

Khan's commentary on the Bible, although incomplete, was a rare attempt by a Muslim to use the Bible as a source of spiritual guidance for Muslims. Khan studied Hebrew with a Jewish tutor to aid him in his task of biblical interpretation. Aware of the work of Muslims who demolished the Bible as unreliable and corrupt, and whose aim was to refute Christianity, Khan set out instead to attempt 'reconciliation' (Ridgeon, 2001: 7). He always wrote with two audiences in mind: on the one side the British, to whom he wanted to represent Islam as a rational, reasonable faith and Muslims as loyal subjects; and on the other hand Muslims who 'rejected British imperialism' (Ridgeon, 2001: 5). Aware of the Pfander–Kairanwi exchange as well as of what missionaries said about Islam, Khan also represents a response to Muir's and to Christian views of Islam and so he can be said to have participated in Christian–Muslim encounter. In writing about the gospels, he was critical of the views of some of the European scholars whom al-Kairanwi had cited, arguing that a scholar such as F. C. Baur could not be regarded as a man of faith. He rejected the view that the gospels were second-century forgeries (Ridgeon, 2001: 8). Where he departed radically from previous Muslim opinion was on the issue of *tahrif*. Contending that the gospels 'confirm the Qur'anic message', he was inclined to accept their veracity (Ridgeon, 2001 7). Instead of arguing for textual corruption, he asserted that *tahrif* could also refer to verbal misinterpretation and to mistakes made in transmitting the texts. The latter can be investigated by study of the earliest manuscripts. The former can be identified by a comparison with the Qur'an. In his view, the Gospels do contain elements of the original *injil* revealed to Jesus, although they are not identical with this scripture. While other Muslims argued that the Bible is not God's word, Khan defended its revelatory status, even extending the term '*wahy*' (revelation) to the apostles, although their writing may not be altogether accurate: 'the revelation prior to the Qur'an, such as that bestowed on . . . the apostles was of an inferior status because it did not represent God's words, but only the form of the content' (Ridgeon, 2001: 7).[6] Nonetheless, for Khan, the Bible remains a text that Muslims can use for spiritual nourishment. Convinced that the Bible points to Muhammad, he cited, among other verses, Genesis 17:20; Genesis 21:12; Deuteronomy 18, 15–18 and, from the Gospels, John's references to the *Paraclete* (*Essay on Prophecies Respecting Muhammad as contained in both Old and New Testaments*: 9–12).

Khan on the Trinity, Jesus and the Crucifixion

On both the Trinity and the status of Jesus, Khan's views did not differ much from those of Ibn Taymiyyah and al-Kairanwi but his style is much more irenic, although he could also make bold claims for Islam, such as 'Islam . . . is the perfection of religion, and because of this perfection Islam is the last religion . . .' (Khan, 2002: 302). Like the above, he considered the Trinity to be an innovation introduced after the apostles, 'in opposition to the eternal truth and contrary to the pure precepts inculcated by Christ' (*Essay on whether Islam has been beneficial or injurious to human society in general*: 38). The Qur'an affirms that Jesus is a Word and a Spirit from God, but denied that he is God. However, influenced by Ibn al-Arabi, Khan entertained the possibility that the terms 'word' and 'spirit' of God might also mean 'son of God', which could be identified as an eternal attribute of God (8). Yet this did not make Jesus and God partners in a Trinity with the Holy Spirit, or with Mary (citing Q5:116) because Jesus functioned under the 'authority of God' (9). Jesus' temptation by Satan only makes sense if he was a man (9; Khan cites Matt 4:10). Khan did not believe that Jesus died on the Cross, although he allows that a crucifixion may have occurred, after which Jesus' body, still alive, was hidden and the story of the ascension circulated. Nor was Jesus' death necessary for salvation, since 'there is no concept of original sin in Islam' (10). By the sixth century, the message preached by Jesus was so corrupt that God had to send Muhammad (9), who 're-established the worship of the Unity of the Godhead and revived that pure religion inculcated by Christ himself', and 'warned the then-called Christians of their errors and invited them to accept true religion – a religion preached by Christ' (ibid.). Muhammad had forbidden use of the cross, the worship of images, 'declared that God has no son, and in opposition to the doctrine of the Trinity preached, inculcated and propagated the worship of the one and only God' (24–5). Thus, Christians and Muslims should be friends: 'No religion upon earth is more friendly to Christianity than Islam, and the latter has been to none more beneficial and advantageous to Christianity' (37).

Khan's use of the Qur'an

In interpreting the Qur'an, Khan allowed allegory to explain material that otherwise implied the type of supernatural occurrence that he considered incompatible with reason and science, rejecting 'all the myths and stories that have been incorporated in the commentaries' on the Qur'an (Dar, 1957: 265). The presence of allegory in the Qur'an enables fresh interpretation in the light of new knowledge, since an 'increase in human knowledge' can 'reveal meanings and significance which had never occurred to the people of bygone ages' (Dar, 1957: 266–7). He argued that only the spiritual teaching of the Qur'an is binding on Muslims; its legal and social content can be adapted to circumstance, provided that this conforms 'with the fundamental spiritual values of Islam' (Dar, 1957: 268). Stressing the common Abrahamic origin of the two faiths, Khan supported the above statement by citing 'those Qur'anic verses' (that is, the verses of friendship) 'which portray Christianity in positive light' while he 'failed to mention the negative descriptions which appear in 5:14–15 and 5:51 (Ridgeon, 2001: 5). On the other hand, he was not suggesting that the Christianity practised in his own day was identical with the faith taught by Jesus. Some commentators describe Khan's writing as both 'defending Islam' and as 'hurling counter-attacks on Christianity' (Dar, 1957: 128). Ridgeon (2001) cites Khan's own words, that 'perhaps no one has written such severe books as I have against the Christian religion, of which I am an enemy' (5). His aim, says Dar, was to present Islam's incomparable claims to 'superiority over all other creeds' (135). Yet he appears to have wanted to reconcile rather than to refute. He wanted Muslims to benefit from Western education, and to cooperate with the British administration in India. He appointed distinguished English scholars to teach at Aligarh, which he wanted to be a Muslim Cambridge. His curriculum placed eastern and western subjects side by side. Among those influenced by his views, Khuda Bakhsh (1877–1931) expressed the opinion that Islam was compatible with all true religions, 'and especially Christianity, which he frequently praised' (Smith, 1946: 32–2; see Bakhsh, 1926).

Van Gorder's comment about Sufis' positive views of Jesus predisposing them to engage with Christians in dialogue with Jesus at its centre raises the problem that, while Muslims generally treat Jesus with respect, Christians find it difficult to reciprocate on Muhammad. Perhaps the real problem is not Muslim reluctance to place Jesus at the centre of dialogue, or in some cases to move some way towards a Christian view of Jesus, but Christian reluctance to speak well of Muhammad, of whom Khan hoped that some day it would be said that he had been 'a preacher of truth and righteousness' (1870: xxii). Does anything in this chapter help Christians to re-evaluate their view of Muhammad?

Chapter 7

Contemporary Christian and Muslim Confrontation

Confrontation has strong supporters among Christians and Muslims. Two of the most accessible examples of contemporary Christian–Muslim confrontation are the rival internet sites www.answering-islam.org and www.answering-christianity.com. The Muslim site, run by Osama Abdullah, owns the domain for www.answering-islam.com, so anyone who types that address into their browser will be directed to the Muslim site. The Christian site does not publish the names of all of its authors, stating that several members of the team have received death threats for criticizing Islam, since anyone who 'voices critique of Muhammad is an enemy of Islam, and this deserves the death penalty'. The site's sub-title is 'A Christian–Muslim Dialog', which implies a conciliatory approach; but the aim is to refute or to rebut Islam. Several articles on this site rebut articles on the Muslim site and vice-versa, so in fact there is a dialogue of sorts between the two. On the Christian site, the section 'Rebuttals to Muslim Polemics' includes responses to the writings of Deedat (1919–2005) and Jamal Badawi as well as Osama Abdullah's site, referring to its contents as 'diatribes'. Several articles by Sam Shamoun respond to Osama Abdullah, while John Gilchrist responds to the writings and speeches of Ahmad Deedat, who engaged in a number of public debates with Christian opponents, including the television evangelist Jimmy Swaggart, the apologist and Campus Crusade for Christ associate Josh McDowell and the Palestinian Christian Anis Shorrosh, among others. The Muslim site's rebuttal page includes responses to what it describes as Shamoun's 'foul mouth' as well as to articles by Shoroush and many other Christians. Shamoun, born in Kuwait, was raised as a Nestorian and is now a Baptist. He has lived in the USA since he was a child. Gilchrist is a South African lawyer. Shoroush has authored several books, including *Islam Revealed: A Christian Arab's View of Islam*, and holds a doctorate from Oxford. Each site accuses the other of rudeness, telling lies and deception.

Another polemical site, run by Jay Smith, is the Muslim–Christian Debate Website, www.debate.org.uk. Smith, a regular speaker at London's Hyde Park Speakers' Corner, debates in public with Muslims, including Jamal Badawi, whom the Christian site describes as 'without doubt the best known Muslim speaker in the West for the last two decades', and a convert, Abdur Raheem Green, who also speaks at Hyde Park and has a webpage on 'we need to unite', www.weneedtounite.com. Badawai, an Egyptian by birth, is a professor at Saint Mary University, Halifax, Canada. He directs the Islamic Information Foundation and is a council member of the Islamic Society of North America. His PhD is in Business Administration. He has a prolific presence on the web. Deedat is no longer alive but his pamphlets remain in circulation, so represent contemporary polemic. His arguments are repeated on many Muslim sites. Two of his booklets will be analysed below, *Crucifixion or Cruci-fiction?* (1984) and *What the Bible Says About Muhammad* (1979). Other writings by him will also be referenced.[1] Pamphlets and videos of his public debates are available on several websites, including 'Islam and Christianity – a comparative analysis' at www.jamaat.net/deedat.htm. Some twenty million print copies of his books are said to be in circulation. Siddiqui (1997), commenting on the lack of anybody within the Muslim world comparable to the Vatican and World Council of Churches offices on inter-religious relations, remarks that were such a desk to be created, there would be pressure to fill it with 'a person who may follow the line of "dialogue" adopted by Ahmed Deedat' (192).

To illustrate the popularity of the ideas and arguments Deedat expounded, links will be established with some of the internet articles published on Osama Abdullah's site. This chapter's analysis of Christian and Muslim contemporary confrontation demonstrates that a great many classical arguments are repeated by both sides. The persistence of traditional themes can be seen by listing the respective topics discussed on each site. Under 'site topics', the Christian site includes: the Qur'an, Muhammad, Women in Islam, 'Who is Jesus?' and Islam and Terrorism. The Muslim site lists Bible, Trinity and Jesus, Women and Morality, Islamic Justice and Government as well as Terrorism and Paedophilia. Discussion about terrorism and paedophilia introduce a new emphasis: the former in the main stimulated by 9/11 and other recent acts of terror perpetuated by people who described themselves as Muslim; while discussion of paedophilia was stimulated by Ergun Mehmet Caner's and Emir Fethi Caner's *Islam Unveiled* (see below). However, behind these foci stands classical debate about Islam as an inherently violent faith and about Muhammad's sexual conduct. One development is that there is more face-to-face encounter than previously occurred, and that much of the literature is intended to be read by the Other; Zebiri's comment about much Muslim anti-Christian polemic being mainly consumed by Muslims may be right, but this material does reach a Christian readership (1997: 89). The Christian site reproduces many classical texts, including Muir's abstract of the *Risalah*, his own writing, books by Pfander, William St Clair-Tisdall and Samuel Zwemer as well as by W. H. T. Gairdner, whom I have categorized as a conciliator. Much of the politeness that characterized classical confrontation is also absent; the *Risalah* began by invoking happiness and a long life on the caliph, and with an avowal of friendship, while Pfander's writing, as Muir put it, displayed 'an uncommon exuberance of language, a richness of diction, a perfect facility in the Persian idiom, and a degree of ease in adopting elegant and appropriate illustration', which astonished Muslim readers, some of whom suspected that an accomplished Persian had 'assisted their translation' (Muir, 1897: 30–1). In contrast, the Christian website refers to some Muslims who attribute it to 'Jews who intentionally propagate wrong information about Islam' and respond that it is a 'Muslim paranoia to accuse Jews to be behind anything that they do not like'. The Christian site, under 'responses to Osama Abdullah's site', speaks about 'lies', 'misrepresentations', 'attacks' and 'hoaxes'. The Muslim site refers to Sam Shamoun's 'foul mouth' and to the Christian site, which it calls 'anti-Islamic', as 'spreading lies'. Under a link to a video of a debate between Shamoun and Sami Zaatari on the Trinity, the Muslim site advises viewers to exercise discretion. It also accuses some contributors of plagiarism, of rehashing other people's work without attribution. When speaking of Jesus as God's son, Deedat implies that Christians believe that God used his penis to impregnate Mary, referring to the expression that the 'Most High would overshadow' Mary as 'gutter language'. In his 1985 Royal Albert Hall debate with Anis Shorrosh, he interpreted the term 'begotten son' to mean that God 'sired' Jesus.[2] 'The Muslim', he said, 'takes exception to the word "begotten", because begetting is an animal act, belonging to the lower animal functions of sex. How can we attribute such a lowly capacity to God?' (*Christ in Islam*, Chapter 5). Crudeness, however, is not only on the Muslim side; the Caners' reference to Muhammad having 'sexual relations with a child of nine' (63), which will be discussed below, was certainly intended to be provocative, if not crude. Spencer (2006), too, presents Muhammad as a 'paedophile', a 'misogynist' and as someone who took 'joy at the assassination of his enemies' while his 'words and deeds' have moved 'Muslims to commit acts of violence for fourteen hundred years' (184, 194)

Among Christian polemicists, the writings of Ergun Mehmet Caner and Emir Fethi Caner have become very popular, winning evangelical book prizes and far outstripping the sales of even the most widely used college-level, non-polemical text, such as John L. Esposito's *Islam the Straight Path*. The Caners are Turkish converts from Islam who teach in the USA. The sub-title of their *Unveiling Islam* is 'An Insider's Look at Muslim Life and Beliefs' (2002). The book's foreword describes it as, in the wake of 9/11, a 'trustworthy guide to the unfamiliar and suddenly threatening world of Islam'. 'All faiths', it states, 'are *not* the same' but 'Jesus is the *way*, the *truth* and the *life*'. Written by the President of the Southern Baptist Ethics and Religious Liberty Commission, Richard Land, the foreword refers to the 'often bloody persecution faced by fellow Christians around the world', which is presumably meant to mean the persecution of Christians by Muslims. The book is intended for a Christian readership, as a guide to Islam but also as a manual to aid their outreach to Muslims. The book claims that its authors 'present a practical strategy Christians can use to open a dialogue with Muslims'. However, the purpose of such a dialogue is to point out Islam's weaknesses as contrasted with Christianity's strengths, to better equip Christian witness to Muslims. The brothers say that their book is not a 'diatribe filled with invective against a world religion' but aims to inform Christians about Islam so that they can 'present Christ more effectively'. Muslims have responded to the book, which, through remarks made by the Southern Baptist President, Jerry Vines in June 2002, based on its contents, have provoked debate. Riots in India following Vine's remarks led to five deaths. The Caners' book, in many respects, is a counterpoint to Esposito's, which they view as liberal and pro-Muslim. Another counterpoint book to Esposito's is Robert Spencer's *The Truth About Muhammad*. Spencer, a lay Catholic and co-author of *Inside Islam:*

A Guide for Catholics, is director of Jihad Watch, and has debated with many Muslims in television and radio broadcasts. His views are so widely known that he was referred to in the 2 September 2006 video 'Invitation to Islam', featuring the American convert Adam Gadahn, who suggested that Spencer ought to abandon his unbelief and turn his sword against the enemies of God by embracing Islam. Gadahn described Spencer and George W. Bush as 'Zionist crusader missionaries of hate'.

The Caners both possess doctorate degrees, Ergun from the University of South Africa, Emir from the University of Texas. Ergun is President of Liberty Theological Seminary in Lynburg, Virginia while Emir is associate professor of church history and Anabaptist studies at the Southeastern Baptist Theological Seminary in Dallas, Texas. In contrast, Deedat was self-taught. Spencer has an MA in Religious Studies from the University of North Carolina at Chapel Hill although his focus was on early Christianity. He has been referred to as an Islamophobe and his *bone fides* as a scholar of Islam have been questioned. Deedat's and the Muslim site's contributions will be discussed first, then the Christian contributions.

It could be argued that in comparing Deedat with the Christian writers selected I am not comparing like with like, since the latter can claim scholarly credentials while the former cannot. However, the Caners and Spencer, like Deedat, also represent what can be described as popular contributions, sales or distribution of which have outstripped those of more academic and certainly more conciliatory writers, whose books have, in contrast, sold in the thousands, not in the hundreds of thousand. In 1986, Deedat received the prestigious King Faisal Award for outstanding services to Islam. Deedat lacked the intellectual capabilities of a Mawdudi or of a Qutb but shared many aspects of their critique of the Christian world, which they associated with the West. Whether regrettable or not, it is a fact that Deedat's views resonate widely with much Muslim opinion. I have to admit that Deedat's name has often surfaced in conversation with Muslims, while the names of Muslim conciliators have rarely if ever been mentioned. To ignore Deedat, or at least the widely used arguments represented by his works, would be to stick one's head in the sand.

Ahmed Deedat: Kairanwi Revisited

Deedat's style has been described as 'flamboyant' and 'rhetorical', as much 'designed to entertain as to edify'. 'He employs', says Zebiri (1997), 'ridicule and sarcasm' as well as 'crude languages and images which seem designed to shock' (47). Deedat acknowledged the influence of al-Kairanwi's *Izhar ul-Haqq* and 'draws on it extensively when impugning the biblical text'. The corruption of Christian scripture is a major theme for Deedat, which is consistent with the classical tradition. However, in pursuing his arguments he goes beyond the classical tradition by speaking about Jesus in terms that can best be described as disrespectful, presumably on the grounds that the Christian Jesus is a fiction not to be confused with the Qur'an's Jesus, whom Muslims respect. He also has a lot to say about the Crucifixion and the nature of Jesus, also dominant themes in Christian–Muslim encounter. The following analysis focuses on these themes.

Deedat was born in India, moving to join his father in South Africa when he was nine. Due mainly to financial necessity, he left school at the age of sixteen, starting to work in a furniture shop. This was near a Christian seminary. He soon encountered missionaries and seminarians who, visiting the store, hurled abuse at Islam. Sir Sayyid Ahmed Khan, explaining the causes of the 1857–8 revolt in India, had written about how 'missionaries' used 'violent and unmeasured language' as they attacked 'the followers and holy places of other creeds' (cited in Dar, 1957: 279). Sometimes, the missionaries were accompanied by colonial police. Nasr (1990b) comments how Christian missionary activity, 'usually combined with political and economic domination', played such a 'major role in determining Muslim attitudes towards Christians' that many Muslims identify Christian mission with colonialism and for that matter 'practically all the activities of Western powers with Christianity' (133). Deedat identified the missionaries' activities as allied with the South African Whites' desire to exercise control over the Black and Asian populations, since once converted to Christianity they would become subject to the authority of their superiors within the Church, who were all White. Ahmed decided to defend Islam against the criticism of the missionaries and started to research the Bible in order to refute it. It was at this point that he first read *Izzar-al-Haq*. He delivered his first public lecture in 1942 to a modest audience. However, his popularity grew rapidly. In 1957 he founded the Islamic Propagation Centre International, becoming its President. Supported by the bin Laden Group, the PPCI's headquarters in Durban is 'bin Laden House'. While this does not imply a direct link with Osama bin Laden, since the Group is run by other members of the bin Laden family, Deedat is reported to have supported Osama and to have shared his anti-Jewish views (according to Jihad Watch, 10 August 2004, 'Islamic Apologist Ahmed Deedat funded by Osama bin Laden'). Deedat wanted to revive Islamic *da'wa* (mission), which he believed was neglected and necessary to counter Christian mission.

Deedat on Jesus' Crucifixion

In *Crucifixion or Cruci-fiction*? Deedat speaks of how offensive he found missionaries who insisted, in their preaching, that despite any 'good works' a Muslim may perform, or despite the quality of the life they live, they are doomed to damnation unless they 'accept the redeeming blood of Jesus, and take Jesus . . . as personal saviour'. Referring to the thousands of different Christian denominations all vying to 'redeem the heathen', he remarks that the Christians cannot hold a 'candle to Muslims' in 'brotherhood, in piety or in sobriety', nor could they teach them anything in terms of hygiene, ethics, morality or hospitality. Christians, he wrote, had been pushing Jesus' crucifixion 'down his throat' as the 'only redeeming factor for mankind' since his teens. All they offered, he said, was the blood of Christ; 'according to St. Paul, there is nothing that Christianity can offer mankind, other than the blood and gore of Jesus.' Paul, he says, as 'every knowledgeable Christian concedes', was 'the real founder of Christianity' and not 'Jesus Christ (Peace be on Him)'. Muslim attribution to Paul of corrupting an originally pure and monotheistic Christianity was noted in Chapter 2. Deedat then argued that Christianity stands and falls on the Crucifixion, without which there would be no blood through which salvation could be obtained, 'Because', said the missionaries, 'salvation comes "only through the blood of Jesus"'. In a nut shell, said Deedat, 'No Crucifixion – No Christianity'. For Deedat, it is axiomatic that the Crucifixion did not occur because the Qur'an says that it did not happen. Citing Q5:171, with English and Arabic script in parallel, he concludes that those who claim that Jesus was crucified lack knowledge of what took place and followed instead their own conjecture. The gospel's account of the crucifixion is 'guess work', 'fiction'. This also makes the resurrection a hoax and a lie. The gospel writers, he said, 'invent shocking statements', and foist 'flagrant, deliberate fabrications' onto Christians. The gospels, he says, would not be accepted as evidence by any court of law, since they cannot be traced back to their original authors. Christians have unjustly persecuted Jews for 2,000 years for killing Jesus but 'for a surety they killed him not'.

Referring to the notion that all people are born into sin and so require the death of a sinless victim to redeem them, as compared with the Muslim belief that 'every child is born sinless and innocent', Deedat attributed the Christian view to 'Mithraic legends' which they borrowed. He represents the gospel, which Taymiyyah had represented as *hadith* rather than as scripture, as faked substitutes for the original *injil*; Taymiyyah had it that even if as *hadith* the gospels were still unreliable, their compilers may have believed what they wrote and so did not intentionally deceive (236). For Deedat, the gospel writers deliberately deceived. While he used 'peace be on him' as a sign of respect for Jesus, he develops an alternative narrative that depicts Jesus as a prankster, a failed revolutionary whose disciple, Peter, did not carry a sword to 'pare apples and bananas' but to 'maim and to kill'. Among other Christian writers, he finds support for some of his views in Schirrmacher (Chapter 14, 'Crucifixion'), such as that Jesus ate because he had not died, and therefore had a physical not a spiritual body, in Luke 24:41–43, else this would have been some sort of pretence. According to Deedat, Jesus entered Jerusalem on Palm Sunday with every intention of leading an armed revolt against Rome. He accepts the Christian understanding that Jesus fulfilled prophecy by riding a donkey, citing Zechariah 9:9. However, the popular uprising which Jesus expected 'fizzled out like a damp squib, despite all the "Hosannas" and hoorays to the "Son of David"'. 'All this ballyhoo', says Deedat, was 40 years premature. Jesus therefore, who had nonetheless 'proved himself a skillful strategist and planner', tried to rethink the situation, which is why, after the meal in the upper-room, he withdrew to the Garden of Gethsemane, where he deployed his disciples in inner and outer defensive positions, eight at the entrance to the courtyard, three to 'wait and watch' on the inside. Deedat stresses that these disciples were armed. Jesus, he says, was not the 'prince of peace . . . who couldn't hurt a fly' of Christian piety but a would-be revolutionary, who told his 'soldiers' to slay his enemies (Luke 19:27) and who brought a 'sword' and 'fire', not peace (Matthew 10:34; Luke 12:49–

51). According to Deedat, Jesus expected to be arrested as a rebel but thought that the arrest would be a 'clandestine' operation and that, by defending the Garden, he could easily resist. What he had not foreseen was the betrayal by Judas, the sleepiness of his disciples and the number of soldiers involved in his arrest, the 'band of men' referred to at Mark 14:43, which overwhelmed him. This was why he counselled Peter to put away his sword, since it would have been 'suicidal for his sleepy warriors to offer even a pretense of resistance'. The crucifixion was neither planned nor expected but an accident. However, says Deedat, Jesus did not die on the Cross but survived the ordeal. Deedat says that Jesus would not have been nailed but tied with leather straps to the Cross and that he was not stretched on the Cross long enough to die. There was no resurrection, simply a recovery. Deedat draws on some of the explanations of Jesus' resurrection offered by nineteenth-century writers and discussed by Albert Schweitzer, whose *Quest of the Historical Jesus* he cites.[3] Jesus was taken down from the cross before he had died by secret disciples, including the Roman Centurion who had cried, 'Surely he is the Son of God,' and taken to a place of safety. Mary did not go to the tomb to anoint a dead body but to massage a living one; *masaha*, says Deedat, can also mean to rub or to massage. That is why, when she went back after two days, she was surprised when she could not see Jesus in the tomb. Jesus was already up and walking and played a prank on her by surprising her from behind, asking 'Why are you weeping?' She mistook Jesus for a gardener because, fearing the Jews, he was disguised as one. Jesus told her not to touch him because although he appeared 'normal to all intents and purposes, he had, nevertheless, been through a violent, physical and emotional ordeal. It would be excruciatingly painful if he allowed her any enthusiastic contact.' Deedat does not believe in the Ascension, either. Jesus died a natural death. Here, he parts company from the majority of Muslims, who understand Q3:55 to refer to Jesus being taken up into heaven.

Deedat on Tahrif

In extensive writing on the Bible, Deedat accepts the view that it is corrupt, contradictory and full of errors. In his public debates, he cites from different translations to prove the Bible's unreliability. In contrast, he depicts the Qur'an as wholly reliable. Like al-Kairanwi, he refers to Christian sources to confirm the human, not divine, origin of the Bible. In *Is the Bible Still God's Word?*, he cites from Kenneth Cragg's *The Call of the Minaret* where he says that the Gospels came through 'the mind of the Church behind the authors' and so 'represent experience and history' (citing p. 277[4]). He cites passages which he considers to be pornographic, depicts the Bible as preoccupied with illicit sex, and suggests that it should be banned, citing Bernard Shaw's view that it is the most dangerous book in the world and should be kept under lock and key. Passages cited include Genesis 35:22, 38:15–20, 2 Samuel 13:5–14, 16:21–23 and Ezekiel 16:23–24, ridiculing the claim that such passages are profitable for 'reproof, correction or instruction unto righteousness' (2 Timothy 3:16). These 'juicy snippets', he says, are 'sexually stimulating but . . . spiritually . . . damning'. He is closer here, perhaps, to Ibn Hazm on the Bible as an 'accursed book' than he is to Ibn Taymiyyah, for whom, although corrupt, the Bible was not totally corrupt, so passages could still be cited as predictions of Muhammad. On the other hand, while emphatic that the Bible is a catalogue of errors, Deedat also cites the Bible both to prove that it does not support Christian belief in Jesus as God's son and in the Trinity, and as predicting Muhammad. I am tempted to ask that, if best kept under lock and key, how can the Bible be used to convince Christians that, as it points to Muhammad, they ought to embrace Islam?

Among many contradictions and errors in the Bible, Deedat pointed to 2 Samuel 24:1 which says that God told David to 'number' Israel, while 1 Chronicles 21:1 says that Satan did; 2 Chronicles 36:9 which says that Jehoichin was 8 'when he began to reign', while 2 Kings 24:8 says he was 17; and 2 Samuel 10:18 which says that David slew 700 Syrians, while I Chronicles 19:18 has 7,000. The Muslim site has material of a similar genre and, of course, al-Kairanwi had made much of discrepancy in biblical numbering. In an article rebutting Shamoun, the Muslim site maintains that both God in the Old Testament and Paul in the New permit lying, citing as examples Samuel lying to Saul's men and Paul at Romans 3:1–8 and Philippians 1:15–18. Elsewhere, the site claims that the Christian scriptures were complied 300 years after Jesus' time. By then, Christians had 'gossiped so much and lied and fabricated so much that they made an entire bible/religion out of it all'. It is interesting that Deedat consistently accused the writers of the Christian and Jewish scriptures of lying and of fabrication but cites from both liberally in constructing his own arguments. His version of the 'crucifixion' is almost wholly based, for example, on his own interpretation of the gospels. Turning to the issue of predictions of Muhammad in the Bible, Deedat again identifies no few, all of which, presumably, are valid and reliable even if contained in a book which should be banned. However, this is one area were polemics has developed since the days of John of Damascus and al-Kindy, both of whom claimed that Muhammad had not been predicted and so lacked an essential qualification of a true Prophet. Contemporary Muslims cite numerous biblical passages. The Muslim site has a whole section dedicated to this topic.

Predictions of Muhammad in the Bible

In his tract, *What the Bible Says About Muhammad*, Deedat begins by pointing out that since Christians find just about everything that happens to have been predicted in the Bible, it surely cannot be silent on Muhammad, 'the greatest benefactor of mankind'. Indeed, says Deedat, the Bible predicted Muhammad in such passages at Deuteronomy 18:18, which applies to Muhammad much more convincingly than to Jesus. Moses did not 'die for the sins of the world', as Christian claim Jesus did, or go to hell for three days. Muhammad, not Jesus, is the prophet 'like unto Moses'. Muhammad, like Moses, married and had children. Muhammad, like Moses, gave new laws to his people, while Jesus claimed to introduce nothing new, citing Matthew 5:17–18. Deedat also points out that while Jesus' birth was miraculous, Moses' and Muhammad's were natural. Jesus was 'rejected by his people' while Moses and Muhammad were 'accepted as prophets by their people'. Turning to the New Testament, Deedat argues that John the Baptist predicted Muhammad, because he was asked whether he was the Messiah, Elias or 'that prophet'. The 'that prophet' referred to the prophet predicted at Deuteronomy 18:18. Thus, Muhammad is 'that prophet' and Jesus the expected Messiah. He does not comment on whether Elias has returned as expected.

Jesus and the Trinity

When Deedat turns to discuss *Christ in Islam*, he follows traditional Muslim opinion in stating that the Qur'an vindicates Jesus of all the charges made against him, such as that he claimed to be God's son and demanded worship. Rather, these are lies and false doctrines manufactured by Christians about him. Christians exaggerate Jesus' significance, citing Q4:171. Jesus was a word and a spirit and a sign from God but he was neither God, nor God's son nor the Second Person of the Trinity. The Trinity is a blasphemy that the Qur'an totally repudiates. 'I and the Father are one' (John 10:30) does not mean that Jesus is God but that Jesus' will was identical with God's purposes. Jesus prophesied the coming of Ahmed (the Paraclete, citing Q61:6). Jesus' miraculous birth does not make him God's son. Rather, this means that, like Adam, Jesus had no physical father (or mother too, in Adam's case). He cites Q3:59. Jesus' real message was 'believe in God and His Commandments', just like Muhammad's. Jesus did perform miracles but he did so by a power that was not his own, as Ibn al-Arabi had argued. Jesus' miracles are no proof of divinity, since even 'false prophets can perform miracles'. When speaking of the Qur'anic Jesus, Deedat is respectful. In contrast, when speaking of the Christians' Jesus, he used phrases such as 'Jesus had doubly miscalculated', 'the prank that Jesus was playing' went 'too far' and Jesus had been 'most reluctant to die'. Far from remaining silent like a lamb being led to the slaughter, Jesus presented a 'masterful defense' before his accusers. Christians are deluded when they apply Isia 53:7 to Jesus, claiming that he did not open his mouth. The only miracle that Jesus predicted of himself was that of Jonah (Matt 12:40), that people would think him dead when he was still alive. Neither the crucifixion nor the resurrection nor ascension was predicted of Jesus or by Jesus. When describing his many encounters with Christian clergy and scholars, Deedat relishes his own self-proclaimed victory, depicting them as rather stupid, despite their doctorate degrees, in their inability to answer his questions.

Contemporary Christian Confrontation

The contemporary Christian confrontationists discussed here, like their Muslim counterparts, stand in continuity with the classical tradition, although there are some new emphases. Many of the anti-Islam arguments that their predecessors employed feature prominently in their writing. Unlike the *Risalah* and the *Mizan*, however, the Caners' book, like John of Damascus' writing, is not intended for Muslims but for Christians as a manual on how they should deal with Muslims. His aim is not to commend Christianity but to undermine and attack Islam. One telling sentence arguably sets the Caners apart from some earlier confrontationists, although not from all. They write: 'Christians and Muslims do not worship the same God, unless Muslims wish to agree that Jesus is God and Lord' (206). This removes any possibility of identifying common ground, or of Muhammad having received any legitimate inspiration or revelation from God. John of Damascus, for his part, had recognized some common ground between Islam and Christianity: both religions were monotheistic and opposed idolatry. The Caners make their exclusivist view explicit when they state that: 'Only through the blood of Jesus, spilt on the cross, can someone be saved' (19), which sounds like the type of preaching against which Deedat reacted. Their father, who did not embrace Christianity, as far as they know, 'entered a Christless eternity' when he died (20).

Spencer's book is less explicitly Christian than the Caners. While the Caners' book is a manual for missionaries and other Christian workers somewhat in the style of St Clair-Tisdall's *A Manual of the Leading Muhammadan Objections to Christianity* (1904), Spencer's goal is to influence policymakers to take the 'threat' of Islam more seriously. However, he strongly suggests that the God of Islam and of Christians is different when he writes that although the Qur'an 'claims that the deity of Jews and Christians is the same as that of the Muslims (29:46)', since 'traditional Islam rejects such Christian doctrines as the Trinity, the divinity of Christ, and others, and castigates Judaism along with Christianity as a renegade perversion of Islam, it seems prudent to me . . . to continue to use the Arabic world "Allah" to refer to the Islamic deity in English' (17). Muhammad, says Spencer, 'had only a dim grasp of the Christian doctrine of the Trinity', citing Q4:157 (114). Thus, Spencer distinguishes the Christian from the Muslim God.

Both the Caners and Spencer suggest that writing their books was potentially a risky enterprise. Spencer refers to reaction to the cartoons published in Denmark in early 2006, to the murder of Dutch filmmaker Theo van Gogh in September 2004 following his depiction of the treatment of Muslim women in *Submission* and to the attempted murder of Nobel Literature Prize laureate Naguib Mafouz in 1994 as examples of what can happen when anyone is perceived to have criticized Islam. The Caners write about the persecution they experienced as converts from Islam and the experience of others who, 'for the sake of the Gospel . . . are being bullwhipped into submission, tortured, imprisoned, beaten, battered, and broken' (15).

Major Themes: Continuity and Discontinuity

Both books revisit many classical issues. These include Muhammad's moral character and use of violence, a theme which pervades both texts, and the composite and borrowed origins of the Qur'an as Muhammad's creation, while specific incidents in Muhammad's life are highlighted as proof that it is one matter to 'discuss Muhammad's life' and another to 'emulate him' (Caner and Caner, 2002: 64). Spencer (2006), whose main interest is how Muhammad's example has encouraged – in his view – violence, states: 'the words and deeds of Muhammad have been moving Muslims to commit acts of violence for fourteen hundred years' (194). Neither the Caners nor Spencer are interested in presenting or in defending Christian concepts but in demolishing Islam. Thus, the Trinity and Jesus' divinity do not feature prominently, although they are referred to as points of departure between the two faiths. The Caners assert that although 'Trinity is a difficult mystery to explain' it is 'fully taught in the Bible and can be defended by anyone with a functional understanding of what the Bible teaches'. They also assert that while it is 'not within the scope of this book to defend the fact of Jesus' life, death and resurrection', the 'eyewitness testimony in the four gospels is much more credible than the legends about Jesus that Muhammad and other Muslims assembled centuries later' (2002: 210). They do not deal with Muslim rejection of the gospel accounts as 'eye witness' or of the Bible in general as corrupt and unreliable. Where the two texts differ from earlier Christian examples of polemic is partly context and partly emphasis. Both texts are set firmly in a post 9/11 context. Post 9/11 has seen a flurry of books about Islam. Many of these have been written by authors with no particular track record of scholarship of Islam, such as Hal Lindsey. The Caners refer to 9/11 on page 15. Land's Foreword does this on page 11, the first page of text. The 'Introduction' begins with a description of a broadcast by bin Laden claiming credit for 9/11 with 'effervescent glee' (23). Spencer's (2006) whole agenda is to expose the mantra 'Islam is peace' that in his view 'controls American policy' as a fallacy (1). 9/11 provides his immediate context, since subsequent to the acts of terror committed on that day, 'Muhammad became more controversial than ever before in the Western world' and 'many of the questions on which his example was invoked and discussed are still relevant to the War on Terror' (169). Incidentally, the Muslim site denies that Muslims were in any way connected with 9/11, which it describes as an 'inside job'.[5] The emphasis on Muhammad's use of violence in both texts is traditional, as are many of the incidents discussed as examples of Muhammad's moral culpability, such as his multiple marriages and extermination of enemies. Both texts refer to the slaying of 'the poets' (Caner and Caner, 2002: 50; Spencer, 2006: 162–3), since Muhammad brooked no criticism or any 'opposition to his rule' (Spencer, 2006: 162).

The Caners' chapter on Muhammad is called 'Muhammad: The Militant Messenger'. Chapter headings in Spencer include 'War is Deceit' (7), 'Casting Terror into their Hearts' (8) and 'Victorious Through Terror' (9) as he constructs his case that Islam was from the very beginning propagated by threat, violence and terror, and thus 'warfare and booty were among the chief preoccupations of the Prophet of Islam', which is reminiscent of al-Kindy's verdict that Muhammad's 'chief object and desire' was waging war and marrying beautiful women (53, 90, 100, 107, 120). The Caners also have it that on the one hand Muhammad was 'less cruel than many other warriors in the Arabia Peninsula' and was 'an incredible tactician'. On the other hand, he 'allowed his leaders to use barbarous tactic to subdue the enemy' and 'seldom gained conversions except through coercion' (54), echoing al-Kindy's conviction that Islam was spread by the sword. Both books reject the legitimacy of Muhammad's prophetic call, which follows from their assertion that Allah is different from the Christian God. Obviously, if different from God, Allah can not exist, at least for monotheists. The Caners' sub-heading for their discussion of Muhammad's call is 'The First Revelation: Divine or Demonic?' (41). Citing the 'Satanic Verses' incident, they claim that Muhammad 'oscillated between revelations from Satan and Allah' (44). The 'tortured prophet repeatedly believed himself to be demon possessed', and on several occasions 'changed Allah's wisdom for his own'. Describing Muhammad as the 'human author' of the Qur'an, they state that it 'cannot be trusted, since its human author was careless and inconsiderate with the revelation' (45). One of the most 'troubling admonitions in the Qur'an', which, they say, teaches 'a woman's genetic inferiority' (133), is that it 'allows marital punishment' (138, citing Q4:34). In Islam, they say, 'the wife is considered the husband's sex object' (137, citing Q2:223). In their chapter on the Qur'an (4) they highlight 'conflict with the Bible', including the reference at 5:116 to a Trinity of father, mother and son and denial of Jesus' crucifixion. Spencer has much more detail on the composition of the Qur'an, which he attributes to borrowings from Judaism, Christianity and Zoroastrianism. Muhammad was even told to consult with Jews and Christians (Q10:94; Spencer, 2006: 51) while the 'suspicion that Waraqah taught Muhammad significant portions of what' he represented 'as divine revelation . . . has haunted Islam' (53). In company with Muir and earlier writers, Spencer has it that Muhammad fabricated revelation to further his agenda and personal goals, thus 'on more than a few occasions the circumstances of these revelations seemed to manifest Allah's anxiety to grant his prophet his heart's desires, as in the notorious story of . . . Zaynab bint Jahsh', the example used by al-Kindy (50) and even earlier by John of Damascus, who described 'the Woman' as 'the type of precept' that Muhammad had given in his 'discourse' (139). The Caners follow earlier polemicists in highlighting alleged contradictions in the Qur'an (91–93), which could be seen as a tit-for-tat response to Deedat on the Bible. The Caners refer to Muhammad's marriage with Zaynab and to the 'revelation' that he received to justify this but do not overly censure Muhammad on this occasion, choosing instead to concentrate on his marriage with Aisha at the age of six and his consummation of their marriage when she was nine. 'Many', they say, 'gloss over this act' but 'how a prophet of noble character could wed someone so young . . . remains a mystery' (59). Pfander had also referenced this as a moral defect. This new emphasis on the age at which Muhammad consummated his marriage with Aisha resulted in what Spencer calls 'an immense controversy' in the USA. In July 2002, Jerry Vines, former President of the Southern Baptist Convention, using the Caners' book as his source, said: 'Christianity was founded by the virgin-born Jesus Christ. Islam was founded by Mohammed, a demon-possessed pedophile who had twelve wives, and his last one was a nine-year old' (cited by Spencer, 2006: 170).

The Charge of Paedophilia

Picking up on the accusation of paedophilia, itself a development in Christian anti-Muslim polemic, Spencer admits that this particular charge is anachronistic but suggests that once Muhammad's action has been 'forcibly removed from its historical context and proposed as a paradigm for human beings of all times and places', Muslims 'even in modern times' have a licence to take 'child brides' (171). Spencer discusses paedophilia in his chapter on Muhammad's legacy (169). He characterizes this as one of misogyny, violence and intolerance of other religions. He also highlights 'draconian punishments'. On misogyny, he recounts the *hadith* that there are more women in hell than men, the differential in inheritance law between men and women (Q4:11), and the verse on the need for two female witnesses when one man's evidence will suffice (Q2:282), as well as men being allowed up to four wives while women are allowed only one husband (4:3). True, says Spencer, Muhammad could sometimes be kind and gentle, but there are so many examples of intolerance and violence in his biography that Muslims can justify acts such as 9/11 as emulating him today. These examples, too, he says, are not to be dismissed as the 'twisting or hijacking of Islam' since they are 'amply attested in early Islamic literature' (189). Similarly, the Caners write:

> Were the men who flew planes into the towers and into the Pentagon acting out the wild ranting of a cultic leader who had bastardized the peaceful religion of Islam? Or did they offer their lives because they believed orthodox Islamic doctrines? The authors of this book assert that Islam does in fact have an essential and indispensable tenet of militaristic conquest. The terrorists were not some fringe group that changed the Qur'an to suit political ends. They understood the Qur'an quite well and followed the teachings of *jihad* to the letter. (Caner and Caner, 2002: 184)

Muslims today, says Spencer, like to cite a verse such as Q2:62 to 'stress commonality between Islam and Christianity' but the 'preponderance of the testimony that' Muhammad 'left in the Qur'an and Hadith favors not tolerance and harmony . . . but just the opposite' (177). 'It is', he says, 'nothing short of staggering that the myth of Islamic tolerance could have gained such currency' (182). The issue of paedophilia has become a topic of what I call tit-for-tat exchange. Almost certainly as a rejoinder to Vines and others who accuse Muhammad of this crime, the Muslim site has a section dedicated to the subject. However, while the site does discuss the age at which Muhammad married Aisha, pointing out that this was not unusual at the time or unacceptable to Arab culture, it concentrates on citing Bible passages involving the killing of children, rape and other examples of what it calls 'x-rated pornography in the Bible'. This is almost certainly influenced by Deedat's opinion that the Bible, as pornographic literature, should be banned. The site counter-attacks by asking why paedophilia is so rampant among the Christian churches, picking up on charges against Catholic priests in particular. Answering this question 'requires no fifty page article', since the Bible itself is responsible for their sexual deviancy. The Bible, the article continues, does not directly command 'its followers to become pedophiles, rapists and homosexuals' but is so corrupt that Christians deem nothing sacred.

Jihad as Interpreted by the Caners and Spencer

Islam as a religion of violence featured quite prominently in classical Christian polemic but these contemporary writers have, arguably, more to say on this issue than on any other, perhaps even more than on Muhammad's sexuality. Three chapters in the Caners book discuss violence, namely 12, 13 and 14, entitled 'The Illusion of Religious Liberty: Terrorism from Within', 'The Bloodshed of Jihad' and 'Clash of Cultures', respectively. They cite in full the *fatwa* by bin Laden and his associates issued 23 February 1998 declaring war on the USA (181–4), then continue that the Qur'an 'supposedly from the very mouth of Allah takes a dim view of the nonbeliever' (Caner and Caner, 2002: 185), citing Q2:191, 2:193, 3: 85 and 8:13–17 as evidence that Islam does not allow the 'toleration' of unbelief. On pages 188–9 they cite several of the verses of opprobrium, such as 4:171, 5:14, 5:17 and 5:51. They do not include any of the verses of friendship. Next, they discuss rewards for *jihadic* behaviour, citing Q4:74, 'Let those who fight in the cause of Allah who sell the life of this world for the Hereafter . . . to him who fights in the cause of Allah – whether he is slain or gets victory – soon shall We give him a reward of great value' (190). Continuing to discuss *jihad*, they reject the view that it can be understood as an internal, spiritual struggle rather than as a 'physical struggle' (194), arguing that just as Muhammad found 'spiritual victory in physical success', so 'modern Muslims . . . do so whenever called upon'. In their earlier discussion of *jihad* in the context of Muhammad's career, they wrote:

Muhammad himself gave the example for *jihad* (fighting: holy war). There was no governmental call for warfare, only individual desire that led to the greatest rewards in heaven. Ethical values seemed to play little or no role. Whatever the Muslims did was justified, since the cause was just. Muslims believed that they received forgiveness for all their sins only by fighting in jihad. Is it any wonder, then, that holy war continues to be a prophetic call? (48).[6]

The Caners and Spencer argue that Islam is not a religion of peace and that acts of terror and of violence perpetrated by Muslims in the name of Islam are directly justified with reference to the example of Muhammad, whose life cannot be taken as a paradigm for all humanity, as Muslims argue. The greatest difference, the Caners claim, between Jesus and Muhammad is that Jesus 'shed his own blood on the cross so that people could come to God' while Muhammad 'shed other people's blood so that his constituents could have political power throughout the Arabian Peninsula'. Since Muhammad is 'held to be the "excellent exemplar for him who hopes in Allah and the Final Day" (surah 33: 21), we need', they continue, 'to look no further for explanation of violent acts within Islam than at the character of its founder' (49). Similarly, in summing up the policy implications of his expose of Muhammad's life, Spencer writes, 'stop insisting that Islam is a religion of peace', continuing 'this is false, and falsehoods are never productive' (182). Neither comment on the fact that even al-Kindy remained a Christian within the Arab world, as have quite large communities until today, which of itself questions the claim that Islam presents unbelievers with the choice of death or conversion.[7]

Islam and Political Correctness

The Caners and Spencer wrote in the context of a post 9/11 critique of what has been called political correctness in writing about Islam. Spencer is also the author of *The Politically Incorrect Guide to Islam* (2005). One reviewer describes Spencer's *The Truth About Muhammad* as trading 'platitudes for scholarship, delusions for reality' about the true nature of Islam. The book is a 'threat to "religion of peace" propaganda that lulls the West into submission' (Michelle Malkin). Daniel Pipes describes the book as countering the 'near-hegemonic hold' that the 'pious narrative of Muhammad has gained' even in the West. In constructing his biography of Muhammad, Spencer swipes several times at Karen Armstrong's book on Muhammad, which he describes as hagiography (6; see 70–1, 82–3, 170, 132). He also criticizes Carl Ernst for describing Muhammad as a 'charismatic person known for his integrity' (4). Throughout his book, Spencer criticizes the view that a 'tiny minority of extremists have supposedly hijacked their religion' and argues that such Muslims are good Muslims. The Caners intended audience is less those who make US policy than Christian evangelists but they too set out to redress what they see as the 'truth' about Islam, which others misrepresent. Either, they write, 'Islam is correct' or 'Christianity is correct', since they cannot 'both be correct' (16), an assumption that Pfander had shared. On the other hand, the Caners do not engage in polemic with authors or texts that they take to misrepresent Islam but rely on their own expertise as former Muslims to 'tell it like it is'. Spencer, as Director of Jihad Watch, has a more political agenda. Jihad Watch aims to influence policy makers to take the threat of militant Islam more seriously, including initiating a new Manhattan project to free the USA from dependence on Arab oil, making 'western aid contingent on' Muslims renouncing 'jihad ideology', revising immigration policies to include 'hard questions about the applicant's views on pluralistic societies, religious freedom, women's rights and other features of Western societies challenged by elements of Muhammad's teachings and Islamic law' (Spencer: 192–4). Another admirer of his book, Bat Ye'or, whose own work denounces Islam for systematically destroying Christian and Jewish communities, praises Spencer's 'extensive scholarship and clear style, together with his forceful argumentation', all of which makes the book 'essential reading to understand the crucial issues of the twenty-fist century'. Spencer also runs Dhimmi Watch, a site dedicated to bringing 'public attention to the plight of the *dhimmis*, and by doing so, to bring them justice'. It posits that humiliating restrictions and human rights violations are enshrined in Islamic law. The Caners take it as axiomatic that Christians are 'taught to live at peace by the living and written Word of God' while 'Muslims are taught by the Qur'an and Allah's messenger to "fight and slay the Pagans wherever you find them" (surah 9: 5)' (174).

Pipes,[8] who runs Campus Watch and the Middle East Forum, has been outspokenly critical of what he calls 'political correctness' when writing or speaking of Islam. In his *Militant Islam Comes to America* (2002) he argues that critical scholarship of Islam has been 'shut down' (xvii). He especially singles out John L. Esposito for criticism, describing the *Oxford Encyclopedia of the Modern Muslim World* as a 'monument of apologetics' (xvi, 104–8) and as the supreme example of 'political correctness'. Esposito, whom he describes as a 'liberal democrat' (89), misled policymakers when his 1992 book *The Islamic Threat: Myth or Reality* dismissed the threat-thesis, and President Clinton in misadvising him (45–6). Campus Watch describes Esposito as the foremost apologist for Islamism.[9] The fact that his Center for Muslim–Christian Understanding at Georgetown has been funded by the Saudi royal family has not escaped criticism.[10] Pipes argues that militant Islam may not be Islam per se but it nonetheless represents a threat to the American way of life, since Muslims who live in America are committed to making America Muslim, some by any means. He cites Ismail al-Faruqi, whom Esposito described as 'a pioneer in the development of Islamic studies in North America', as saying that 'Nothing could be greater than this youthful, vigorous, and rich continent [of North America] turning away from its past evil, and marching forward under the banner of Allahu Akbar' (113). Faruqi participated in Christian–Muslim and Muslim–Jewish dialogue. Militant Islam is a danger to the USA because it stands opposed to the values and freedoms on which the USA was built. However, both Pipes and Spencer argue that moderate Muslims can promote a type of Islam that teaches 'against Muhammad's warlike example' (Spencer, 2005: 193), and hating the 'prospect of living under the reign of militant Islam . . . can envisage something better' (Pipes, 2002: 256). Militant Islam, says Pipes, is extricable from Islam, since it does not represent Islam's 'eternal essence' (251). Nor does Pipes represent the War on Terror in terms of a clash of civilizations, pointing out that Islamists are just as violent towards 'Muslims who do not share' their outlook at they are towards Americans and Israelis (249). 'Militant Islam', he says, 'is an aggressive totalitarian regime that ultimately discriminates barely if at all among those who stand in its path' (249).

Assessment

Both the Caners and Spencer say that they are not writing diatribes against Islam. Similarly, in revising Pfander's *Mizan*, Tisdall claimed that he had tried to maintain a 'conciliatory tone' and to avoid 'needless offence' (in Pfander, 1910: 4). However, just as comments by Pfander that traditions on such matters as Muhammad's relations with his wives are 'not pleasant reading' but serve to cast light on 'Muhammad's moral character' (332) and his claim that the Qur'an encourages unlimited lust (297) are hardly likely to attract Muslim approval, so the Caners' and Spencer's depictions of Muhammad are very unlikely to appeal to Muslim readers. The Muslim site 'Unveiling Islam' includes a response to the Caners' book. The author describes the book as representative of a mindset that, 'taking advantage of the prevailing negativism towards Islam' portrays the religion as 'a violent and evil religion and the holy Prophet Muhammad as a false prophet'. The author repudiates that the perpetrators of 9/11 were acting as good Muslims, citing Q4:29, which prohibits suicide.[11] The reviewer takes specific issue with the Caners' assertions about apostasy and *jihad*. On apostasy, they claim that Islam demands the killing of apostates (19), while their depiction of *jihad* was described above. The author cites Q2:256, 10:99 and 18:29 to illustrate that belief or disbelief is a matter of free choice, and *hadith* to illustrate that apostasy was not punishable by death except when 'combined by other circumstances' and criticizes the Caners for citing only one *hadith* on this matter. Citing numerous Qur'anic passages and *hadith*, the author states that *jihad* is not synonymous with war but is primarily understood as a spiritual struggle for self-purification (Q29:6) and to attain nearness with God (Q26:69). It can also involve arguing in order to persuade unbelievers of the truth of Islam (29:8). Other Muslims point out that the word 'jihad' is not used in any of the 'sword verses' that permit war, in certain circumstances (famously, 9:5 and 9:29).[12] Reaction to Spencer, mentioned above, includes the accusation that he is a 'Zionist crusader missionary of hate'. In an exchange with Jamal Badawi, Spencer responded to Badawi's offer of a million dollars to anyone who could prove that the Qur'an mentions 'holy war' by citing Q9:5 and 9:29 and challenging Badawi to make him a rich man – he would soon be flying off in the Jihad Watch's Learjet.[13] Badawi replied that none of these passages employ an Arabic word that can be translated as 'holy war' and that no such phrase or word exists. Spencer acknowledged that this as this is technically true he was not, in fact, a rich man after all.[14] In this lengthy response, Spencer discusses other Qur'anic verses that only permit fighting against aggression or oppression, such as 22:39–40. However, referring to Sayyid Qutb and bin Laden as well as Ibn Kathir, among others, he argues that many Muslims support the view that the Qur'an not only permits but demands aggressive expansion.

Confrontationists on both sides generally refuse to listen to alternative explanations, even though both are happy to cite what they perceive to be sources sympathetic to their view by the 'other side'. Spencer cites Qutb but not the very influential Yusuf al-Qaradawi, who has condemned terrorist attacks, as have the Grand Sheikh of Al-Azhar and the Imam of the Grand Mosque in Mecca. Generally, the polemicists' Islam is monolithic, and Muslims have a single opinion.[15] In referring to the *Oxford Encyclopedia*, Pipes (2002) rants against the entry on women in Islam for its feminist bias, dismissing this out of hand (105), thus it is perhaps not surprising that in describing Muhammad's misogyny, Spencer pays no attention whatsoever to Muslims who deal differently with the material under review. Many Muslims dismiss the genuineness of the misogynist *hadith*, and argue that the spirit of the Qur'an embraces gender equality. When Pipes (2002) complains that what matters is not 'how things should be, but how they are' (106) he ignores the possibility that 'how things are' has nothing to do with a correct interpretation of the Qur'an but with male chauvinism. Both classical and contemporary Christian polemicists refer to such incidents in Muhammad's career as the killing of the poets without stopping to consider why, in the context of what was in fact a war, such action may have been taken. Lings (1983) points out that at least one such poet was not merely a poet but a leading member of a tribe that opposed Muhammad, who was mustering up support for his enemies (160). Criticism of Muhammad's multiple marriages or of Aisha's age when their marriage was consummated does not evoke among Muslims the expected response. Muslims do not regard these episodes as evidence of Muhammad's moral culpability. Rather, aware as they are of these incidents, they continue to venerate Muhammad as the best example for human life. Christians have been hurling these incidents at Muslims for centuries but there is little if any evidence that Muslim opinion on Muhammad is likely to change. Muslims point out that since Muhammad married he is a better example to follow for those of us who live life as married men and women than is Jesus, who did not marry. Many Muslims do not interpret the Qur'an as permitting multi-marriage in any circumstances but as limiting this to specific and rare situations. Sayyid Ahmed Khan supported this view. Of course, other Muslims do argue in favour of polygamy. Muhammad is certainly given special licence but Muslims emphasize the political and social reasons for his marriages. Many argue that marriage, even polygamous marriage, is better than adultery.

Classical and contemporary Christian polemicists emphasize that Islam is a religion of violence, spread mainly if not exclusively by the sword, that it is intolerant of minorities and of dissent, and suppresses women and freedom of speech. Muhammad is held to be morally culpable, making nonsense of the claim that his example should be emulated by all humanity. Satanic inspiration is at least hinted at by quite a few writers, including the Caners. All represent the Qur'an as the work of Muhammad, who is often charged with fabricating 'revelations of convenience' (Spencer, 2006: 58). Attribution of much of Islam to borrowing from Christianity and Judaism is also a common theme. The Qur'an is represented as a human work, containing what the Caners describe as 'odd teachings' and 'contradictory statements' (90–1), while the Bible is represented as wholly reliable. Muslim polemicists, such as Deedat, attack the Bible and reject it as containing anything worthwhile. Christian polemicists attack the Qur'an yet both sides liberally cite the other's scripture to support their arguments, implying that they must be of some validity. The contention that Christians and Muslims worship a different God leaves no scope for any accommodation between the two religions. Perhaps the only developments that can be identified in this chapter are less courtesy on both sides, the specific charge of paedophilia, the Bible as pornographic and, in the post 9/11 context, the almost complete identification of militant Islam with Islam *per se*, since even if this is denied by occasional reference to 'moderate Muslims', it is more than implied by the assertion that Muslims who carry out suicide attacks do so on the authority of Muhammad (see Spencer, 2006: 186–91; Caner and Caner, 2002: 184). It is debatable whether the contemporary confrontationists match classical confrontationists in terms of the quality of their scholarship. While the Caners and Spencer have a better grasp of the Qur'an than John of Damascus and the Martyrs of Cordoba did, they probably fail to surpass either al-Kindy or Pfander. The Caners claim insider knowledge but present Islam as a purely mechanical system, lacking any genuine inner dimension. They describe the Islamic view of salvation as 'mathematical righteousness', a matter of accumulating enough good deeds rather than a complete surrender to the goodness and mercy of God. They cite a tradition that God will deliver some of the damned from hell not 'because of their own merit but to demonstrate his compassion' but report this critically, failing to recognize any beauty here, as Ahmed Khan complained of Muir (Caner and Caner, 2002: 150, citing Geisler and Saleeb, 1993: 126). 'Prayer', they write, 'is not a personal conversation between a human and God' but 'an external practice saturated with formal procedures and required customs' (124). Yet for millions of Muslims, prayer is an intimate time spent close to God, and represents a profound inner experience of spiritual renewal. In describing the five pillars of Islam, they do not refer to the importance of right intent, the absence of which negates the value of any obligatory act, or to the concept of *taqwa*, God-consciousness, which permeates Muslim devotional life. Failure to consider how Muslims view incidents they choose to censure permeates classical and contemporary polemic. Conciliators may pay Sufi Islam too much attention; the Caners only refer to this spiritual tendency in passing (36, 165, 208, 251).

Chapter 8

Contemporary Christian and Muslim Conciliation

The Contributors

This chapter discusses four Christians and four Muslims. Three of each faith are classified as conciliatory, one as a cross-category example. The Christian conciliators are: Jomier, a Catholic; Khodr, a Greek Orthodox; and Cragg, a Protestant. This choice deliberately spreads across the main ecclesiastical communities. Khodr, Metropolitan Bishop of Mount Lebanon, is one of many examples of a conciliator who lives within the Muslim world, not in Europe or North America. Jomier and Cragg spent a great deal of their lives in the Arab world, in which both have been missionaries. Cragg cannot easily be dismissed as a liberal. The cross-category Christian contributor is Phil Parshall, who represents a more conservative approach yet cannot be classed as polemical. Parshall, who spent many years as a missionary in the Muslim world, is a disciple of McGavran. Of the Christian writers, Khodr and Jomier are the only ones whom I have not met, or heard speak. It is interesting, in passing, to note how quite a few bishops have contributed towards a conciliatory approach to Islam, starting with the Patriarch Mar Timothy I, through Paul of Antioch, Nicolas of Cusa, William of Tripoli to Bishops Khodr and Cragg. Bishops are the lead theologians for their communities, and when their communities live in intimate contact with Muslims, the question 'how should we understand our faith in relation to Islam?' naturally arises. The fact that bishops have taken a lead in developing a more conciliatory approach tends to suggest that it is not only marginal figures that pursue this, since bishops, even if liberal, are certainly not marginal.

My Muslim conciliators are Askari, a Shi'a, Muhamed Talbi, a Sunni and Amir Hussain, who describes himself as a Western Muslim. This selection, as does my choice of Christian exemplars, gives a geographical spread. It also covers the two main traditions. Khurshid Ahmad is my cross-category contributor. He does not engage in polemic and inclines towards conciliation, yet shares some of the assumptions of more confrontational writers. Ahmad has held political office in Pakistan, and is no marginal figure. Of the four Muslims, Ahmad is the only one whom I have not met, or heard speaking at some seminar or conference.

Zebiri (1997) comments that those 'Muslims who express the most positive appreciation of Christianity' have usually 'participated in interfaith dialogue' (162). This is true of many contributors. Contributors discussed in this chapter have participated in various Christian–Muslim consultations, some convened by the World Council of Churches and by the Vatican. Ahmad took part in the 1976 Tripoli dialogue, co-sponsored by the Vatican and the World Islamic Call Society, an agency of the Government of Libya. Some of the Muslims know some of the Christians. Cragg and Ahmad took part in a conference at the Centre for the Study of Islam and Christian–Muslim Relations in Selly Oak, Birmingham, UK in 1976. Ahmad was present at the 1976 WCC's Chambésy dialogue on 'Christian Mission and Muslim Dawa'.[1] Ahmad and Askari were together at Cartigny in October 1976 discussing the next steps in Christian–Muslim relations. Talbi and Askari were both at the multilateral dialogue in Colombo, in April 1974, discussing the possibility of a 'world community'. Talbi expresses appreciation for Jomier, among other Christian scholars of Islam (1990: 86). Hussain acknowledges a long list of Christian teachers, including three former moderators of the United Church of Canada, and describes himself as having 'strong ties with the United Church' of which his 'late wife, Shannon L. Hamm, who died in 1992, was a member' (2006: 13). Siddiqui (1997) is a useful resource because he tracks the development of formal dialogues, their agendas and deliberations. The WCC established its Sub-Unit on Dialogue in 1971.[2] Khodr was a participant in the WCC Central Committee meeting at Addis Ababa in 1971 when the decision to set the Sub-Unit was taken, and wrote one of the papers that subsequently 'became the basis of the "Interim Policy Statement and Guidelines"' on dialogue adopted at that meeting (Siddiqui, 1997: 47). The Vatican's Pontifical Council for Inter-religious Dialogue was established in 1964[3] and has two sub-committees on Christian–Muslim relations: the Catholic–Muslim Liaison Committee, whose Muslim members represent several Islamic organizations, including the World Muslim League[4] and the World Muslim Congress,[5] which meets annually, and a joint committee with Al-Azhar University, Cairo, established in 1998. The Catholic Church and the Muslim world share similar views on a number of moral issues, such as abortion, homosexuality and promiscuity, which has enabled co-operation between Catholics and Muslims at several international conferences, such as the United Nations Conference on Population and Development that met in Cairo in 1994 (see Fitzgerald, 2006). The issue of Christian mission and of Islamic *da'wah* has been a major theme in both WCC and Vatican-sponsored dialogue, and will feature in this chapter. Another major event in terms of Christian–Muslim relations was the signing of the Alexandria Declaration on 21 January 2002 by prominent Muslim and Christian leaders with Jewish counterparts in which they commit themselves to a peaceful and just solution to the Israeli–Palestinian issue.[6] Muslim, Christian and Jewish leaders also signed the Commitment to Global Peace at the historic World Summit of Religious and Spiritual Leaders convened by the United Nations and financed by Ted Turner of CNN in August 2000.[7]

Siddiqui usefully describes individual participation as well as institutional in Christian–Muslim dialogue, on both sides. He conducted interviews with Ahmad, Askari and corresponded with Talbi, and comments (1997) that Askari, Shi'a, pursues an approach that crosses 'denominational lines' and uses 'Sunni[8] theological materials extensively in their academic pursuits' (81). Issues that have dominated this survey of Christian–Muslim encounter again surface in this chapter, including the status of scriptures, Trinity, and the status of Jesus and of Muhammad. What interests us here is whether modern conciliators have moved forward on any of these issues, building on classical contributors. Have Christians found ways to appreciate Muhammad? Have the Muslims anything new or different to say about Jesus, or about the integrity of the Bible? Has any progress occurred on the Trinity or on the inter-related question, 'Who is God?'

The Contributions of Jacques Jomier, OP and Bishop Kenneth Cragg

Daniel (1997) compares Jomier's role in France with Cragg's in England, describing him as a 'meticulous scholar'. Cragg, he says, has 'taught Christians to learn their own religion from the Qur'an'. Cragg's 'writings are probably the most penetrating analyses of Islam in English', although he 'will never compromise what he has to say for the sake of easy reading'. Cragg's style has been described as 'Cragg-speak'. Cragg's encounter with Islam provokes such deep and profound thought that he wrests every ounce of meaning he can from his choice of vocabulary, which sometimes perplexes his readers. Jomier, says Daniel, 'is less severely uncompromising with his readership' (329). Jomier and Cragg pursue their sympathetic and conciliatory engagement with Islam without abandoning their concern for mission. Cragg first went to the Middle East in 1939 as a missionary of the British Syria Mission,[9] serving in Beirut where he also taught at the American University. Between 1970 and 1974 he was assistant Anglican Bishop of Jerusalem. Jomier went to Cairo with his Dominican order to help establish the Institute for Oriental Studies (founded in 1945) after gaining his doctorate.

Cragg aims to facilitate a Christian appreciation and understanding of Islam, not to enter into disputation, or to deal with controversial issues, although inevitably some feature in his writing. Many compare him with Gaidner, who was also based in Cairo, suggesting that he builds on Gairdner's earlier work, for which Cragg has expressed appreciation (see Tebbe, 2002).[10] Cragg is a prolific author and it is not possible to analyse his approach with reference to a single text, although *The Call of the Minaret*[11] (original edn 1956; third edn 2000), his first major monograph, is still an accessible introduction to some of his basic ideas. Jane Smith's essay on Cragg[12] summarizes his main ideas with references to about eight of his books, while Mahmut Aydin has substantial discussion in Chapters 4 and 5 of his online book of Cragg on the Qur'an and on Muhammad respectively. Jomier operates within the Post-Vatican II context and is guided by the words of *Nostra Aetate* that the Church regards Muslims with esteem, since they also worship the 'one God, Living and subsisting in Himself', and that ancient animosity and quarrels between Christian and Muslims should be forgotten so that Christians and Muslims can work sincerely for mutual understanding and to preserve and 'promote peace, liberty, social justice and moral virtue' (1989: 132).

He cites the full text of what Vatican II said about Muslims and refers to the 'new perspective of Catholic theology since 1950' (143). His text mentions Christian–Muslim meeting sat Al-Azhar (141), Cordoba (143) and Tripoli (141).[13]

Cragg's theological background was evangelical, so when he first went to the Middle East his aim was to convert Muslims. However, as he encountered Islam, he became convinced that God speaks through Islam as well as through Christianity. Consequently, Christians as well as Muslims have a duty to listen to God's message through Islam, since God's words address all humanity. His *Call* does not follow a standard format for introductory texts on Islam, with chapters on the Prophet, historical development, the five pillars, the Qur'an and Islamic Law, for example. Rather, it uses the cry of the muezzin to explore what it is that Muslims are being invited to do when they hear the call to prayer in terms of faith and practice. Taking the call to prayer as the 'epitome of Muslim belief and action', he sets out to 'seek in it the clue to Islam, and from that clue to learn the form and dimension of a Christian relationship to what it tells' (x). The call to prayer thus transcends religious boundaries and, as he also argues of the Qur'an, speaks to Christians as well as to Muslims. Cragg's own denomination has endorsed dialogue. In 1988, the Lambeth Bishops' Conference (Resolution 20) affirmed the four principles of dialogue developed by the British Council of Churches. Resolution 21 approved the document, *Jews, Christians and Muslims: The Way of Dialogue*, which contains more than a little evidence of Cragg's influence.

Jomier's *How to Understand Islam* is more conventional in format, and much shorter. Chapters include Islam's emergence, expansion, dogmas, law, piety and 'Christianity as Islam Sees It', Christian–Muslim relations and Muslim apologetic. Like Cragg, Jomier sets out to enable Christians to develop a positive appreciation of Islam, not to refute or to demolish it. Cragg may have started out thinking of Islam as a false system but in his encounter with Muslim piety discovered that he could not easily dismiss Muslims as seekers only. He encountered Muslims whose intimacy with God could not be denied. If God is speaking to Christians through Islam, he asks, how can apparent differences be reconciled, since it cannot be that God is 'the author of confusion' (Cragg, 1984: 11). Cragg's engagement with Islam is certainly intellectual and theological but at bottom it is also deeply spiritual. Most of all, he has engaged in the dialogue of religious experience. The identity of Allah with the Christian

God, for Cragg, is a fundamental assumption: 'The differences, undoubtedly real, between the Muslim and Christian understanding of God, are far reaching and must be patiently studied', he writes, 'but it would be fatal to our mutual tasks to doubt that one and the same God' is adored by all (2000: 30). Jomier does not simply subscribe intellectually to *Nostra Aetate's* affirmation that Allah and the Christian God are One but recognizes that Muslims enjoy a genuine relationship with God. Muslims' 'experience of God', he writes, 'lies within Islam' (142). Typically, Cragg's recognition of valid spiritual and devotional content and experience in Islam produces a statement such as:

> We wish to hear at the Minaret what it is that greets every rising sun and salutes every declining day for millions of our contemporaries and thus to enter with them across the threshold of the mosque into their world of meaning. For it is a world that deserves to be penetrated with understanding and for which, as we believe, there is endless significance in another world of faith, whose trustees we are and whose interpreters we would become. (2000: 28)

Jomier writes that the 'esteem in which Muslim society holds prayer has an influence on the opinion that Muslims have of other religions' so that 'not only do Muslims often accuse Christians of being impure (because they do not practice ablution), but, at present they are accused of not praying at all' (58). In contrast, the Caners dismiss Muslim prayer as purely mechanical. As he approaches the Mosque, the Qur'an, Muslim prayer, Cragg sees these as sacred ground, revered by millions. Wishing to respect the objects of Muslim reverence, he takes off his shoes as he approaches what Muslims deem to be holy, reflected in the title of his 1959 book. It is difficult to conceive of the Caners echoing these sentiments. Since Islam's God is not their God, for them, the muezin's call to prayer can evoke nothing meaningful in a Christian's heart. Both Cragg and Jomier consider the issue of a Christian appreciation of Muhammad to be of central concern. Cragg addressed this in *Muhammad and the Christian* (1984) and in Chapter 3 of *The Call*, Jomier in his chapter on 'The Problem of Muhammad'. The following sections examine these writers on Muhammad and the Qur'an, which they take to be too closely related to be considered separately, on the Trinity and the central question 'Who is God?', on the Bible and on the Crucifixion.

Cragg and Jomier on the Prophet and his Book

In approaching the Qur'an, Cragg's strategy is to suspend judgment, so that Christians can learn to appreciate how Muslims understand their own scripture. The Qur'an, says Cragg, 'can never be authentically known in neglect of the sensitivities, the emotions, the property in it, of Muslims' (1984: 11). In his extensive writing on and translation of the Qur'an, Cragg tries to listen to Muslim voices, to 'see the Qur'an, as it were, in its own mirror' (1971: 17–18). Critics point out, though, that he tends to ignore material that is 'not compatible with the content of the Bible' while also interpreting points of dispute in 'the light of Christian teaching' (Aydin, 1993: 4: 14).[14] This has been described as a tendency to Christianize Islam, ironic given that Cragg's aim, one shared by too few Christians, is to reflect Muslim self-understanding. Zebiri (1997) cites some Muslim criticism of Cragg (221; see also Kerr, 2002: 13). One critic accuses him of perpetuating a colonialist deconstruction of Islam in as much as he takes Islam to pieces, then reassembles it in a way he finds more compatible with Christianity. Colonial Orientalists such as Muir, of course, deconstructed then reassembled Islam in a way that underscored the superiority of Christianity and of Western civilization. On the other hand, other Muslims express appreciate for Cragg's scholarship, especially of the Qur'an, suggesting that non-Muslims can contribute to its exegesis, a right that Cragg claims on the basis of the Qur'an's own 'claim to universality' (Zebiri, 1997: 214). Esack, whose approach to the Qur'an is close to Cragg's, describes Cragg, whom he cites on the first page of his 2005 book, as a scholar 'whose work' he 'has found inspiring' (3, 7). Rahman (1984) described Cragg as 'a man who may not be a full citizen of the world of the Qur'an, but is certainly no foreigner either – let alone an invader!' (81). Esack says that Cragg and others set out to compensate for 'past scholarly injuries inflicted on Muslims' and to foster a 'greater appreciation of Islamic religiousness' (ibid.). Indeed, Cragg has a profound sense of the need to make amends and writes of restoring what Islam itself misses, which he describes as a 'call to retrieval' in as much as Islam needs to 'retrieve' what it fails to say about 'the Christ to whom Islam is a stranger' (2000: 220). This was a 'failure in love, in purity, and in fervor, a failure of the spirit' (219). Like Gairdner, Cragg believes that Muhammad did not encounter Orthodox Christianity. Christians therefore failed to bear authentic witness to him, with the result that the Qur'an emasculates

Jesus (235) and disqualifies what for Christians stands at the heart of their understanding of God (219). Jomier (1989) speculates that the Christians with whom Muhammad may have had contact were 'marginal to the mainstream Christianity at the time' (6). He does not dismiss the possibility that some popular stories found their way into the Qur'an, observing that while Muslims maintain that 'Muhammad did not know any' of these, 'some documents claim that there were people at Mecca, including members of Muhammad's own family, who knew these stories' (144–5). It is possible too that Waraqah represented the type of Christianity which early Muslims regarded as true (108). 'Divine action', he continues, discussing the specific question of Muhammad's sincerity, 'is in no way incompatible with the role of the human sub-conscious', since 'Christian theology thinks that God often acts by using human beings, their knowledge and psychology as his instrument' (145). Muslims find 'enough' in the Qur'an, so 'why should they feel the need to look for anything else?' Some of the Qur'an's 'finely-chiseled phrases . . . send a shiver through those who hear them', such as 31:34: 'And no one knows in what land he will die' (134). He describes the Qur'an as 'suffused with an atmosphere of prayer' (149).

In attempting to reassess Muhammad from a Christian perspective, Jomier (1989) suggests that Christians can affirm that God's Holy Spirit was to some degree at work through Muhammad (142). Pointing out that the Grand Sheikh of Al-Azhar asked Christians to 'respect Muhammad', Jomier put it to one of the delegates at an official consultation that while Christians agree that the 'manner of speaking which was current in the middle ages is now inadmissible', the questions remains 'How do Muslims want us to respect Muhammad, while remaining Christians?', since if they respect Muhammad 'as Muslims do, they would become Muslims' (141). While aware that some Christians have affirmed outright belief in Muhammad as a prophet, Jomier is concerned to enquire what such a statement implies for Christians. For Jomier, there is no question but that Muslims enjoy though Islam a genuine relationship with God or that salvation is possible for Muslims. Even if Christianity is regarded as the 'official way of salvation', he says, Christians can acknowledge that some people, through no fault of their own, 'do not succeed in discovering this way'. God, however, saves them 'in other ways'. God's grace is thus not 'bound in a limiting way to the sacraments' of the Church. Indeed, he says, Christians should recognize that 'within Islam numerous believers are in a relationship with God that grace has brought about in them' (147). Referring to al-Ghazali, he comments that some Muslims also extend the possibility of salvation to non-Muslims (131). Jomier's explanation of Muhammad is that he was a charismatic reformer, who challenged the Christians of his time to be faithful to the Gospel. God, he says, raises such reformers up to oppose 'a fossilized church', such as in the case of the Protestant reformation, when it was 'very clear' that 'a reform was needed' (147–8). He does not hesitate to describe Muhammad as a 'great politician and religious genius' (144) but suggests that for Christians to describe him as a 'prophet' is problematic because they will 'always use the word 'prophet' with qualifications' (146–7). Islam's origin stems from Muhammad's 'real and profound religious experience' (143). Viewing Muhammad as what he calls subjectively sincere, Jomier says that from a Christian perspective, the fact that Muhammad's message contained errors (143), such as its denial of the Crucifixion, needs to be tackled. He also comments that at certain points in his life, Muhammad acted in ways that would have to be described as 'harsh': he 'took vengeance on a number of his enemies', 'arranged the political assassination of Jews' and 'could not bear poets to write against him' (144). Here we have an echo of Christian polemic.

Jomier (1989) also suggests that Christians could regard Muhammad as a prophet in the Old Testament sense, although he does not elaborate (143). Cragg makes a similar suggestion but gives more detail on what this recognition means. Jomier and Cragg both accept that God worked though Muhammad. The Qur'an emerges in their thought as an inspired text but one which developed through and engaged with Muhammad's sub-consciousness, which explains the presence of material such as the docetic view of Jesus resembling those in the non-canonical gospels (see Jomier, 1989: 109). Influenced by the Christian conviction that God does not override but employs the mind of his human instruments, these writers tend to understand the Islamic revelation as an event in which the relationship between the messenger and the messenger's book was so intricate that is it impossible to separate them. In Christianity, the word of God was incarnated in a human being, then that 'word' was attested to by other human beings, who wrote the gospels. In Islam, the primary word from God is the Book, but that book was communicated through, and cannot be understood apart from, the life of a man. Cragg understands the Qur'an as the record of Muhammad's religious experiences. Controversially, since Muhammad denied being a poet, Cragg likens Muhammad's inspiration to that of the poet: 'The Qur'an, in its power and quality, is a thing of surpassing poetical worth', he says, 'its genesis must be understood in terms of literary inspiration'. 'The mystery of its origins', he continues, 'cannot be fathomed without sounding the depths of language' (1971: 41). Like Jomier, Cragg rejects the Muslim contention that the Qur'an is verbatim God's words. For him, it is a product of religious experience generated at the very juncture where God meets messenger, and contains 'a parallel quality of active mind and spirit in both directions of his medial position between the eternal and the temporal, between the word given and the word declared' (1971: 19). 'There need', he says, 'be no serious doubt that the voice in the Book is authentically the voice of the prophet' (2000: 88). He does not actually argue that Muhammad wrote the Qur'an physically but he does interpret *ummi* (unlettered) to refer to Muhammad as 'not yet scriptured'. It would be unfair to contend that a successful merchant was illiterate (1971: 56).

A few Muslims have articulated views that approach Cragg's idea that the Qur'an is both a word from God, and Muhammad's words. Notice the difference, however, between the traditional Muslim formulation that the Qur'an is the word *of* God, rather than *from* God. Nonetheless, Rahman wrote that:

the Qur'an is the Word of God (Kalam allah). Muhammad, too, was unshakeably convinced that he was recipient of the Message from God, the totally other. This 'Other' through some channel 'dictated' the Qur'an with an absolute authority. Not only does the word Qur'an, meaning 'recitation', clearly indicate this, but the text of the Qur'an itself states in several places that the Qur'an is verbally revealed and not merely in its 'meaning' and ideas. (1966: 31)[15]

Influenced by Rahman and acknowledging Cragg as a sympathetic Christian scholar of Islam, Esack speaks about the 'grey area' that Muslims have been reluctant to explore, that is, the area between 'the Prophet's life and the Qur'an' (2005: 101). First, there is an issue whether a clear line can really be drawn between Qur'an and *hadith*, given that some *hadith* are classed as revelation (115). Second, if the Qur'an entered Muhammad's 'heart', 'does this not assume that that heart – located in his unique person which, in turn, was located in sixth-century Arabia – did not impact upon what entered it and later emerged from his tongue as uttered revelation?' (116). Cragg thinks that Christians can gain much from reading the Qur'an, with its emphasis on the sovereignty of God, on God's mercy and on justice.

Cragg suggests that prophetic meanings can 'seem retrogressive by simple time criteria' (1984: 92). Thus, Muhammad can be understood as a type of Old Testament prophet, considered from the point of view of what he calls 'cultic' rather than 'chronological time'. Should we not, he says, 'look backward into the great Old Testament prophetic tradition . . . to find in Muhammad a strange, and yet unmistakable, shift in the whole concept and expression of prophethood?' (2000: 83). Rather than having a universal message, however, which Muslims insist is true of Muhammad, his message was specifically intended for those people who lack a faith, which resembles Paul of Antioch's view. Again, Esack's approach is similar. He argues in favour of the universal validity of Muhammad's message and mission but suggests that Muhammad's message varied from community to community, calling those with no faith, pagan or idolatrous faith to Islam and people of the book to return to their true paths (1997: 173). Of course, many Muslims claim that the true path of Christianity is Islam. As Jomier comments, 'since Christianity and Judaism were corrupt', it was Muhammad 'whom God charged with establishing the religion in all its purity' (109). However, Esrack does not maintain that Christians must convert. In Esack's view, Christians and Jews need to practise what they preach in terms of love of enemies, going the extra mile, ministering to the needy, and freeing the oppressed from oppression (1997: 170). Cragg's concern to understand the process by which the Qur'an entered the world does not necessitate a detailed examination of what Christian polemicists see as moral problems in the life of Muhammad, to which Jomier also only makes passing but not judgmental reference. Cragg suggested that 'too much' is made of such issues as Muhammad's 'plural marriages', 'opportunist tactics' or 'repressive measures', and 'too little' of his 'solicitude for orphans and magnanimity to certain foes'. 'He has proved', he continues, 'both for good and ill profounder than much criticism and eulogy' (2000: 84). He comments, however, that setting forth Muhammad's life 'without offending modern Muslim susceptibilities is difficult' (76). He describes the 'massacre of the Banu Quraizah' as marking the 'darkest depths of Muslim policy' and as negatively contrasting 'the magnanimity of Muhammad when subsequently he faced their Meccan allies in the "siege" after his reconquest of the holy city' (79). Cragg, however, is primarily concerned with Muhammad's combination of temporal and religious authority, which he sees as more Old Testament-like than New. He sees the *hijra* as marking a turning point, from warner to warrior. In a passage that actually resembles Muir, he writes about how surahs 'exhorting to friendly relations with the "people of the book" . . . give way to flat disavowal and explicit condemnation' (Cragg, 2000: 76–7; see Muir, 1894: 440). Unlike Muir, though, he does not argue that a moral declension occurred but that the decision 'for a religious authority armed with the sinews of war and means of government' set the subsequent tone for Muslim society (85), in contrast to Jesus' decision, which was that 'of the Cross – no less conscious, no less formative, no less inclusive' (85). Comparing Q5:82 and 9:30–31 he remarks that 'it is hard to resist the impression that Muhammad's attitude changed when he . . . failed to receive the . . . welcome he . . . expected' from Christians and Jews (234).

Jomier and Cragg on the Bible, Jesus and the Trinity

Jomier describes the Muslim charge of *tahrif* but says that the 'accusation of falsification is leveled at specific groups' and can be understood to refer to 'false interpretation rather than falsification of the text'. Ahmad Khan argued in favour of the latter, while Esack points out that the Qur'an only castigates a 'section' of 'the people of the book' and is actually silent on 'the extent and nature of distortion' (see Q2:109; 3:113; 5:66; Esack, 1997: 173). Referring to Muhammad's challenge to the Jews to read the Torah in order to find confirmation of the truth of the Qur'an (3:93), Jomier (1989) remarks that 'the whole force of the argument is lost if the Jews have only a falsified text' (156). Discussing the pseudo-gospel of Barnabas, he comments on its popularity, as does Nazir Ali (13–14). Jomier suggests, however, that Barnabas is 'the wrong solution to a real problem' for Muslims because its depiction of Jesus contradicts the Qur'an's, since Jesus 'asserts in it that he is not the Messiah and declares that Muhammad will be the Messiah' (157). In the Qur'an, Jesus is called the Messiah, a title that has never been applied to Muhammad. Both writers refer to Muslim claims that the Bible predicted Muhammad. Jomier observes that it is difficult to come to an agreement on this, since 'everything depends on the principle by which one justifies' the operation of sifting through biblical texts. Christians will continue to apply John's Paraclete to the Holy Spirit;

Muslims are likely to continue to apply this to Muhammad. Cragg (2000) comments on the anomaly, noted in this book, that on the one hand the Bible is said to be corrupt while on the other some passages are held to be 'free of corruption' (257). The problem, he says, stems from the fact that for Muslims the 'biblical scriptures do not square with the Qur'an'. Since they believe that their 'original form' did square with the Qur'an, the conclusion is that they must now be corrupt (254; see Jomier, 155). Cragg suggests that the Christian argument that manuscript evidence exists that corroborates that the Bible has not 'undergone changes since the fourth century' falls on deaf ears, making 'little impression on dogmatic prejudice' (254).

On Jesus, the Cross and the Trinity, Jomier and Cragg assert that the Qur'an is mistaken. Jomier refers to the possibility of interpreting Q4:157 to allow that Jesus was crucified but points out that even if this is accepted, the cross still does not occupy, for Muslims, 'a place in the history of salvation' since for them God 'gives his forgiveness directly to anyone who asks for it' (109). Jomier remarks that Muslims regard themselves as true Christians and 'think that the Qur'an provides all the indispensable knowledge about Jesus' (108). Cragg on the cross follows a similar argument. The cross is a central theme for him. He is saddened beyond measure that Islam has no place for this event. He takes the Cross as historical fact, arguing thus that on this issue the Qur'an cannot be right, reversing Ibn Taymiyyah's argument. 'History', says Cragg 'is plain enough' and 'if Muslims do not follow it, it is because their prejudgment has intervened arbitrarily to break it' (267). The tragedy is that Muslims cannot conceive of a God who fails to 'rescue his servant from the hands of his enemies', since their God is a God who 'turns the tables, opens the trapdoor, and confounds all foes' (268). Muslims fail to see the Cross as that act through which God identified with human suffering and reconciled the world to himself (272).

On the Trinity, Cragg stresses that while Muslims see this as a 'violation of faith in God's unity' (278) Christians understand Trinity as expressing and illuminating divine Oneness. 'Muslims who debate tritheism', he says, 'are not discussing Christianity' (279). Neither the apostles nor the Church father posited multiple deities (280). Trinity, he argues, must be understood as rooted in how Christians experience God. No other language can explain 'what Christ had been to them and done for all humankind' than that of God being present in and through Jesus (283). Cragg suggests that this way of speaking of God is not totally alien to Muslims, since they also accept that the 'book itself is God's speech' and that God communicates to humanity through 'messengers and spirits'. The difference is that Christianity 'takes these activities and gathers them into its understanding of the nature of God' (284). Jomier says that Muslims tend to regard Trinity as a type of mathematical formula. Few Muslims regard Christians as monotheists, he says (154, 108). In response, Jomier comments, Christians have tried to show Muslims that God's oneness is 'compatible with a degree of multiplicity, that of divine attributes' thus attempting to draw a parallel between the Trinity and aspects of Muslim theology. Arabic terms for 'nature and substance' have 'shocking connotations . . . when applied to God' and so should be avoided. One helpful way of expressing Trinity, he says, might be to say that 'the divine essence is one, while the three consubstantial persons are only subsistent relations' (154).

George Khodr's Contribution

Khodr's lifelong involvement in Christian–Muslim relations is an important example of a Christian commitment to Muslim–Christian rapprochement within the Arab world. He has not written extensively on Christian–Muslim relations but his contribution to the 1971 WCC meeting made a seminal contribution to thinking about dialogue. There are parallels between his thinking and Roman Catholic contributors, including Jomier and Paul Knitter. Khodr has participated in many dialogues. For example, Askari and Khodr were both participants at Ajaltoun in March 1970 and at Broumana in July 1972. In September–October 1987 Khodr co-chaired a dialogue on religion and society on the island of Crete. In his paper, 'The Economy of the Holy Spirit', Khodr argued that the Bible recognized 'faith' outside Israel and the Church, citing Acts 14:17, 17:23 and 17:28. Paul affirmed that in the 'real world' a 'false God has no existence' (38). While the Church Fathers saw the many pagan Gods as 'demons fighting against the Lord' they also spoke about the *logos spermatikos* 'present even before Christ's coming', referring to 'Justin's famous notion' (39). The Fathers such as Justin and Clement could 'respect the wisdom of antiquity', albeit with reservations (40). The idea that the Christian world is one of 'peace, light and knowledge', while the non-Christian world as one of 'war and darkness' followed from the first approach

(41). It informed the belief that non-Christians could only attain salvation by becoming Christian. Hence, the world needed to be evangelized or even dominated by the Christian world. Khodr sees a link between colonialism and this attitude since it posits that 'the rest of the world remains a-historical until it adopts Western experience which, moreover, by implacable logic and technological determinism, is destined to dominate the world' (41). For Khodr, the Church is God's 'breath of life for humanity'. It represents what human life ought to be, the 'image of the humanity to come' (43). It is God's instrument in the world, not 'over against the world, separate from it' but 'part of the world'. It is intended for the nations, yet how God will use the Church to redeem the nations is part of the divine mystery. The church, then, is the 'cosmos', the *oikonomia*.

Khodr's background as a Christian in the Muslim world informs what follows. Orthodox Christians have developed an understanding of mission that differs from that of Western Christianity. The West has associated mission with individual conversion; the East has tended to think in terms of redeeming the world. Indeed, Christ died to redeem the world (John 3:16)[16] and his resurrection fills the whole earth (Col 1: 17, 45). This makes possible the salvation of those who are outside the Church, since the Spirit is present everywhere and 'fills everything by virtue of an economy distinct from that of the son' (46). Applying His energies and operating 'in accordance with His own economy', the Spirit can make Christ become 'an inner reality' even for those who do not name His name. Other religions can thus be seen as 'points where His inspiration is at work' (46). All 'who are visited by the spirit are the people of God' and the 'great religions' can be described as 'training schools of the Divine Mercy' (47). The missionary task is to 'Name Him whom others have already recognized as the beloved' (49). Adding numbers to the church is not the issue, since people will 'come in of their own accord once they begin to feel at home in it as the Father's house' (48). Meanwhile, missionaries should 'identify all the Christic values in other religions' and show 'them Christ as the bond which unites them and His love as their fulfillment'. Jomier, as noted, speaks of the Holy Spirit's activity within Islam, and of Muslims enjoying a genuine relationship with God. Knitter (1996), drawing on Khodr, argues that by affirming the Spirit as the free-ranging aspect of the Trinity, Christians can 'Accept that the kingdom of God beyond the church is independent; that is, not to be submerged or engulfed or incorporated into the economy of the word represented in the Christian churches' (113–14). The spirit has its own 'hypostatic independence' (113) and while it can never be 'understood without reference to Christ' it can 'never be reduced to the Word, subordinated to the Word'. The conversion of the Other become less vital although witness to how Christians understand the world in relation to its Creator can still be pursued. Similarly, Esack's concept of the 'believer' as anyone who opposes oppression, who works to eliminate poverty and discrimination, whether they formally associate with the Muslim community or remain Christian, or humanist, removes conversion from the equation. He emphasizes the *humanum*, the need to discover new ways of becoming human through solidarity with the poor (1997: 202, citing Gustavo Gutierrez).

Phil Parshall: A Cross-category Example?

Parshall, a life-long missionary, writes primarily as a missiologist. His understanding of mission as aiming to convert Muslims is different from Cragg's and Jomier's. Parshall (2002) affirms that 'God is only to be known and experienced through his son, Jesus Christ' (27). Cragg (2000) does say that a 'Christian mission that renounces the making of Christians has forsaken both its genius and its duty' (325), but his own object has been rather the conversion of Islam as a whole, the hope that it will adopt Christ crucified and risen as restoring what, in his view, Islam lacks, a 'place for pardon and peace', for 'divine mercy in action for human remaking' (274). He shares with Massignon the idea that simply being present among Muslims, offering them hospitality and friendship, is a form of Christian witness. Yet in his approach to Islam, Parshall is closer to Cragg than to the Caners. He repudiates polemic. He unhesitatingly affirms that Christians and Muslims worship the same God. Parshall writes, 'It seems to be unfair to declare the God of Islam to be absolutely different from the God of the Bible', even if 'Islam presents an inadequate and incomplete . . . view of God' (2002: 27). Parshall speaks of being 'challenged', 'annoyed' and 'dumbfounded' by Islam but says that he considers it a privilege 'to have spent half of' his life living among Muslims. When he writes about Muslim prayer and fasting Parshall sounds more Cragg-like than Caner-like, even though Christianity's refusal to 'enforce a universal liturgy' has a liberating aspect (101). As have many Christians, he interprets

Sufi Islam as evidence of a spiritual hunger in Islam (104), but he clearly sees a genuine experience of God in Islam. He has himself observed the month of fasting (109). 'Christian neglect of fasting', he says, is a matter of concern.[17] Sharing Muslim prayer is more problematic: 'most of the content of the ritual is acceptable to the Christian . . . yet there are a few items of such weighty theological significance that I conclude any true believer who permanently participates in the prayer ritual is indeed compromising his faith in Christ' (1985: 182–3). After citing Cragg's *Call*, Parshall comments that if 'Christians are to go beyond the mosque' physically as well as spiritually, then they must 'equal or excel the Muslims desire for and practice of prayer' (1985: 233). Parshall thinks that Christians should avoid calling Jesus 'son of God' unless 'surrounding it with as great deal of sensitive explanation' (1985: 201). In speaking of the Trinity, any allusion to sexual union must be denied and its metaphorical rather than literal aspect should be emphasized. My own discussions of Trinity and of the concept of Jesus as God's son have never proved fruitful but more often than not, certainly in Bangladesh, my Muslim acquaintances end by saying that at least we worship the same God. This was never disputed.

On *tahrif*, Parshall refers to manuscript evidence in favour of the Bible's authenticity but points out that 'it is obvious that there is a very significant human component in the Bible' (85). Muslims have 'no fewer theological problems' vis-à-vis the Qur'an except that they 'choose to ignore their existence'. Yet he avoids entering what he calls a 'counter-debate' on the question, 'Is the Qur'an the word of Allah?' as 'counterproductive'. 'It would', he says, 'only generate a tremendous lot of heat and little, if any, light' (86). Jay Smith, with a similar Fuller background to Parshall, does engage in such debates, including Deedat-style encounters.[18] Parshall wants to persuade Muslims to accept Jesus as their saviour but he chooses different tactics in order to do so. He can often see positives where polemicists only see negatives. For example, referring to the concept that Islam is fatalistic, he comments that the Muslim 'propensity towards resignation to Allah's will appears to have produced a resilient race of people' in the Bangladeshi nation (142). Parshall's discussion of Muhammad explores his role within official and popular Islamic spirituality. He comments on how Muslims exceed the Qur'an in all but deifying Muhammad. He raises the issue of Muhammad's sexuality, his marriage to Zaynab, citing Q33:37–38, which was 'given divine sanction by this startling quranic verse' and describes

Muhammad's marriage with Aisha as 'the next most criticized' (257). Yet, asking whether Muhammad consciously used his 'alleged "revelations"' to 'manipulate his own disciples and achieve his ends' he cannot declare Muhammad insincere, pointing out how he was reviled and persecuted for his 'belief in the legitimacy of his mission' (160). While leaving the issue ultimately in God's hands, Parshall concludes that Muhammad was not a spiritual person in 'a classical New Testament sense' but *he was* 'a God-seeker, sincere and devoted, attempting to carry out what he believed to be Allah's will' (261), which takes this evangelical Christian missionary a long way from the Caners. Like Cragg and Jomier, he locates Muhammad, culturally, in the Old Testament, suggesting that while his morality falls short of Jesus', when compared with Noah, Moses, David or Solomon, he is no worse than any of these great men of God (260).

Parshall on Muslim Culture and Conversion

Parshall distinguishes Muslim culture from Islam *per se*. Aspects of the former can be retained by converts. In Bangladesh, he established Messianic Muslim communities. Such converts leave the Mosque but remain within the wider community. Parshall encouraged these converts to keep the fast but not to practise *salat* (prayer), at least not in the mosque. Trained at Fuller, where McGavran taught, Parshall subscribes to the view that instead of extracting converts from their culture into mixed congregations, possibly using a common language that is a not a shared mother tongue, forming homogeneous churches is preferable. McGavran argued that people find it easier to become Christian 'without crossing racial, linguistic or class barriers' (1990: 163). For Parshall, this enables Muslims to maintain their all important relationship within the community, especially with their extended families (1985: 178). Parshall is willing to explore further the degree to which Muslim converts can continue to practise Muslim rituals, which raises the question whether such a movement would represent an 'Islamic sect' (1985: 193). In his view, for 'total integration as an Islamic sect to occur', several dangers would be encountered. These include over exaltation of Muhammad, the 'denial by Muslims of the Christian view of biblical authority' (194) and the danger that syncretism would result. Travis (1998) developed a scheme for describing the relationship between different types of communities of Christian converts and their former religious environments. His sixth category are converts who stay within their Mosque communities as secret Christians while outwardly appearing to be Muslim, the opposite of how some Jews and Muslims disguised their faith in post-1492 Spain.[19] Cragg does not approve of such converts – 'no sincere believer will be hidden and unknown', he says – yet he is open to the possibility of converts 'not ceasing to belong with Muslim need, Muslim thought and Muslim kin', leaving open such issues as 'forms of prayer and fasting that will be invaded by new liberty and new meaning' (2000: 318). Arguably, Parshall has moved away from the contention of such pioneer exclusivists as Kraemer, for whom 'to *decide* for Christ and the world He stands for implies a break with ones religious past', thus everything in a convert's religious past must be abandoned (1938: 291). Christian converts too often throw off so many of their previous clothes that they 'end up as Christians with much less spiritual discipline than they had as Muslims' (1985: 225), hence keeping the fast is to be encouraged.

Askari, Talbi and Hussain: Contemporary Muslim Conciliators

Askari has developed an understanding of faith as a category that is independent of the religious label, or identity, of any individual. This is similar to how Rahner understands faith. In several articles, Askari expresses the view that we are all pilgrims walking towards the Absolute and that none of us can claim possession of all knowledge or understanding, that we grasp the Absolute absolutely. This, he says, would be impossible for finite, mortal beings and also dangerous, since any creed that claims to be the exclusive channel to God would become arrogant and even antagonistic towards others. Thus, 'all religions and all approaches within each one of them, are relative to Absolute Truth – they are all just approaches, and the only conviction common to all of them is that there is an Absolute Truth' (Askari and Hick, 1985: 191). Recognizing that absolute truth claims give people psychological security, he suggests that this becomes problematic when transferred into the arena of politics. Polemics, suppression and oppression then follow (Siddiqui, 1997: 118). On the one hand, he does not argue that all religions are the same, since they ask different questions and propose different answers. On the other hand, he thinks that as we are all pilgrims on the path, instead of trying to convince the Other, we should listen to and learn from them as they reciprocate. Dialogue, at bottom, means that we recognize each others as seekers. He suggests that Christians need Muslims and Muslims need Christians; Muslims 'compromise their own response to God' by rejecting the Bible, while Christians help to restrain Muslims from reducing Islam to mere legalism, reminding them of themes less prominent in Islam such as 'the dimension of the tragic, or suffering, of submission in silence without resistance, of confronting self-righteousness, of upholding the values of poverty, of going inward, of partaking of burdens, seen and unseen, of the other' which sound like Cragg (2000: 205–6). Askari also wrests as much meaning as he can from the words he uses. The 'person of Christ' or the 'revelation in a person' as contrasted with Islam's 'revelation in words' reminds Muslims not to worship the Book (Zebiri, 1997: 169). Jesus is a 'sign' for Muslims and Christians in the 'realm of the deep relation between man and God' (ibid., citing Askari, 1992: 42). Those who succeed in rising above particularities towards the universal enter into a zone that Askari calls the trans-religious. Such people have moved from the 'from the letter to the spirit, from the outer to the inner' (Siddiqui, 1997: 115).

Askari is less interested in the minutiae of such issues as Trinity or even the corruption of the Bible than in religious experience and in spirituality. When I was his student at Selly Oak, I was moved by his exegesis of one of the gospel stories. He never gave any hint that he thought the gospels were forgeries, unreliable or simply of no interest for Muslims. Siddiqui says that Askari prefers to avoid these issues (112), although notes that in doing so Muslims would not be following their tradition. Here, Askari refers to, and disagrees with, Ibn Hazm. On Unity versus Trinity, my view is that Askari sees these as different but not ultimately irreconcilable articulations of who God is, but regards the totality of God as surpassing human understanding. Both are true, even wholly true, but not the whole of the truth. The human is a central motif for Askari. We are all human, all children of God. This emphasis on common humanity enabled him to engage with humanist thought. In *Towards a Spiritual Humanism* (1991), he says that even the question 'Does Humanity Exist?' cannot be answered quickly, 'because humanity also is an unfinished becoming', a 'journey, and it is the most difficult journey because here the path and the traveller are one' (130). He writes 'my believing is an unfinished business', a 'door opening towards the beyond' (129). His open-ended, unfinished view of believing and of the religious quest sits uncomfortably with the claim that Christianity and Islam represent complete, perfect, exclusive channels to the divine.

Talbi, like Askari, has taken part in formal dialogues including Colombo, April 1974 and Chambésy, March 1979. In addition to his contribution to religious discourse, he is a distinguished historian and human-rights activist. Talbi's most accessible writing on dialogue is in Griffiths (1990). This article shows his awareness of Catholic thought in particular; he cites with approval from *Nostra Aetate* (92). Talbi argues that the Qur'an at such verses as Q2:62 endorses religious pluralism, which, he says, is confirmed by 5:69 and 2:111–12. Citing 29:46, he argues that the Qur'an invites Muslims to 'discuss and to enter dialogue with men in general, and especially with the faithful of the biblical religions' (83).[20] To engage in dialogue is to obey the Qur'an, which attributes other religions' existence to God's revelation of different paths for different communities (100; see also Q5:48, 10:18–19; 39:46). Talbi is also interested in the *humanum*, citing *Nostra Aetate*, 'What is man? What is the meaning and purpose of life?' (95). He suggests that these questions are excellent themes for formal dialogue. Christians, he says, have sincerely tried to atone for past polemic and misunderstanding by making strides in their knowledge of Islam. He suggests that theological development in Islam has been unequal (85), too often losing contact with the world (86). Islam needs to 'overcome its difficulties', he says, citing Arkoun, a leading advocate of re-thinking Islam (see Arkoun, 1994).[21] Polemics should be avoided: 'it is rare that disputes do not lead to a set-back and an abdication of the mind' (88). Dialogue, however, will also be counter-productive if it is 'conceived as a new form of proselytism, a means of undermining convictions', a charge that has been levelled at Cragg (88). The issue of Christian mission constantly surfaces in dialogue. At Tripoli and Chambésy, Christians were challenged to desist from mission or dialogue would cease. Muslim speakers 'called for a moratorium on Christian mission in Islamic areas and, further, for corporate penitence for the sins of proselytism by which Muslims had been assaulted and provoked' (Cragg, 2000: 200). Subsequent discussion has focused on methods that might be mutually acceptable and on those 'which are to be avoided' (see Siddiqui, 1997: 187).[22] Talbi concludes by observing that God's plan is an 'unfathomable mystery', so Christians and Muslims should accept their 'differences and disagreements, and by competing with one another in good works, shorten the time in which the trial of our disagreements will come to an end' (101).

Hussain has written a gentle, passionate, personal and persuasive call for Christian–Muslim friendship. Written by a Canadian-born Muslim, his book represents a contribution by someone whose primary experience of Islam is outside what would normally be described as the Muslim world. Hussain shares with Askari the idea that Christianity and Islam complement each other. His book is a type of apology, discussing such topical issues as the roles of women and men, violence and *jihad* and 'After 9/11: Muslims in an uneasy limelight'. Hussain discusses what he calls 'problematic verses', such as 60:104 and 5:77–81, commenting that these do not represent a blanket condemnation of people of the book but a reminder to them not to commit excesses. Surah 107 sums up, he says, what God expects from humans and makes it clear that 'no one group of people has a guaranteed ticket to heaven', including Muslims (183). Yet Muslims and non-Muslims who do 'the right things, worship God and observe their duties to the people around them will be rewarded by God'. Hussain and all three Muslim writers can be said to elevate praxis above dogma. What we do is more important than what we believe, which contrasts with Ibn Taymiyyah, for whom salvation was inextricably linked with recognizing Muhammad as God's messenger. Hussain suggests that common Christian and Muslim regard for Jesus and Mary can be a focal point in dialogue, despite differences of belief (191). Like Talbi, he cites *Nostra Aetate* on Muslims (194). He describes Sufism as a 'romance with God' (161) Dialogue between contemplative traditions reminds us to focus less on the vessel than on what it contains; that is, on the 'water of life, rather than remaining confined to our separate understandings of God' (176).

Like Talbi, Hussain argues that God purposefully chose 'not to create a humanity with no differences' and affirms that the Qur'an regards pluralism as part of the divine plan, and thus Muslims ought to 'return to the pluralistic vision of the Qur'an and . . . establish co-operative relations with other religious communities' (197). 'The emerging paradigm of Christianity', he says, 'is leading more and more Christians' to explore commonalities between the two faiths, so much so that 'some contemporary Christians find they have more in common with some Muslims than they do with more traditional fellow Christians' (215). I can personally affirm that I have more in common with Esack and Askari than with the Caners, with whom

I am not confident that I share very much at all, even though they and I are Baptist. Hussain refers to Vines' remarks on Muhammad (66) and to such controversial incidents as the Danish cartoons, commenting that the real issue is not freedom of speech, but 'who has the power to create stereotypes, and how those stereotypes affect the way we treat people' (67). Writing as a member of a minority community in the West, he raises important issues here about the limits of free expression vis-à-vis how stereotypes can reinforce prejudice and discrimination against minorities, especially when they are perceived as somehow different from, and even a threat to, the majority. As pluralist societies think about issues of inclusion and empowerment, finding ways to safeguard against misrepresentation and ridicule becomes critical.

Cross-category Example: Ahmad

An exponent of Mawdudi's thought, Ahmad has interpreted someone widely credited as inspiring jihadist Islam. Mawdudi saw Christianity as totally bankrupt. Why, then, would one of his most accomplished disciples engage in dialogue with Christianity? Partly, for Ahmad, it is a matter of strategy, just as Parshall's irenic approach to Islam is strategic. Parshall thinks it more fruitful than polemic. Ahmad thinks that Islamic economics, governmental systems, laws and traditions can answer the problems of the West as well of those of the Muslim world. However, he wants to win the intellectual debate, not to bring about a worldwide Islamic military take-over of the world. In Pakistan he has been a strong advocate of *Shariah* law, suggesting that Christians would benefit from having their rights enshrined therein, although Christian have been outspoken in opposing this (Siddiqui, 1997: 135). Writing in 1995, pre-9/11 but post-Huntington's clash theory, Ahmad (1999) refutes the idea that Muslim states pose a threat to the West: 'As far as the military power and political strength of the Muslim world are concerned, they are weak and dependent on the West. Where is the question of a military threat from the Muslim world?' (69). The Muslim world is not interested in claiming other people's territories, he says (68). However, nor do Muslims want to be tied to the West's apron strings. They resent the West's hegemony on the rest of the world (72) and its unwillingness to recognize the legitimacy of other paths to democracy (80). When Muslims try to exert self-determination, their efforts are misrepresented as 'religious extremism' 'Islamic fundamentalism', 'Militant Islam' and 'blind anti-Westernism!', when all they want to do is to control their own destiny and put their own house in order (68). They do not condemn the West in its entirety but want to take from the West what 'is good and reject what is unsuitable' (68). In this context, Ahmad argues for acceptance of pluralism within international relations: 'The 21st century should become a century of new opportunities for the exchange and cross-fertilization of ideas, ideologies and cultures.' There would not only be freedom of expression', he says, 'but also acceptance of a plurality of ideologies, cultures and faiths' (73). The West, he argues, has overemphasized secularism, which has 'corrupted man's moral roots' and led to 'an individualism that is not prepared to fulfil its social obligations' (73).

Through the Islamic Foundation, which he founded in Leicester, UK, Ahmad has pursued a critical engagement with the West, rather like an advocate of a particular political philosophy.[23] In fact, the Jamaati-i-Islam has pursued constitutional politics in the Sub-Continent: it has been a partner in government in Bangladesh; in Pakistan Ahmad served as Minister of Planning in Pakistan, and two full terms in the Senate. He has also participated extensively in dialogue. He was a member of the Advisory Board in Selly Oak, 1976–78 when I was there as a student, and Askari as a teacher. He served as Vice-President of the Standing Conference on Jews, Christians and Muslims in England (1974–78) and has lectured in Rome at the Pontifical Institute for Arabic and Islamic Studies. His straightforward definition of dialogue is that it is better to talk with, than about, each other (Siddiqui, 1997: 125). He appreciates Vatican and WCC dialogue initiatives but says there has been a lot of repetition, with no sign of a breakthrough, so it is too soon to pass judgement (Siddiqui, 1997: 129). One of Ahmad's most significant contributions to Christian–Muslim dialogue was his editorial in the October 1976 issue of the *International Review of Mission,* which published the proceedings of the 1976 Selly Oak conference. 'The role of Christian missions in the Muslim world is regarded by the Muslims to be at the root of estrangement between the Christian and the Muslims worlds', he wrote (367). Yet, despite wars and 'moments of stress and strain', Christians and Muslims have lived 'side by side in the Muslim world, on the whole, in peace and harmony with each other since the final revelation of Islam in the seventh century' (367). He called for a halt in 'gross misrepresentation' of Islam and of Muhammad, for missionaries to stop taking advantage of the weakness and helplessness of Muslims who are disadvantaged, 'exploiting their weakness' by targeting them for 'economic assistance, medical aid and education', to desist from subverting Islam through promoting nationalism, socialism, secularism and modernism and to cease treating Muslims as political rivals. At the conference itself, there was 'a respect for the viewpoint and feelings of others', and an 'acceptance of facts whether pleasant or unpleasant'. 'With such an approach', he concluded, 'man can move towards a new world of mutuality and co-existence' (369).

Conclusion

Has Progress Occurred?

In conclusion, I assess what has been achieved by Christian–Muslim encounter and take the opportunity to add some personal ideas to this attempt to understand relations between the two faiths. What progress has been made during 1,400 years of Christian–Muslim encounter? Has any progress occurred? Ahmad suggested that over the 30 years or so of formal Christian–Muslim dialogue there has been a lot of repetition with no breakthrough in sight. However, what would represent a breakthrough? Here, we are thrown back to the question with which this book began. Would a breakthrough involve Christians admitting that, yes, the Bible is corrupt, that the Trinity is a fabricated doctrine and that Islam, after all, is the best religion? Or, would a breakthrough involve some sort of internationally binding concord between Muslims and Christians that they will cease any effort to convert others, or at least desist from controversial or coercive methods of proselytism? Throughout these chapters, the same issues have surfaced again and again. Often, Christians and Muslims have given the same or similar answers to the questions posed of them. One substantial development is the creation of formal mechanisms to promote better understanding and dialogue. Chapter 8's discussion involved scholars from both sides who can be said to belong to a community of dialogue. Many of them have met. They are aware of each other's writing and increasingly speak the same, rather than a different, language. This community extends into academia, where several of our contributors have or have had membership. Yesterday, the recognized scholars of Islam in the West taught in isolation from Muslims. Today, most departments of Islamic Studies or of Religious Studies have a Muslim as well as a Christian faculty. This extends to religiously affiliated institutions, such as Hartford Seminary where the Duncan Black MacDonald Center for the Study of Islam and Christian–Muslim

Relations, the oldest centre for such study in the USA, has two Muslim and one Christian faculty. Scholarship of Islam in relation to Christianity is no longer a matter of us writing about them but of both us writing about ourselves. This has added a new dimension, and can be identified as progress. One unfortunate tendency is for universities to prefer Muslim over non-Muslim scholars of Islam. This gives the impression that only a Muslim can properly teach about Islam, which might discourage a non-Muslim from gaining their doctorate in the field, anticipating that when they apply for jobs, they will lose out to insiders.[1] Issues such as the role of women in Islam, how the Qur'an is to be interpreted, war in Islam and even certain incidents in Muhammad's life that attract non-Muslim censure can be discussed together, enabling Christians to listen to Muslim explanations that do not for them compromise Muhammad's legacy, or moral integrity. On the other hand, the publication of official statements and the creation of agencies for dialogue is not universally supported. Many evangelical churches and evangelicals within mainstream churches, even those that have officially endorsed dialogue, remain committed to a more confrontational approach. The work of the WCC's Sub-Unit was criticized at the Nairobi Assembly in 1975 for compromising mission and for possibly encouraging syncretism. Some Muslims point out that the Churches speak with forked tongue. On the one hand, they have committed a modest amount of money and resources to promoting dialogue, while on the other they spend much more money on missionary activities.[2] The Pontifical Council is a respected and even prestigious body within the structures of the Vatican but pales into insignificance besides the much larger Congregation for the Evangelization of Peoples, formerly *Sacra Congregatio de Propaganda Fide*, founded 1622 with its own historic headquarters (built 1644).

The Nature of God

Initially, Christian–Muslim encounter was hampered when Christian used words that Muslims found repugnant, implying a physical and even sexual begetting of Jesus, or which seemed to compromise God's Unity. When Christians such as Paul of Antioch started to use language derived from Islamic discourse on God's attributes, Ibn Taymiyyah rejected this because he knew that Christians really meant three gods, not One God with plural attributes. The passage of time has allowed at least one Muslim to entertain such language in application to Jesus and God, although he posits God as being 'above all relations' while Jomier describes the 'three consubstantial persons' as 'subsistent relations', so some clarification here is needed.[3] In Muslim thought, however, God is said to be none other than God's mercy and God's power; yet these are also distinct from each other, while obviously related to God and, therefore, to each other. The real problem for Muslims is the idea that Jesus, who was a man, was also God, and so that God could enter, or incarnate, human body. This idea has been described as repugnant to Muslims, yet why should a God who can say, 'كن' (*kun*, be), and 'it is' (Q3: 47; 59), not be able to enter a human body? Christians have never believed that the whole of God became human, only that an aspect of God did. Jesus was wholly (*totus*) God but not the whole (*totum*) of God. If God is absolute, how can we dictate to God what God can and cannot do? In fact, many Christians no longer believe in a literal incarnation (see Hick: 1977).[4] For many, the incarnation expresses the conviction that *somehow* God was present *through* Jesus but that the *how* of this presence is a *mystery* as well as a *metaphor*. Personally, I affirm that *Jesus was God* without being able to explain this. I do not know whether Jesus was ontologically God, or whether he was so intimate with God that the distinction between who he was and who God is became blurred, which Muslims describe as a harmony of Jesus with God's will. Applying the same approach to the Qur'an, I can go further than Cragg or Jomier, for whom, in the end, it was Muhammad who wrote the Qur'an, and draw closer to Muslims by affirming that *somehow* God made God's word enter Muhammad, and pass through him into what became a physical, material object, a book. The actual processes of *incarnation* and of *bookification* can be regarded as mysteries while their reality or truthfulness can be affirmed. Fundamental in much Christian–Muslim discourse is the contention that when Christianity and Islam differ, they cannot both be true. Yet it can be true that God is One and also a Trinity if the totality of God is beyond all human language. Both can express truth about God, both can be *wholly true* of God yet neither can be the *whole truth* about God. The fact that Islam and Christianity do not always agree can remind Muslims and Christians that God is ultimately beyond number, beyond language, beyond fallible and finite human understanding. Yet I also believe that this God reveals enough about God's-self to enable us to enter into a meaningful relationship with God. This is the meaning of revelation, the drawing back, by God, of the divine curtain. Has progress occurred, then, on the issue of 'Who God Is?' It seems to me that when such scholars on both sides acknowledge that ultimately all our formulations about 'Who God is?' fall short of God's totality, some progress can be identified. If neither Muslims nor Christians insist on the absolute nature of their doctrinal articulations, movement towards God and away from either of our formulations takes place.

Has Progress Occurred on the Status of Muhammad?

Among Christian polemicists, the same charges of fabricating scripture, opportunism, use of violence and sexual misconduct feature in today's literature, as they did in John of Damascus. Some conciliators recognize Muhammad as a prophet, a larger number accept that he was sincere, even if his sincerity was subjective. Few go so far as to exonerate him of any criticism. Yet when Jomier and Cragg describe Muhammad as a type of Old Testament prophet, is this meaningful to Muslims, for whom Muhammad confirmed not only the Old but the New Testament? Is a Muhammad whose sincerity and desire to serve God is recognized but who is *not named* as a Prophet, acceptable? No more so, perhaps, than a Jesus who is recognized as a Prophet and as a word and a spirit from God but who is *not named* as the one who died on the Cross to redeem the world. The idea that Christians must respect Muhammad exactly as Muslims do, or that Muslims must respect Jesus exactly as Christians do, implies that we ought simply exchange faiths! More helpful are recognitions by such Muslims as Esack, Talbi and Nasr that if both Christianity and Islam are from God, then God must be speaking to all of us through both faiths. This is also Cragg's view. He asks whether God can be 'the author of confusion'. Much Christian–Muslim discourse has tried to unravel the mystery of apparent contradictions – is God One, or Three, or Three in One, did Jesus die on the Cross, is the Bible corrupt when it differs from the Qur'an, or vice-versa? Could it be that God is deliberately speaking to us *differently* in each tradition, not because God is playing a game with us or authoring confusion but to remind us that we cannot, while remaining human, grasp the *totality* of who God is? It could be that paradox is essential to the nature of God, who is at one and the same time transcendent and immanent, just and merciful, simple yet complex, singular yet possessing plural attributes, distinct from creation yet intimately involved in, and even present within, creation. How could any single articulation exhaust the nature of God? Apparent paradox or contradiction simply says that God has not exhaustively described God's-self through what God has revealed to a single people. Applying this to the question of who Muhammad might be for Christians, and who Jesus might be for Muslims, can any progress be achieved?

As a Christian, I affirm that Muhammad was God's instrument through which revelation was channelled. I have less difficulty than Jomier in calling Muhammad a prophet, because as long as it remains clear that my primary loyalty is to Jesus I do not think Muslims will assume that I have converted. I argue that having a primary loyalty, or what I would call a defining paradigm of being in relationship with God, which is how I view Jesus, does not preclude me from recognizing other sources of divine revelation. My loyalty to Jesus does not prevent me from acknowledging that Muhammad can teach me much about God's will for humanity. Here, I draw on Lewis Bevan Jones' contention that God's revelation in Jesus is *definitively* but not *exhaustively* revealed, and that there remain 'regions unknown, which faith can never exhaust' (1939: 76). Thus, the Holy Spirit has continued to inspire Christians and non-Christians, including the New Testament authors, and leads us into further truth (John 16:13). I do not find the notion that there could be another prophet after Jesus problematic, since he himself spoke of prophets who would arise, who should be judged by their fruits (Matt 7:20). This is only problematic for those who say that Muhammad has been so judged, and found wanting. I warm to the idea that Jesus is the definitive spiritual guide, something that the Sufi designation 'the seal of sanctity' implies but that although he taught a general ethic, Muhammad's social discourse provides the detail. I can look to Jesus as my spiritual guide but I struggle for much guidance from Jesus on how much I should pay employees, or even on war, which, sadly, is sometimes a pragmatic necessity, or on human sexuality, for that matter. It seems to me that once Christians affirm that explicit faith in Jesus is not necessary for salvation, but that God saves whomsoever he wills to save, then the need for Muslims to name the Name is removed. This removes the expectation that a Muslim will revere Jesus as Lord and Saviour who died for him on the Cross. Rather, honouring Jesus as a prophet – a

Christian tradition also affords him – as a word and as a spᵢ… om God fulfils all righteousness.

The Bible and the Qur'an

Willingness to accept that God is the author of the Qur'an removes the problem of crediting Muhammad instead. Of course, I cannot absolutely rule out a human element. Generally, I do not think that God overrides human consciousness. That would seem to negate free will. However, just as a Mary who cooperated with God in bearing Jesus, so a Muhammad who co-operated with God in bearing the Qur'an maintains human freedom. Nasr thinks it unlikely that Muslims will shift in their opinions on the Qur'an, or subscribe to the type of redaction and source criticism that Christians have carried out on its text.[5] On the other hand, in calling for an examination of the Qur'an within the social and political and religious context of its revelation, Muslims such as Rahman, Esack and others openly borrow from Christian opinion (see Zebiri, 1997: 222). Recognition of the role of metaphor and allegory, too, opens up the possibility of different interpretations, some of which challenge a more exclusive theology and an attitude of intolerance towards the religious Other. Cragg and Jomier and other Christian writers regard the Qur'an as a *word from God*, from which Christians as well as Muslims have much to learn. Certainly, this is a different view than that of polemicists, for whom it is a jumbled, confused, fabricated book of error. Cragg and those who approach the Qur'an in a similar way have moved some way towards Muslim reverence for this Book. When Ahmad Khan suggests that the corruption to which the Qur'an refers may be one of meaning not of falsification, the Bible emerges as a Book from which Muslim can also learn. Askari 'not infrequently draws on biblical illuminations' and 'is one of the few Muslims who have made some attempt at Biblical interpretations' (Zebiri, 1997: 165). Here, from the Muslim side, some movement can be discerned on the issue of the Bible's reliability. Many Muslims will no doubt continue to pursue Deedat-style polemic and maintain that it is a catalogue of error, pornography and full of contradiction. Parshall admits that some of the errors identified by Deedat exist (2002: 63) but suggests that it can still be considered inerrant. When all facts are known, and original autographs are investigated and 'correctly interpreted', it will be found to be true 'in all it affirms'

(84). For Parshall, this includes doctrine, ethics and the social, physical and life sciences. I do not need to claim as much. For me, the Bible and Qur'an are not repositories of all knowledge or even historical documents but religious and theological discourse.[6] I do not think that all the history in the Bible is necessarily error-free, or that I can find scientific facts there: but I do believe that it is truthful when it speaks about who God is, and about God's will or plan for the world.

Was Jesus crucified?

Our earliest Christian writer, John of Damascus, identified the Crucifixion as a divisive issue. Nineteenth and twentieth-century writers continue to wrestle with its absence in Islam. A few Christians argue that the Qur'an does not emphatically deny the Cross.[7] As Zebiri (1997) points out, 4:157 'is not grammatically straightforward or entirely free from ambiguity' (216). Ibn Taymiyyah, however, took it as axiomatic that Jesus did not die on the Cross and that the gospels are factually wrong, although he did not impute the disciples with deliberate deceit. Cragg takes it as axiomatic that, as an historical fact, Jesus did die on the Cross and that the Qur'an is in error. Yet the Qur'an does not actually say that Jesus *did not die*; it says that the Jews *did not kill him*. I argue that indeed the Jews *did not kill Jesus*, since according to Christian teaching *my sin* and *your sin killed him*. Deedat is right to say that Christians have unfairly accused Jews of deicide, although it could equally be argued that if human salvation depends on Jesus' death, *someone had to kill him* in order for God's plan to proceed. Zwemer (1912: 181) and Cragg (2000: 267) both argue that restoring the Cross, or enabling Islam to retrieve the Cross, is the most important task for Christians vis-à-vis Islam. 'The Muslim reinterpretation of the Cross', Cragg says 'offends deeply against all that the gospels disclose about the self-giving of Jesus' (267). Cragg identifies why the Cross is abhorrent to Islam as 'the presupposition that hostility to the prophets should not succeed in slaying them' (2000: 266). Askari, in suggesting that Islam can learn from the motif of sacrifice and suffering in Christianity, appears to have retrieved at least the metaphor if not the fact of the cross. Ayoub (1978) explored the significance of vicarious suffering in Shi'a Islam and draws some parallels with Christian belief. It is not altogether true that Islam lacks any notion of suffering as within

God's plan.[8] Drawing once more on the possibility that paradox is somehow involved here, is there any way to make sense of a Jesus *who did* and yet *who did not die* on the Cross? Phased like that, the answer is probably no; but rephrased as 'is there any way to make sense of a Jesus *who was* and yet *was not killed* on the cross to redeem all humanity', an answer might be available.

In describing Khodr's 'economy of the spirit', I touched on what might be considered an alternative soteriology to that of the Cross. The Western church emphasizes *Jesus' death* as the great act of redemption, while the East stresses the *whole of Jesus' life*, starting with his birth. Orthodox Christianity is closer here to Islam and to Judaism, neither of which accept the notion of original sin. Ware explains: 'Human beings after the Fall . . . possessed free will and were still capable of good action' (1993: 225). Jesus came to save the world, not just humans *not so much by dying*, although his death is not denied, *but by living*, by *sanctifying* the whole of human life. In him, the *divine became human* so that *the human might become divine* (2 Peter 1:4). Through Jesus' life, God engaged with the human condition, making it holy, renewing life, setting forth the paradigm of the life of love and action lived in tune with God's will. Cragg says that the Cross was no 'afterthought, no sudden tragedy' (2000: 271): yet I am inclined to think that it was not foreseen. Rather, given the opposition that Jesus faced, such a death was probably inevitable and a life lived in selfless service of others found a fitting end in willing self-sacrifice on a cross, in that Jesus did not resist. Deedat, of course, disagreed. The Cross remains central to the Christian story as a metaphor of resisting evil and oppression, yet I am not convinced that my salvation, any more than that of a Hindu or a Muslim, derives from the Cross. My sanctification stems from the fact that Jesus lived, not from the fact that he also died. There have been some Christians for whom Jesus' death was not central to their faith, such as those who identified with the Gospel of Thomas. This is different from denying that Jesus did die but it does raise the issue of how significant or essential the Cross is for human salvation. The possibility, entertained by several Christian writers, that there is indeed salvation outside the visible church, just as Esack says that salvation is available outside formal Islam, questions the need for explicit belief in Jesus' 'blood'. Jomier speaks of Muslims being saved, as Muslims, by God's grace. God's grace, I would suggest, is strong enough to save us all without any price or substitution or sacrifice being paid. The view, often articulated by Christians, that divine justice demanded a perfect sacrifice in order for God, who is omnipotent, to forgive sins seems to limit God, to reduce God to something other than all powerful. I believe that God restrains from constantly intervening in human affairs to honour human free will, and waits for us to assume our proper roles as co-creators with God. However, voluntary self-restraint is different from the view that the necessity of a sacrifice is somehow built into the universe so that even God must withhold mercy and grace. I believe that Jesus did die on the Cross but question whether he was killed, since he voluntarily chose to accept this fate. The Qur'an's apparent although not unambiguous denial of the Cross challenges Christian over-emphasis on Jesus' death.

Asymmetrical Relations, Politics and Tripartite Dialogue

Churches have issued declarations, guidelines and statements on a new approach to Islam. To some degree, this creates asymmetry in relationship with Islam, since no comparable official bodies exist to reciprocate. It can be argued that just as dialogue with Jews has altered Christian thinking, so has dialogue with Muslims and that this new thinking has been officially embraced. As a result of dialogue with Jews, the historic teaching of contempt for Jews has been repudiated. Many Lutheran churches have apologized for what Luther said about Jews. Displacement theology has yielded to the affirmation that the Jewish covenant remains valid: the Christian covenant is either a different covenant, or the Church has been grafted on to the original one (Romans 11:17). Similarly, statements affirming that Muslims are within God's plan have followed from Christian–Muslim encounter. Some reciprocal statements from Muslim organizations expressing respect for Christians would be very welcome as a way of progressing dialogue. However, it is not clear how such an initiative would be undertaken (see Zebiri, 1997: 36).

This raises the issue of politics and the extent to which purely theological or theoretical dialogue can or ought to be conducted in a social and political vacuum. Many Christians have legitimate concerns about the plight of Christians in some parts of the Muslim world, just as Muslims are concerned about the welfare of Muslims in the non-Muslim world and will want to discuss human rights and related issues. When I worked at the British Council of Churches, one member of my committee, a former Muslim, was very outspoken about what he called reciprocity. In his view, the ill treatment of Christians in the Muslim world should be censured by restrictions on Muslim life in Europe, such as denying planning permission for mosques. I did not agree, since two wrongs do not make a right. However, in Islam, the close relationship between religion and state means that legal issues, punishments for adultery, apostasy, for abusing the Prophet or indeed for theft, cannot be separated from religion. Nor can the churches' complicity or conceived complicity in Western cultural and economic domination of the rest of the world be altogether ignored. Cragg comments that 'several Muslim states in the United Nations have withheld their signature from the Universal Declaration of Human Rights because of its insistence that freedom of religion means freedom to become as well as to remain' (2000: 309). Christians will want to raise concerns related to the freedom of people in the Muslim world to choose to become Christian, especially given the contemporary success of Muslim mission in the non-Muslim world. Muslims are free to make converts in the USA; Christians cannot legally worship in Saudi Arabia. Muslims will want to criticize Christians for failing to 'discipline and control . . . imperialism' or to correct 'exploitation' (293). 'Trade relations' are perceived by many Muslims to be too preoccupied by 'sales' rather than with 'people' and 'society' (Cragg: 241). The elevation of the individual in Western society concerns many Muslims, who may wish Christians to listen to their view of society as community. Even recognizing that the Churches are not especially powerful, Christians often are (Cragg, 2000: 293). Cragg argues that Christians do share some guilt for Western hegemony, and should make 'retrieval' (240). Cragg sees Islam's combination of religion and state as problematic because it makes the ideal, in which 'goodness must arise through moral and religious forces' the legal, 'enforceable standard of behavior' (145, 296). Human sin means that we fall short of such standards, hence it is preferable to separate these two levels, the political and spiritual (145). Nasr critiques Christianity's lack of law (1994: 35, 69); Cragg thinks that this leaves Christians free to critique laws made by the state, to give praise where praise is due, to suggest better, fairer or more humane laws when the law is seen as wanting. While the *ummah* and society are identical, the Church, says Cragg, is not identical with the whole society but stands, 'militantly', within it (296), again suggesting asymmetry between the

Muslim and Christian reality. Cragg argues that if church and state are identical, Christians lose their ability to critique the political and social realms. The 'church of grace', he says, 'does not suppose that humanity is perfectible by law' (295). Dialogue, then, will also need to tackle how Christians and Muslims understand the state, religious freedom and dissent. Discussion of secularism, already promoted by the WCC (see Mitri, 1995) may be a fruitful area. Such Muslims as Tibi (2001: 113–14), Mernissi (1994: 65) and Soroush argue that a secular society is not necessarily an irreligious one and that in any society where Muslims constituted a majority, 'its government would take on a religious hue' or it would hardly qualify as democratic (Soroush, 2000: 61, 126). He is convinced that a state 'grows more religious as it grows' freer (145).

Around the world, there are examples of tripartite dialogue between Jews, Muslims and Christians, not least of all among peace activists from all three faiths in the Middle East. Organizations such as the Three Faiths Forum, UK, the Children of Abraham, Michigan and many other tripartite alliances bring Jews, Christians and Muslims together, recognizing a common respect for Abraham. One weakness of Christian–Muslim encounter is that while some international mechanisms exist, no solid network on the local level has yet been formed. In contrast, local branches of the Council for Christians and Jews are widespread. Some wish to see the now well-established structures for Christian–Jewish dialogue open up to Muslim participation. Sometimes, this is appropriate. There is, though, some reluctance. Issues specific to Christian–Jewish relations remain on the agenda and, given the worldwide differential between the Jewish and Muslim populations, Muslim participation could swamp the Jewish presence. Given Muslim hostility towards Israel, which is sometimes deflected onto any Jew, the issue of justice for Palestinians might dominate the dialogue, to the exclusion of other important issues. It might be better to encourage the formation of a comparable network of Christian–Muslim Councils, although tripartite initiatives should not be discouraged.

The Dialogue of Life

One development, arguably an example of progress, is the recognition of each others' spiritual life. Amir, who can worship in churches as a Muslim, writes of singing hymns which 'speak to his soul' (14). When a conservative, evangelical, Church Growth exponent such as Parshall can speak movingly of Muslim spirituality, progress can be claimed. Another possible development, which could be described as progress, is collaboration on issues of social justice. Several Muslims have advocated collaboration as a priority, including Nasr in his visit to the Vatican.[9] Zebiri (1997) comments that while 'for Christians theology is the foremost religious science, Muslims tend to highlight praxis rather than doctrine and give priority to jurisprudence' (9). Sometimes, such collaboration involves a setting aside of some of the above theological issues, an agreement to differ until God informs us about 'that on which we differ' (Q5:48). At times, in the face of conflict or calamity or disaster, such issues lose their apparent significance. There are many places around the world where Christians and Muslims collaborate. Much goes unsung. I have heard stories of Christians and Muslims helping each other in times of natural calamity in Indonesia, where both communities have rebuilt mosques and churches. In mixed communities, Christians and Muslims work together in civil society, on school boards, on local councils, in national Parliaments, as well as through some formal Christian–Muslim alliances. Internationally, they co-operate in the World Conference on Religion and Peace and in other interfaith bodies. WCRP collaborates closely with the United Nations, which has contracted it to work in several areas of conflict where religious identity is a factor. I do not believe that our works save us – salvation is by God's grace – but nor do I believe that evil lives, or standing idly by while others suffer, pleases God. What we do, not what we say, best witnesses the quality of our faith. I am sure that there are people who are totally convinced that they are saved whose lives belie this belief. Knitter, speaking about missionaries who want to add numbers to their churches at any cost, suggests that to do so while ignoring social evil in the societies in which they work does not please God (1996: 121). Even though successful in Church growth terms, this type of mission is a failure. I agree with Esack, whose theology was forged alongside Christians in the anti-apartheid struggle,[10] that what God most wants us to do is to liberate the oppressed. I add to this: feed the hungry; restore sight to the blind; proclaim the acceptable year of the Lord. My missionary mandate is Luke 4:18–19, not Matthew 28:19–20. I am convinced that God will judge me by what I do, not by what I believe. Calling Jesus 'Lord' is hypocritical if my life does not mirror his (Luke 6:46).

Notes

Introduction: Confrontation versus Conciliation, Debate versus Dialogue

1   'Other' is widely used, especially in post-colonial writing, and in writing about alterity, or 'Otherness', to refer to those who are different from us. The term was first used by Hegel. In contemporary usage it denotes how we stigmatize others, so that all Muslims or all Hindus or all Black people share the same characteristics which are radically different and less desirable than our own.

2   Many Muslims have claimed this after 9/11, which they 'blame on a Jewish or Christian conspiracy against Islam' (Ahmed, 2003: 34). For example, see 'The Primary Conspiracy Against Islam' at http://www.islamcity.com/forum/forum_posts.asp?TIP=365. See also Tibi (2005) on how fundamentalist Muslim regimes are deflecting criticism 'of their failures with domestic problems . . . by their successful presentation of a Western conspiracy (*mu'amarah*) directed against Islam' (79). Many Muslims, including children, have told me that 9/11 was committed by Jews.

3   In Bangladesh, for example, Bengalis whether Christian (who are a tiny minority of some 0.5 per cent) or Hindu (approximately 14 per cent) or Muslim revere three writers: the Muslim Nazrul Islam (1899–1976), the Hindu Rabrindranath Tagore (1861–1941) and the Christian Michael Madhusudan Datta (1824–1873). Nazrul expressed what almost all Bangladeshis hold to be true: 'No avatar or prophet ever said that I have come for the Hindu, I have come for the Muslim, I have come for the Christian. They all said, we have come for humanity – like light, for everyone' ('Hindu–Muslim' (1926)). All three poets stressed the oneness of the human family and the shared values of humanity's religious traditions.

4   Many borders were determined by the victors of World War I, who divided the Ottoman Empire up between them.

5   Khurshid Ahmad, for example, who is discussed as a cross-category example in Chapter 8.

6   Jesus said, 'Why do you look at the speck of sawdust in your brother's eye and pay no attention to the plank in your own eye?' (Luke 6:41 NIV).

7   Available at www.wcc-coe.org/wcc/what/interreligious/77glines-e.html

8   Available at www.wcc-coe.org/wcc/what/interreligions/77glines-e.html. The Vatican has also published its own guidelines *Guidelines for Dialogue Between Christians and Muslims*, New York/Mahwah, NJ, Paulist Press, 1990.

9   Available at www.vatican.va/roman_curia/pontifical_councils/interelg/documents/ rc_pc_interelg_doc_19051991_dialogue-and-proclamatio_en.html

10   Available at ht_decl_19651028_nostra-aetate_en.html

11   See *Dialogue and Proclamation*, 3:42. The document also describes the 'dialogue of theological exchange', sometimes called the dialogue of ideas and that of 'religious experience' where people 'share their spiritual riches'.

1   The Bible: An Agenda for Dialogue or Diatribe?

1   This is referred to as displacement theology.

2   This association was made at an early period. Ibn Ishaq records Abu Talib saying, 'Did you know that we have found Muhammad, a prophet like unto Moses as described in the oldest books, and that love is bestowed on him bestowed on him (alone) of mankind', dated approximately 614 CE (Guillaume, 1955: 160).

3   In the Arabic Bible, Παράκλτος was translated as أحمد (Ahmad), a diminutive of محمد (Muhammad).

4   The Arabic word for God, الله (Allah), has no number. Grammatically masculine, it is also used by Arab Christians. While some Christians regard Allah as a different God from theirs, linguistically the God of Islam and of Christian Arabs is identical.

5   The 'three paradigms' of exclusivist, inclusivist and pluralist were developed by Race (1983) as models that can describe most Christian theologies of religion. They can, with caution, be applied to Muslim views; see Goddard (2000: 158). Newbigin (1989) famously suggested that his position had elements of all three. Like any classificatory system, including my conciliation–confrontation categories, the paradigms have their limitation.

6   Samuel Marinus Zwemer (1867–1952), the 'apostle to Muslims', was a missionary in the Arab world from 1891 until he became a professor at Princeton Theological Seminary in 1930. He was a prolific writer on Islam, and on how to 'win' Muslims for Christ.

7   There is another aspect, however, to Justin. He pioneered the concept of the *logos spermatikos* (seminal reason) as the generative principle of all wisdom

and truth. In his *Second Apology*, he wrote: 'whatever either lawgivers or philosophers uttered well, they elaborated by finding and contemplating some part of the Word', that is, the Logos (Ch. X). 'Whatever things are rightly said', he continued, 'are the property of us Christians' (Ch. XIII). The Stoics and other Greek philosophers spoke of the *logos spermatikos* in a similar way. Justin had studied philosophy and continued, as a Christian, to wear the philosopher's gown.

8   Muir's book is dated but represents what many conservative Christians still think about Islam, and in contrast to much that has been written qualifies as a serious and in some respects groundbreaking study of Islam's primary sources, considered by one eminent scholar, Albert Hourani, to be 'still not quite superseded' (1989: 34).

9   Written in Latin, they preferred this to anything in Arabic. Southern (1978) comments: 'They were fleeing from the embrace of Islam: it is not likely they would turn to Islam to understand what it was they were fleeing from' (25–6).

10   Kraemer and Karl Barth (1886–1968), who influenced him, were both reacting to the crises in the German Church during the Hitler years, when too many Christians were prepared to regard what Hitler said as God speaking through culture. Stressing a radical discontinuity between the revelation in Christ, and all human culture, Barth and Kraemer challenged identification of Nazism with God's will. Aquinas's mistake had been to regard revelation in too intellectual terms (1938: 114). Religion represents human seeking; revelation is God's finding of humanity. Revelation, not religion, is incorruptible.

11   Clement of Alexandria (d. 202 CE) wrote in *The Stromata* that, before the coming of Christ, 'philosophy was necessary to the Greeks for righteousness', which served them as a 'type of preparatory training'. 'God', said Clement, 'is the cause of all good things', although especially 'of the Old and the New Testament'. Philosophy 'was given to the Greeks directly and primarily, till the Lord should call the Greeks' (Book One, Chapter V).

12   Hocking (1873–66) chaired the Laymen's Commission on US Protestant missionary work (1932), which concluded that Christians should see themselves as 'brothers in a common quest' with those of other faiths (31), thus 'the Christian will therefore regard himself as a co-worker with the forces within each religious system which are making for righteousness'. For Kraemer, humanitarian work was only of value if it led to conversion (1938: 433). He rejected the report.

2   The Qur'an and Christianity: Affection or Hostility?

1   The latter, however, is used in this book for convenience.
2   Christian scholars also attribute reference to Jesus speaking from the cradle, such as Q3:46 to Gnostic influence or as a direct borrowing from the *Arabic Infancy Gospel*, where verse 1 has Jesus say, 'I am Jesus, the Son of God, the Logos, whom thou hast brought forth . . . sent by my Father . . . for the salvation of the world'.
3   Possible translations include 'was shaped for them', 'contrived for them' and 'fashioned for them'.
4   Taha (1900–85) in his *The Second Message of Islam* argued that the earlier Meccan verses with their message of equality, self-defence and tolerance cancel or abrogate such later Madinan verses as 9:5 and 5:51, not vice versa. Later verses, such as those that insist on male superiority or reduce non-Muslims to second-class status, were merely temporary concessions to human weakness and historical circumstance. Thus, 2:62 cancels 5:51, 22:39–40 cancels 9:5 and 9:71 cancels 4:34, for example.

3   The Traditional Christian Confrontational Approach Towards Islam: Classical Contributions

1   Available at www.answering-islam.org/Books/MW/john_d.htm
2   Which has Muhammad the 'heresiarch' preach to 'irrational animals', 'subject' Zaynab 'to his lust' claiming 'divine inspiration', fabricate revelation after attending 'assemblies of Christians' and predict that he would rise from the dead. Instead, dogs consume his corpse, 'appropriate' for a prophet who 'committed not only his own soul, but those of many, to hell'. Gabriel was a 'vulture', sent by the 'spirit of error' (Wolf). In the Song of Roland, Muslim souls go straight to hell, those of Christians killed in battle against them straight to heaven.
3   Traditional Muslim belief that Muhammad was 'unlettered' (*ummi*) protects him from the charge of having composed or compiled the Qur'an; see Q7:156; 62:2. Christians have disputed Muhammad's illiteracy. Nasr compared the necessity of Muhammad's unletteredness with Mary's virginity: both ensure that God's word enters the world without any human contamination (1994: 44).
4   After narrating and ridiculing an absurd story about a she-camel, implying that this is from a chapter of the Qur'an, John says that only 'brutish' people could believe such a tale.

5   See Daniel (1997), 'The Imputation of Idolatry to Islam', 338–43.

6   The Qur'an was aware of the charge of fabrication, 'And the infidels say, "This Qur'an is a mere fraud of his own devising, and others have helped him with it"' (25:4).

7   Daniel (1997) comments that, 'among medieval critics of Islam, ways of copulating assumed an importance' that now seems 'out of all proportion'. This centred on Q2:223; see 'res turpisima', 351–3.

8   See http://answering-islam.org.uk/Books/Al-Kindi/

9   Some Muslims contend that the *asalamu alaikum* should only be used to greet Muslims. A few prefer to greet non-Muslims with a less courteous salutation.

10   Available at www.answering-islam.org/Books/Pfander/Balance/index.htm.

11   Muir's analysis of the literary exchange between Pfander and Kairanwi was published in *The Mohammedan Controversy* (1897). Muir did not report the verbal debate. For a detailed analysis see Powell (1993).

12   John does not name Zaynab, describing her as the 'beautiful wife' of Zayd, a 'comrade' of Muhammad. Zayd was Muhammad's adopted son (Sahas, 1972: 139). The Spanish *Life* describes Zayd as 'a certain neigbour' of Muhammad.

4   Classical Christian Conciliatory Approaches towards Islam

1   Alphonse Mingana (1878–1937) translated and published the dialogue between the Caliph and the Catholicos in volume two of *Woodbrook Studies* (1928), having brought a MSS to England. Day two of the discourse, on which this analysis is based, is available at http://darkwing.uoregon.edu/~sshoemak/102/texts/timothy.html.

2   Tradition turned El Cid (d. 1099) into a Christian crusader but he actually worked for Muslims as well as for Christians, crossing the frontier between the various states (see Fletcher, 2003: 89).

3   See Daniel (1997), 'Martyrs and Killers', 344–46.

4   Available at the internet site of its translator, Jasper Hopkins, cla.umn.edu/sites/jhopkins/

5   Cusa wrote of 'One religion in a variety of rites', *Una religio in rituum varietate*. See Pratt, 113.

6   Massignon submitted two doctoral theses in 1922, which both 'pioneered the modern study of sufiism'. One was his study of al-Hallaj. The other was his *Essais sur les origins de lexique technique de la mystique Musulmane* (Paris: Geuthner), which demonstareed that Sufi terminology is 'rooted in the Qur'an and early Islamic exegesis' (Kerr, 2002: 14).

7   Massignon was married, so could not be ordained in the Western tradition.

5 The Traditional Muslim Confrontational Approach towards Christianity

1   Khadduri thinks the pact the 'work of later generations since it departs from the instructions of tolerance and protection otherwise ascribed to Umar' (1955: 194).

2   Kraemer claimed that while Christianity, like any other religion, became corrupt it was uniquely self-critical and self-correcting (1938: 109, 145). Ibn Taymiyyah characterized Christianity as prone towards corruption, while Islam enjoyed divine protection: 'Whenever there is error in the *tafsir* [exegesis] of the Qur'an or in the transmission or incorrect interpretation of a *hadith*, God has raised up someone from the community who clarified it' which showed 'proof for the error of the one who made it, and the falsity of the liar' (1984: 238).

6 Classical Muslim Conciliatory Approaches towards Christianity

1   *Dhimmis* refers to protected, non-Muslim communities.

2   Luther had harsh words for the Turks, wrote a preface for a work of anti-Muslim polemic but also suggested that the threat to Vienna could be divine punishment for Christian laxity as 'God's rod and the devil's servant', echoing an early explanation of Muhammad's success (1967: 170).

3   Some scholars think that the word Sufi derives from *suf*, wool, because the first Sufis wore wool.

4   The book is identified as Volume I. Khan, though, did not write a second volume.

5   Each of the 12 essays in *Essays on the Life of Mohammed* is separately paginated, so I reference the chapters by name.

6   Paul of Antioch has referred to the Apostles as messengers. Only rasul receive revelation. Here is some common ground between Ahmad and a medieval Christian conciliator.

7 Contemporary Christian and Muslim Confrontation

1   Tracing original publication dates is difficult as most of Deedat's pamphlets were lectures given on numerous occasions. Videos and text versions are easily

available on the internet. I have used electronic versions in this chapter, where pagination is not given. Where possible, hard copy editions are referenced in the Bibliography as well as internet versions.

2 His critics note that this does not refer to the Greek source. 'Begotten' (see John 3:16) is a translation of μονογενής, which means 'type' or 'kind', as in 'only kind' rather than 'to beget', or 'father'. It has no sexual connotation. The same word is used in the Nicene Creed, ''Ιησοῦν Χριστόν, τόν Υἱὸν τοῦ Θεοῦ τὸν μονογενῆ, τὸν ἐκ τοῦ Πατρὸς γεννηθέντα πρὸ πάντων' ('Jesus Christ, the only begotten son of God, begotten of his father before all worlds').

3 For example, H. E. G. Paulus (1761–1851) had Jesus survive the Cross, aided by secret disciples. F. E. D. Schlieiermarcher (1668–34) also hints that Jesus survived the crucifixion (see Bennett, 2001: 103). K. F. Bahrdt (1741–92), who pioneered the notion that Jesus was an Essene, also posited secret assistants and that Jesus survived the cross. Deedat also argues that Jesus had secret disciples. There is some similarity between Schweitzer's Jesus and Deedat's: Schweitzer's Jesus too had not planned to die on the cross.

4 This quotation is p. 249 of the 2nd edition, published in 2000.

5 I once heard a senior Muslim diplomat remark that bin Laden is currently being secretly protected by the Bush regime, on whose behalf he directed 9/11.

6 Muhammad, of course, was the acknowledged ruler and so was the 'government'. In fact, in the legal tradition, governmental sanction for *jihad* was required. It could not be initiated by a private citizen. Also, it has always been regarded as a collective duty (*fard al-kifaya*) not an individual one (*fard ayn*). Indeed, some men ordinarily should not engage in *jihad* (Q4:71) but remain behind to look after the vulnerable and as a reserve in case of need. See Bennett, 2005: 233–4.

7 Nor do they refer to the classic work of Sir Thomas Arnold, whose *The Preaching of Islam* (1913) demonstrated that while Islam's spread has been due to a variety of causes, 'one of the most powerful factors at work in the production of this stupendous result' was 'the un-remitted labors of Muslim missionaries' (3). Some nineteenth-century writers thought that Christian missionaries could learn lessons from Muslim missionaries in terms of respect for existing cultures. See, for example, R. B. Smith's 'Mohammedanism in Africa', *Nineteenth Century*, 22: 791–816 (1887). From the Christian missionaries, said Smith, Africans 'imbibes the conviction that to be a good man he must be like the white man, not as his equal but as his parasite' (810), while in Islam he discovers an 'energy, a dignity, a self-reliance and a self-respect which is all too rarely found in their pagan or their Christian fellow-countrymen' (800).

8 Pipes (2002: 145–55) argues that some Muslims are 'sleepers', living quiet lives waiting to be activated like Cold War KGB spies. Here, he draws on the

traditional accusation that Muhammad allowed deceit during war. See Spencer, 'War is Deceit', 103–22. See Khan, 1984: 52: 157–8 on telling lies and deceit during war.

9   See also Stanley Kurtz, 'Exposing Esposito: How the academy infected intelligence', *National Review* online, www.nationalreview.com/contributors/kurtz120301.shtml 3 December 2001.

10   See article on solomonia.com 'Bin Talal in, Christians out', comparing the University's acceptance of Muslim funding with its expulsion of evangelical Christians from the campus: www.solomonia.com/blog/archives/009384.shtml

11   See www.unveilingislam.org/1-Response-Unveiling-Islam.html

12   Some Muslims do argue that these verses abrogate earlier verses permitting only self-defence, thus sanctioning aggression to spread the rule of Islam; but other Muslims locate these verses in the context of an ongoing war which, temporarily halted by an armistice, was later continued. This view does not regard these verses as permitting unprovoked aggression or territorial conquest.

13   'I'm Rich, I'm Rich' www.jihadwatch.org/archives/005055.php 14 February 2005.

14   'I am Not Rich' www.jihadwatch.org/archives/005440.php 22 March 2005.

15   Although the Caners do discuss 'Islamic Sects and Splinters', including Sh'ia.

8 Contemporary Christian and Muslim Conciliation

1   The WCC's *Current Dialogue*, issue 36, December 2000 focused on Christian-Muslim dialogue, available at www.wcc-coe.org/wcc/what/interreligious/cd36-00.html. Hans Ucko's editorial highlights the need for consideration of human rights vis-à-vis Christian minorities in Muslim countries and the role of religion in conflict situations, including the religious 'legitimization of violence'. The question about the motive of dialogue in relation to missionary activity remains crucial, he says. Brown (1989) surveys 20 years of WCC sponsored Christian–Muslim dialogue, usefully listing those who participated. Michael Fitzgerald of the Pontifical Council also surveyed Christian-Muslim relations in 'Christian–Muslim Dialogue: A Survey of Recent Developments', focusing on Catholic involvement (10 April 2000) available at www.sedos.org/english/fitzgerald.htm.

2   Known since 1980 as the Office on Inter-religious Relations and Dialogue.

3   Originally called the Secretariat for Non-Christians, it was raised to the higher status of a Council in 1988.

4   Rabitah (World Muslim League) was formed in 1962. See Siddiqui, 1997: 180–84.

5   Mu'tamar (World Muslim Congress) was formed in 1926. See Siddiqui, 1997: 175–79.

6   Text available at www.bc.edu/research/cjl/meta-elements/texts/cjrelations/ resources/documents/interreligious/alexandria2002.htm

7   Text available at http://www.millenniumpeacesummit.com/resources/nr/Commit ment%20to%20Global%20Peace.pdf

8   I have heard Askari speak in Sunni mosques where his authority and knowledge of Islam were clearly respected.

9   This subsequently became the Lebanon Evangelical Mission and then part of Middle East Christian Outreach, see http://www.aboutmeco.org/Crossroads/ Crossroads-(July-2006).html.

10   Gairdner was a playwright. Cragg has translated M. Kamal Hussein's novel, *City of Wrong* (1994).

11   This is a very comprehensive text, covering a wide range of topics, including Arabic literature (212 f.), the status of minorities in Islam and the issue of Muslim toleration (205), the 'old and simplistic thesis that Islam was spread by the sword' (229), the Palestinian issue (209) and the unity of religion and state in Islam, Muslims approval for Thomas Carlyle's portrait of Muhammad (172).

12   'Balancing Divergence and Convergence, or Is God the Author of Confusion?: An Essay on Kenneth Cragg', Hartford Seminary online articles, available at http://macdonald.hartsem.edu/smithart2.htm

13   Jomier (2002) reproduces the text of *Nostra Aetate* (101–04) and several other Catholic documents, including 'Dialogue with Muslims from the point of view of the Catholic Church' by Cardinal Francis Arinze (105–10) and 'Muslim and Christian Communities Should be in respectful dialogue' by Pope John Paul II (111–15). Jomier was consulted during the writing of the Vatican's Guideline for Dialogue between Christians and Muslims, see Bormans (1981). See p. 187 above for their comment on prayer.

14   Reference to Aydin are to the pagination of a printed-out chapter from the electronic version, citing the chapter first.

15   Jomier (1989) says that Rahman saw the Qur'an as 'entirely from God yet in a sense entirely from Muhammad', says Jomier (1989: 159).

16   John 3:16 says that God so loved the cosmos that he sent his only son. When the Common Language translation of the Bengali Bible appeared, I was appalled to see that 'cosmos' had been translated as '*manush*', humanity.

17   At a Christian–Muslim colloquium I attended in Toronto in 1989 we discussed prayer and fasting in our two traditions. On prayer, we appeared to occupy a lot of common ground. However, on fasting we Christians could only talk about historic practices especially in the monastic tradition. Muslims present were somewhat puzzled and perplexed by our lack in this area.

18   Parshall holds a D.Miss from Fuller, Smith a Th.M.

19   Parshall's Muslim converts fit the fifth category:
      C1 – Traditional Church Using Outsider Language
      C2 – Traditional Church Using Insider Language
      C3 – Contextualized Christ-centred Communities Using Insider Language and
      Religiously Neutral Insider Cultural Forms
      C4 – Contextualized Christ-centred Communities Using Insider Language and
      Biblically Permissible Cultural and Islamic Forms
      C5 – Christ-centred Communities of 'Messianic Muslims' Who Have Accepted
      Jesus as Lord and Savior
      C6 – Small Christ-centred Communities of Secret/Underground Believers.
      (Travis, 1998: 407–8)
20   Askari also regards the Qur'an as dialogical 'through and through (Siddiqui,
      1997: 113).
21   Present at Cartigny, 1976 on the next steps in dialogue, and at Crete, where
      Khodr was co-chair, in 1987.
22   The final statement from Chambésy 'sought to distinguish proselytism and
      propaganda from genuine and appropriate concern for the expansion of truth
      as sincere witness desired to bring it' (Cragg, 2000: 200). At Chambésy it was
      Ezaddin Ibrahim who issued this ultimatum.
23   See www.islamic-foundation.org.uk

Conclusion: Has Progress Occurred?

1   In contrast, Askari was happy for his Christian colleague David Kerr to
     teach introductory courses on Islam so that he could lead more discursive,
     philosophical seminars and bible studies. As students, we always knew that
     what Askari said was deep and meaningful even when we were perplexed
     by what was meant, so profound was his choice of words. However, that he
     revered and found insight in the Bible as well as the Qur'an was self-evident in
     what he did say.
2   Although some mission agencies have also adopted dialogue. When I worked
     at the British Council of Churches (1986–92) my salary and the budget of
     my committee on inter-religious relations was mainly funded by missionary
     societies. My desk was within the Mission division.
3   See Nasr (1990a: 128) on accepting 'the persons of the Trinity as "aspects" or
     "Names" of God without condition and above relations'.
4   Widely cited by Muslim apologists, such as Jamal Badawi, in support of the
     Muslim view of Jesus.
5   For a classic example, see Tisdall's *The Original Sources of the Qur'an* (1905),
     available at www.answering-islam.org/Books/Tisdall/Sources/index.htm

6   Tibi (2001) comments that for a Muslim to disavow that the Qur'an is an 'inexhaustible encyclopedia of science involves the danger of being accused of unbelief', referring to the popular tactic among Islamists of declaring anyone who dissents from their opinion an apostate. In an attempt to counteract this tactic, in July 2005 179 leading Muslims scholars met in Jordan under the auspices of the King and agreed mutual recognition of eight schools within Islam as valid and that that no member of any school can be declared an apostate.

7   For example, Nazir-Ali, a Christian of Muslim background and an Anglican bishop (1983: 17).

8   Cragg writes of 'segments of Islam' possessing 'far reaching ideas of sacrifice, notably among the Shi'ahs' (2000: 273). Ayoub has taken part in many Christian–Muslim dialogues, including the Crete gathering on religion and society that Khodr co-chaired in September 1987 and the Toronto colloquium at which I was also present (1989).

9   Visiting the Vatican in December 1977, Nasr proposed cooperation on such issues as preventing ecological disaster, energy conservation and confronting atheism (see Siddiqui, 1997: 156).

10   Esack is a scholar activist. Post-apartheid, he was Commissioner for Gender Equality in the Mandela Government.

References

Addison, James Thayer (1942) *The Christian Approach to the Moslem: A Historical Study*. New York: AMS Press

Ahmad, Khurshid (1976) 'Guest Editorial'. *International Review of Missions*. October. Vol. LXV, No. 20, 366–9

Ahmad, Khurshid (1999) 'Islam and the West: Confrontation or Cooperation?' *Muslim World*. Vol. LXXXV, No. 1–2, 63–81. January–April. Online at http://macdonald. hartsem.edu/articles/ahmadart1.pdf

Ahmed, Akbar (1992) *Postmodernism and Islam: Predicament and Promise*. London: Routledge

Ahmed, Akbar (2003) *Islam Under Siege: Living Dangerously in a Post-honor World*. Cambridge: Polity

Akbar, Ahmed (2002) *Islam Today: A Short Introduction to the Muslim World*. London: I. B. Tauris

Al-Ghazali (1979) *Kitab al-Waqiz fi fiqh madhab al-imam al-Shafi'i*. Beirut

Ali, 'Abdullah Yusuf (2002) *The Meaning of the Holy Qur'an*. Beltsville, MD: Amana Publications

Alichoran, Joseph (1996) 'Review of Christians and Moslems in Iraq by Benedicte Landron'. *Journal of Syrian Academic Society*. Vol. X, No. I, 85–90

al–Kindy (1882) *The Apology of al-Kindy*. Edited by Sir William Muir. London: Smith. Online at www.answering–islam.org/Books/Al-Kindi/index.htm

Apostolov, Mario (2004) *The Christian–Muslim Frontier: A Zone of Contact. Conflict or Cooperation*. London and New York: RoutledgeCurzon

Aquinas, Thamas (1957) *On the Truth of the Catholic Faith: Summa Contra Gentiles*. Garden City, NY: Image Books

Arkoun, Mohammed (1994) *Re-thinking Islam: Common Questions. Uncommon Answers*. Boulder, CO: Westview Press

Armour, Rollin (2002) *Islam. Christianity and the West: A Troubled History*. Maryknoll, NY: Orbis

Armstrong, Karen (1992) *Muhammad: A Biography of the Prophet*. San Fransisco, CA: HarperCollins

Arnold, Sir Thomas (1913) *The Preaching of Islam*. London: Constable

Askari, Hasan (1991) *Towards a Spiritual Humanism: a Muslim–Humanist Dialogue*. Leeds: Seven Mirrors

Askari, Hasan (1992) 'The Dialogical Relationship between Christianity and Islam' in Leonard Swidler (ed.) *Muslims in Dialogue*. Lampeter: The Edwin Mellen Press

Askari, Hasan and Hick, John (1985) *The Emergence of Religious Diversity*. London: Avebury

'Ata Ur-Rahim, Muhammad (1977) *Jesus: Prophet of Islam*. London: MWH London

Austin, R. W. J. (1975, 1980) 'Introduction'. *The Bezels of Wisdom*. Marwah, NJ: The Paulist Press, 1–41

Aydin, Mahmut (1993) *Modern Western Christian Theological Understandings of Muslims Since the Second Vatican Council*. Cultural Heritage and Contemporary Change Series IIA, Volume 13. Online at http://onlinebooks.library.upenn.edu/webbin/book/lookupname?key=Aydin.+Mahmut

Ayoub, Mahmoud (1978) *Redemptive Suffering in Islam*. The Hague: Mouton

Baksh, Khuda S. (1926) 'A Muhammedan View of Christianity'. In *An Outline of Christianity: The Story of Our Civilization*, edited by A. S. Peake and R. G. Parsons, Vol. 5, pp. 245–55. London: Eaverly

Barber, Benjamin (1995, 2001) *Jihad v McWorld*. New York: Random House

Benedict XVI, Pope (2006) 'Faith. Reason and the University. Memories and Reflections. Meeting with the representatives of Science. University of Regensburg'. September. Vatican: Libreria Editrice Vaticana. Online at www.vatican.va/holy_father/benedict_xvi/speeches/2006/september/documents/hf_ben–xvi_spe_20060912_university-regensburg_en.html

Bennett, Clinton (1992) *Victorian Images of Islam*. London: Grey Seal

Bennett, Clinton (1996), 'The Legacy of Karl Gottlieb Pfander'. *International Bulletin of Missionary Research*, Vol. 20 No. 2, 76–81

Bennett, Clinton (1998) *In Search of Muhammad*. London: Cassell

Bennett, Clinton (2001) *In Search of Jesus: Insider and Outsider Images*. London: Continuum

Bennett, Clinton (2005) *Muslim and Modernity: An Introduction to the Issues and Debates*. London: Continuum

Bergen, Peter (2002) *Holy War. Inc: Inside the Secret World of Osama bin Laden*. New York: Free Press

Bin-Talal, Hassan (1995) *Christianity in the Arab World*. New York: Continuum

Bormans, Maurice (ed.) (1981) *Guidelines for Dialogue between Christians and Muslims*. New York and Mahwah: Paulist Press

Brown, Stuart (1989) *Meeting in Faith: Twenty Years of Christian–Muslim Conversations Sponsored by the World Council of Churches*. Geneva: WCC Publications

Burikhardt, Titus (1975, 1980) 'Preface'. *The Bezels of Wisdom*. Edited and translated by R. W. J. Ausin. Mahwah, NJ: Paulist Press, xi–xv

Calvin, John (1957) *Institutes of the Christian Church*. Philadelphia, PA: Westminster Press

Caner, Ergun Memhet and Caner, Emir Fethi (2002) *Unveiling Islam: An Insider's Look at Muslim Life and Beliefs*. Grand Rapids, MI : Kregel Publications

Constable, Remie (ed.) (1997) *Medieval Iberia: Readings from Christian. Muslims and Jewish Sources*. Philadelphia, PA: University of Pennsylvania Press

Courbage, Youssef and Fargues, Phillipe (1997) *Christians and Jews under Islam*. London: Tauris

Cracknell, Kenneth (1986) *Towards a New Relationship*. London: Epworth

Cragg, Kenneth (1959) *Sandals at the Mosque*. London: SCM

Cragg, Kenneth (1971) *The Event of the Qur'an: Islam and Its Scripture*. London: George Allen & Unwin

Cragg, Kenneth (1984) *Muhammad and the Christian: A Question of Response*. London: Darton, Longman and Todd

Cragg, Kenneth (1994) 'Introduction' to *City of Wrong* by M. Kamal Hussein. Oxford: Oneworld, 18–30

Cragg, Kenneth (1956, 2000) *The Call of the Minaret*. Oxford: Oneworld

Cragg, Kenneth (2005) *The Qur'an and the West*. Washington, DC: Georgetown University Press

Cromer, Evelyn (1908) *Modern Egypt*. New York: Macmillan

Daniel, Norman (1997) *Islam and the West: The Making of an Image*. Oxford: OneWorld

Dar, Bashir Ahmad (1957) *Religious Thought of Sayyid Ahmad Khan*. Lahore: Institute of Islamic Culture

Deedat,Ahmed (1979) *What the Bible Says About Muhammad*. Lahore: Kazi Publications

Deedat, Ahmed (1981) *Is the Bible Still God's Word?* Chicago, IL: Kazi

Deedat, Ahmed (1984) *Crucifixion. Or Cruci-fiction?* Durban: Islamic Propagation Centre International

Deedat, Ahmed (1990) *Christ in Islam*. Riyadh: International Islamic Publishing House

Denffer, Ahmad von (1983) *Loading Options Ulu m al-Qur'a n : An Introduction to the Sciences of the Qur'a n*. Leicester: The Islamic Foundation

Dennis, James S (1897) *Christian Missions and Social Progress: A Sociological Study of Foreign Mission*. New York: Fleming H. Revell

Ernst, Carl (2003) *Following Muhammad*. Chapel Hill, NC: University of North Carolina Press

Esack, Farid (1997) *Qur'an. Liberation and Pluralism: An Islamic Perspective on Interreligious Solidarity Against Oppression*. Oxford: Oneworld

Esack, Farid (2005) *The Qur'an: A User's Guide*. Oxford: Oneworld

Esposito, John L (1992) *The Islamic Threat: Myth or Reality*. New York: Oxford University Press

Esposito. John L. (1998, 3rd edn) *Islam: The Straight Path*. New York: Oxford University Press

Esposito. John L. (ed.) (1995) *Oxford Encyclopedia of the Modern Islamic World*. New York: Oxford University Press

Fitzgerald, Michael (2006) 'Christian–Muslim Dialogue: A Survey of Recent Developments', Rome: Pontifical Council for Interreligious Diaologue. Online at www.sedos.org/english/fitzgerald.htm

Fletcher, Richard (2003) *The Cross and the Crescent: Christianity and Islam from Muhammad to the Reformation*. London and New York: Allen Lane

Fosdick, Harry Emerson (1952) *Great Voices of the Reformation: An Anthology*. New York: Random House

Friedmann, Yohanan (2003) *Tolerance and Coercion in Islam: Interfaith Relations in the Muslim Tradition*. New York: Cambridge University Press

Gairdner, William Henry Temple (1920, 5th edn) *The Rebuke of Islam*. London. United Council for Missionary Education, online at www.muhammadanism.org/Gairdner/rebuke/rebuke_of_islam.pdf

Gairdner, William Henry Temple (1924) *Mishkat Al-Anwar: The Niche for Lights*. London: Royal Asiatic Society. online at www.answering-islam.org/Books/Gairdner/Lights/index.htm

Geisler, Norman and Saleeb, Abdul (1993) *Answering Islam: The Crescent in the Light of the Cross*. Grand Rapids, MI: Baker

Gilchrist, John (2003) *Sharing the Gospel with Muslims*. Cape Town, SA: Life Challenge Africa

Goddard, Hugh (1995) *Christians and Muslims: From Double Standards to Mutual Understanding*. Richmond: Curzon

Goddard, Hugh (2000) *A History of Christian–Muslim Relations*. Edinburgh: Edinburgh University Press

Gros, Jeffrey, Eamon McManus and Ann Riggs (1998) *Introduction to Ecumenism*. New York: Paulist Press

Guillaume, Alfred (1955) *The Life of Muhammad: A Translation of Ishaq's Sirat rasu'l Allah*. Oxford: Oxford University Press

Hick, John (1973, 1996) *God and the Universe of Faiths*. London: Macmillan; Oxford: Oneworld

Hick, John (ed.) (1977) *The Myth of God Incarnate*. London: SCM Press

Hilali, Muhammad Taqi al-Din and Khan, Muhammad Muhsin (1994) *Translation of the Meanings of the Noble Qur'an in the English Language*. Madinah: Mujamma' al-Malik Fahd li-T iba 'at al-Mus h af al-Shari f

Hocking,William Ernest (chairman of the inquiry) (1932) *Re-thinking Missions*. New York: Harper Brothers

Hocking, William Ernest (1956) *The Coming World Civilization*. New York. Harper Bros.

Hodges, Richard and Whitehouse, David (1983) *Mohammed, Charlemagne and the Origins of Europe: Archeology and the Pirenne Thesis*. Ithaca, NY: Cornell University Press

Hogg, Alfred George (1939) 'The Christian Attitude to Non-Christian Faith'. *The Authority of the Faith* London. International Missionary Council and Oxford University Press, 102–25.

Hopkins, Jasper (1994) *Nicholas of Cusa's De Pace Fidei and Cribratio Alkorani*. Minneapolis: The Arthur J. Banning Press. Online at www.cla.umn.edu/sites/jhopkins/

Hourani, Albert (1989) *Europe and the Middle East*. London: Macmillan

Howarth, Stephen (1982) *The Knights Templar*. New York: Barnes & Noble

Hunter, Sir William W (1871) *The Indian Musalmans: Are They Bound in Conscience to Rebel against the Queen?* London. Trübner

Huntington, Samuel P. (1993) 'The Clash of Civilizations'. *Foreign Affairs*. Summer. Vol. 72, No. 3. 22–8

Huntington, Samuel P (1996) *The Clash of Civilizations and the Re-making of World Order*. New York: Simon & Schuster

Hussain, Amir (2006) *Oil and Water: Two Faiths: One God*. Kelowna, BC: CopperHouse.

Ibn al-'Arabi (1975, 1980) *The Bezels of Wisdom*. Edited and translated by R. W. J. Austin. Marwah, NJ: The Paulist Press

Ibn Hazm (1997) 'On the Inconsistencies of the Four Gospels', translated by Thomas E. Burman, in *Medieval Iberia: Readings from Christian. Muslim and Jewish Sources*. Edited by Constable. Remie, Philadelphia, PA: University of Pennsylvania Press, 81–83.

Ibn Ishaq, Muhammad (1955) *The Life of Muhammad: A Translation of Ishaq's Sirat rasu'l Allah*, translated by Alfred Guillaume. Oxford: Oxford University Press online at www.muhammadanism.org/Jones/Christianity_explained.pdf.

Ibn Taymiyyah (1984) *A Muslim Theologian's Response to Christianity: Ibn Taymiyya's Al-Jawab Al-Sahih*, edited and translated by Tom Michel. New York and Delmar: Caravan Books.

Jomier, Jacques (1989) *How to Understand Islam*. London: SCM

Jomier, Jaques (2002) *The Bible and the Qu'ran*. San Fransisco, CA: Ignatius Press

Jones, Lewis Bevan (1939) *Christianity Explained to Muslims*. Calcutta: YMCA Press

Kabbani, Rana (1989) *A Letter to Christendom*. London: Virago

Kairanwi, M Rahmatullah (2003) *Izhar-ul-Haq. The Truth Revealed*. London: Ta Ha

Kathir, ibn (2000) *Tafsir ibm Kathir*. 10 Volumes. edited and translated by Shaykh Safiur-Rahman al-Mubarakpuri. Riyad: Darussalam

Kerr, David (2002) 'Christian Mission and Islamic Studies: Beyond Antithesis'. *International Bulletin of Missionary Research*. January, 8–15.

Khadduri, Majid (1955) *War and Peace in the Law of Islam*. Johns Hopkins University Press: Baltimore, MD

Khan, Muhammad Muhsin (1984) *The Translation of the Meaning of Sahih al-Bukhari.* New Delhi. Kitab Bhavan

Khan, Sayyid Ahmad (1870) *A Series of Essays on the Life of Mohammed and Subjects Subsidiary Thereto.* London. Trübner

Khan, Sayyid Ahmad (1871) 'Review of Sir W. W. Hunter's The Indian Musalmans'. *Writings and Speeches of Sir Sayyid Ahmad Khan,* edited by Shan Mohammad. Bombay: Nachiketa Publications, 66–82

Khan, Sayyid Ahmad (2002) 'Lecture on Islam'. *Modernist Islam: A Sourcebook.* Edited by Charles Kurzman. New York: Oxford University Press, 291–303

Khodr, George (1981) 'The Economy of the Spirit'. *Mission Trends: Faith Meets Faith No 5,* edited by Gerald H. Anderson and Thomas F. Stransky. Grand Rapids, MI: W. B. Eerdmans, 36–49

Knitter, Paul (1996) *Jesus and Other Names: Christian Mission and Global Responsibility.* Maryknoll. NY: Orbis

Kraemer, Hendrik (1938) *The Christian Message in a Non-Christian World.* Grand Rapids, MI: Kregel Publications

Kraemer, Hendrik (1939) 'Continuity or Discontinuity'. *The Authority of the Faith.* London: International Missionary Council and Oxford University Press, 1–23

Küng, Hans (1993) *Christianity and World Religions: Paths to Dialogue.* Maryknoll, NY: Orbis

Landron, Benedicte (1994) *Christians and Moslems in Iraq: Nestorian Attitudes Towards Islam.* Paris. Editions Cariscript

Lindsey, Hal (2002) *The Everlasting Hatred: The Roots of Jihad.* Murrieta, CA: Oracle House

Lindsey, Hal and Carlson, C. C. (1970) *The Late Great Planet Earth.* Grand Rapids, MI: Zondervan

Lings, Martin (1983) *Muhammad: His Life Based on the Earliest Sources.* Lahore: Suhail Academy

Luther, Martin (1967) 'On War Against the Turks'. *Luther's Works,* edited and translated by Robert C. Schultz. Philadelphia: Fortress Press, 155–205

Maqsood, Ruqaiyyah Waris (2000) *The Mysteries of Jesus: a Muslim Study of the Origins and Doctrines of Christianity.* Oxford: Sakina

Marshall, David (2001) 'Christianity in the Quran'. *Islamic Interpretations of Christianity,* edited by Lloyd Ridgeon. London: Curzon, 3–29

Massignon, Louis (1982) *The Passion of al-Hallaj: Mystic and Martyr of Islam.* Princeton, NJ: Princeton University Press

Mawdudi, Sayyid Abul A'la (1967–79) *The Meaning of the Qur'an* (9 vols). Lahore: Islamic Publications

Mawdudi, Sayyid Abul A'la (1972, 2nd edn) *Purdah and the Stratus of Women in Islam.* Lahore: Islamic Publications Ltd

Mawdudi, Abu'l Ala (1999, 3rd edn) 'Political Theory of Islam'. *Islam: Its Meaning and*

Messages, edited by Khurshid Ahmad. Leicester: The Islamic Foundation, 147–71

McAuliffe, Jane Dammen (1991) *Quranic Christians: An Analysis of Classical and Modern Muslim Exegesis*. Cambridge. Cambridge University Press

McAuliffe, Jane D (2005) 'Readings the Qur'an with Fidelity and Freedom'. *Journal of the American Academy of Religion*, September, Vol. 73, No. 3, 615–35

McGavran, Donald (1990, 3rd edn) *Understanding Church Growth*, revised and edited by C. Peter Wagner. Grand Rapids, MI: Eerdmans

Menocal, María Rosa (2002) *The Ornament of the World: How Muslims. Jews and Christians Created a Culture of Tolerance in Medieval Spain*. New York: Little, Brown & Co.

Mernissi, Fatima (1994) *Islam and Democracy: Fear of the Modern World*. London: Virago

Merril, J. E. (1951) 'Of the Tractate of John of Damascus on Islam'. *The Moslem World*. Vol. XLI, 88–99

Michel, Thomas (1984) *A Muslim Theologian's Response to Christianity: Ibn Taymiyya's Al-Jawab Al-Sahih*. Delmar, NY: Caravan Books

Michel, Thomas (2000) *Paul of Antioch and Ibn Taymiyya: The Modern Relevance of a Medieval Debate*. The D'Arcy Lectures. Oxford University. Online at www.sjweb. info/dialogo/documents/doc_show.cfm?Number=5

Mingana, Alphonse (1928) *Woodbrook Studies*, vol. 2, Cambridge, W. Heffer & Sons.

Mitri, Tarek (ed.) (1995) *Religion. Law and Society: A Christian–Muslim Discussion*. Geneva: World Council of Churches

Moncrief, Charles Scott (1919, 1995) *The Song of Roland*. Edited by Douglas J. Killings, The Online Medieval and Classical Library: omact.org/Roland

Muir, Sir William (1858–60, 1894 3rd edn) *The Life of Mahomet*. 4 volumes. London: Smith & Elder. Online at www.answering–islam.org/Books/Muir/Life1/index.htm

Muir, Sir William (1887) The *Apology of Al-Kindy*. London: SPCK. Online at www. answering-islam.org/Books/Al-Kindi/index.htm

Muir, Sir William (1897) *The Mohammedan Controversy*. Edinburgh: T & T Clark. Online at www.muhammadanism.org/Controversy/pv.htm

Muir, Sir William (ed.) (1923) *The Life of Mohammed from original sources*. Edited by T. H. Weir. Edinburgh: J. Grant

Muir, Sir William (1924) *The Caliphate: Its Rise, Decline and Fall*. Edinburgh: J. Grant. Online at www.answering-islam.org/Books/Muir/Caliphate/index.htm

Nasr, Sayyid Hossein (1987) 'Response to Hans Küng's Paper on Christian–Muslim Dialogue'. *The Muslim World*, April, Vol. 77, No. 2. 96–105

Nasr, Sayyid Hossein (1990a) *Traditional Islam in the Modern World*. London: KPI

Nasr, Sayyid Hossein (1990b) 'The Islamic View of Christianity'. *Christianity Through Non-Christian Eyes*, edited by Paul J. Griffiths, Maryknoll. New York: Orbis, 126–134

Nasr, Sayyid Hossen (1994) *Ideas and Realities of Islam*. London: The Aquarian Press

Nazir-Ali, Michael (1983) *Islam: A Christian Perspective*. Philadelphia, PA: The Westminster Press

New King James Version of the Holy Bible (1982) Nashville, TN: Thomas Nelson

Newbigin, Lesslie (1989) *The Gospel in a Pluralist Society*. London: SPCK.

O'Shea, Stephen (2006) *Sea of Faith: Islam and Christianity in the Medieval Mediterranean World*. New York: Walker

Parrinder, Geoffrey (1977) *Jesus in the Quran*. New York. Oxford University Press

Parshall, Phil (1985) *Beyond the Mosque: Christians within Muslim Community*. Grand Rapids, MI: Baker Book House

Parshall, Phil (2002) *Understanding Muslim Teachings and Traditions: A Guide for Christians*. Grand Rapids, MI: Baker Book House

Peters, F. E. (1994) *A Reader on Classical Islam*. Princeton, NJ: Princeton University Press

Pfander. Karl G. (1910) *The Mizanu'l Haqq: Balance of Truth*. Translated and edited by William St-Claire Tisdall. London: The Religious Tract Society. Online at www.answering-islam.org/Books/Pfander/Balance/index.htm

Phillips, Kevin (2005) *American Theocracy: The Peril and Politics of Radical Religion. Oil and Borrowed Money in the 21st Century*. New York: Viking

Pipes, Daniel (2002) *Militant Islam Reaches America*. New York: W. W. Norton

Pirenne, Henri, Pirenne, Jacques, Vercauteren, Fernand and Miall, Bernard (1938) *Mohammed and Charlemagne*. London: G. Allen & Unwin

Powell, Avril (1992) *Muslims and Missionaries in pre-Mutiny India*. Richmond: Curzon

Pratt. Douglas (2005) *The Challenge of Islam: Encounters in Interfaith Dialogue*. Aldershot: Ashgate

Qutb, Sayyid (1964, 1988) *Milestones*. Delhi: Markazi Maktaba Islami. Online at http://masmn.org/Books/Syed_Qutb/Milestones/ and http://www.youngmuslims.ca/online_library/books/milestones/index_2.asp)

Qutb, Sayyid (1990) 'That Hideous Schizophrenia'. *Christianity Through Non-Christian Eyes*, edited by Paul J. Griffiths. Maryknoll, NY: Orbis, 73–81

Qutb, Sayyid (1976, 1999 3rd edn) 'Islamic Approaches to Social Justice'. *Islam: Its Meaning and Message*, edited by Khurshid Ahmad. Leicester: The Islamic Foundation, 117–30

Race, Alan (1983, 2nd edn 1993) *Christians and Religious Pluralism: Patterns in the Christian Theology of Religions*. London: SCM.

Rahman, Fazlur (1966) *Islam*. London: Weidenfield and Nicholson

Rahman, Fazlur (1984) 'Some Recent Books on the Qur'an by Western Authors'. *The Journal of Religion*, Vol. 16, No. 1, 170–85

Rahner, Karl (1966) 'Christianity and the Non–Christian Religions'. *Theological Investigations*. Vol. 5. New York: Seabury Press, 115–31

Rida, Rashid (1980) *Tafsir al-Manar*. Vol. I. Beirut: Dar al-Ma rifah

Ridgeon, Lloyd V. J. (1999) *Crescents on the Cross: Islamic Visions of Christianity*. New York: Oxford University Press

Riley-Smith, Jonathan Simon Christopher (1987) *The Crusades: A Short History*. New Haven, CT: Yale University Press

Reeves, Minou (2000) *Muhammad in Europe*. New York: New York University Press

Ritzer, George (1993) *The McDonaldization of Society: An Investigation into the Changing Character of Contemporary Society*. Newbury Park, CA: Pine Forge Press

Rodwell, J. M. (1955) *The Koran*. London: Dent

Ruthven, Malise (2002) *A Fury for God: the Islamist Attack on America*. London and New York: Granta

Sacks, Jonathan (2002) *The Dignity of Difference: Avoiding the Clash of Civilizations*. New York: Continuum

Sahas, Daniel J (1972) *John of Damascus on Islam*. Leiden: E. J. Brill

Said, Edward (1978) *Orientalism*. Harmondsworth: Penguin

Salibi, Kamal S. (1985) *The Bible Comes from Arabia*. London: Jonathan Cape

Salibi, Kamal S. (1992) *Who Was Jesus? A Conspiracy in Jerusalem*. London. I. B. Tauris

Schacht, Joseph (1964) *An Introduction to Islamic Law*. Oxford: Clarendon Press

Schirrmacher, Christian (1997) 'The Influence of German Biblical Criticism on Muslim Apologetics in the 19th Century'. *Contra Mundum*. Online at http://contra-mundum. org/schirrmacher/rationalism.html

Schultz, Robert C. (ed. and trans.) (1967) 'On War Against the Turks'. *Luther's Works*. Philadelphia: Fortress Press, 155–205.

Schweitzer, Albert (1998) *The Quest of the Historical Jesus: A Critical Study of its Progress from Reimarus to Wrede*, Baltimore, MD: Johns Hopkins University Press

Sell, Edward (1923, 4th edn) *The Historical Development of the Qur'an*. Tunbridge Wells: People International. Online at www.answering-islam.org/Books/Sell/Development/index.htm

Sells, Michael (1998) *The Bridge Betrayed: Religion and Genocide in Bosnia*. Berkeley, CA: University of California Press

Shorrosh, Anis (1988) *Islam Revealed: A Christian Arab's View of Islam*. Nashville, TN: Nelson

Siddiqui, Ataullah (1997) *Christian–Muslim Dialogue in the Twentieth Century*. New York: St Martin's Press

Smith, Jane (2007) 'Balancing Convergence and Divergence or Is God the Author of confusion? – An Essay on Kenneth Cragg'. Hartford, CT.: Hartford Seminary. Online at http://macdonald.hartsem.edu/smithart2.htm

Smith, Wilfred Cantwell (1946) *Modern Islam in India: A Social Analysis*. London: V. Gollancz

Soroush, Abdulkarim (2000) *Reason. Freedom and Democracy in Islam*. Oxford: Oxford. University Press

Southern, R. W. (1962, 1978) *Western View of Islam in the Middle Ages*. Cambridge, MT: Harvard University Press

Spencer, Robert (2005) *The Politically Incorrect Guide to Islam*. Washington, DC: Regnery Publshing

Spencer, Robert (2006) *The Truth about Muhammad: Founder of the World's Most Intolerant Religion*. Washington, DC: Regnery Pub

Spencer, Robert and Ali, Daniel (2003) *Inside Islam: A Guide for Catholics*. Westchester, PA: Ascension Press

Subhani, Ja'far (1984) *The Message*. Qum: Ansarian Publications. Online at www.balagh. net/english/ahl_bayt/the_message/index.htm

Sweetman, James (1955) *Islam and Christian Theology: A Study of the Interpretation of Theological Ideas in Two Religions*. London: Lutterworh Press.

Taha, Mahmud Muhammad (1987) *The Second Message of Islam*. Syracuse, New York: Syracuse University Press

Talbi. Mohammad (1990) 'Islam and Dialogue: Some Reflections on a Current Topic'. *Christianity Through Non-Christian Eyes*, ed by Paul J. Griffiths. Maryknoll, NY: Orbis, 82–101

Tebbe, James A. (2002) 'Kenneth Cragg in Perspective: A Comparison with Temple Gairdner and Wilfred Cantwell Smith'. *International Bulletin of Missionary Research*. 1 January, Vol. 26, No. I. 16–21

Thoma,. David (2001) 'The Doctrine of the Trinity in the Early Abbasid Era' in Lloyd Ridgeon (ed.) *Islamic Interpretations of Christianity*. New York: St Martins, 78–98

Thompson, Henry O. (1988) *World Religions in War and Peace*. Jefferson, NC: McFarland

Tibi, Bassam (2001) *The Challenge of Fundamentalism: Political Islam and the New World Disorder*. Berkeley, CA: University of California Press

Tibi, Bassam (2005, 2nd edn) *Islam: Between Culture and Politics*. New York: PalgraveMacmillan

Tisdall, William (1895) *The Religion of the Crescent*. London: SPCK. Online at http:// muhammadanism.org/Crescent/Default.htm

Tisdall, William St Clair (1904) *A Manual of the Leading Muhammadan Objections to Christianity*. Online at www.answering-slam.org/Books/Tisdall/Objections/index.htm

Tisdall, William St Clair (1905) *The Original Sources of the Quran*. London: SPCK. Online at www.answering–islam.org/Books/Tisdall/Sources/index.htm

Transparency International (2005) *Global Corruption Report*. Berlin: Transparency International.

Travis, John (1998) 'The C1 to C6 Spectrum: A Practical Tool for Defining Six Types of "Christ–centered Communities Found in the Muslim Context".' *Evangelical Missions Quarterly (EMQ)*, October, Vol. 34, No. 4, 407–8

Van Gorder, Christian A. (2003) *No God but God: A Path to Christian–Muslim Dialogue on God's Nature*. Maryknoll, NY: Orbis

Vander Werff, Lyle L. (1977) *Christian Mission to Muslims: The Record. Anglican and*

Reformed Approaches in India and the Near East 1800–1938. Pasadena, CA: William Carey Library

Vatican (1990) *Guidelines for Dialogue between Christians and Muslims*. New York/ Mahwah, NJ: Paulist Press

Ware, Timothy (1993) *The Orthodox Church*. Harmondsworth: Penguin

Watt, William M (1952) *The Faith and Practice of Al-Ghazali*. London: G. Allen & Unwin. Online at www.ghazali.org/works/watt3.htm

Wolf, Kenneth B. (trans.) (1997) 'A Christian Account of the Life of Muhammad'. *Medieval Iberia: Readings from Christian. Muslim and Jewish Sources*, edited by Remie Constable. Philadelphia, PA: University of Pennsylvania Press, 48–50

Ye'or, Bat (1996) *The Decline of Eastern Christianity Under Islam: From Jihad to Dhimmitude, Seventh–Twentieth Century*. Madison. NJ: Fairleigh Dickinsoin University Press

Zakaria, Rafiq (1988) *The Struggle within Islam: The Conflict between Religion and Politics*. Harmondsworth: Penguin

Zebiri, Kate (1997) *Muslims and Christians Face to Face*. Oxford: Oneworld

Zwemer, Samuel M. (1909) *Islam: A Challenge to Faith*. New York: Student Volunteer Movement for Foreign Missions

Zwemer, Samuel M (1912) *The Moslem Christ*. New York: American Tract Society

Zwemer, Samuel M (1920) *A Moslem Seeker after God: Showing Islam at its Best in the Life and Teachings of al-Ghazali. Mystic and Theologian of the Eleventh Century*. New York and Chicago: Fleming H Revell. Online at www.ghazali.org/books/zwem1.pdf

Index